Contents

THE MAKING OF A WELFARE CLASS?

Benefit receipt in Britain

Robert Walker with Marilyn Howard

The POLICY PRESS

186 134 2357

First published in Great Britain in September 2000 by

The Policy Press
University of Bristol
34 Tyndall's Park Road
Bristol BS8 1PY
UK

Tel +44 (0)117 954 6800
Fax +44 (0)117 973 7308
E-mail tpp@bristol.ac.uk
www.policypress.org.uk

ISBN 1 86134 235 7

Robert Walker is Professor of Social Policy at the University of Nottingham and was formerly Director of the Centre for Research in Social Policy, Loughborough University. **Marilyn Howard** is an independent researcher and a specialist on disability benefits.

Cover design by Qube Design Associates, Bristol
Photograph used on front cover supplied by kind permission of
Mark Simmons Photography, Bristol
Printed in Great Britain by Hobbs the Printers Ltd, Southampton

List of tables and figures

Tables

Figures

Acknowledgements

The New Zealand Treasury originally commissioned the Centre for Research in Social Policy to undertake this review in order to assist national policy making, and contributed generously to the costs of publication.

Special thanks are due to Ron Crawford, who managed the research on behalf of the New Zealand Treasury and supported the researchers; to anonymous referees who suggested that the research should be published and offered many helpful suggestions; to further anonymous referees for The Policy Press who offered creative ideas for transforming a research report into a book; to Sue Maguire and Rachel Youngs who played such an important role in the preparation of the initial research report; to Jennifer Park who prepared most of the graphs and illustrations for the manuscript and who assisted in proof reading; to Suella Harriman and Sharon Walker who prepared the text; to Julie Birch who proof read the initial manuscript and Katherine Thompson who proofed later versions; to Dawn Rushen who guided the project through to publication; to Nick Manning and the University of Nottingham for allowing the lead author time to write up the research as a book; and to the partners and families of the authors who suffered further unwelcome intrusion into their lives.

AA   *Attendance Allowance:* non–contributory, tax-free, non-means-tested benefit paid at one of two rates towards the extra costs which arise from the care needs of elderly and disabled people. May attract *Invalid Care Allowance* for the carer.

AWT   *All Work Test:* a new test of incapacity introduced in April 1995 with *Incapacity Benefit.* The test assessed, for the purposes of determining entitlement to incapacity benefits (*IB, SDA*), and premiums for disability with *Income Support* and *Council Tax Benefit*, whether for medical reasons a person should be expected to work. Normally applicable after 28 weeks of incapacity.

BA   *Benefits Agency:* established in 1991 as the biggest executive agency in government and now one of five agencies in the *Department of Social Security*, with responsibility for the assessment, delivery and administration of all benefits except war pensions (dealt with by a separate War Pensions Agency).

BTWB   *Back to Work Bonus:* introduced as a pilot in October 1996. Bonus may be earned by claimants receiving *Income Support/Jobseeker's Allowance* for three months or more who declare earnings by themselves or their partner above the disregard level. A bonus equivalent to half their earnings above the disregard builds up and is paid in a lump sum of up to £1,000 when either claimant or partner moves into work which takes them off IS/JSA.

CA   *Contributions Agency:* one of five executive agencies in the *DSS.*

CAA   *Constant Attendance Allowance:* for a recipient of Industrial Injuries Disablement Benefit who is assessed as 95% disabled, paid at one of four rates for purposes similar to 'civilian' *AA* /Disability Living Allowance (care).

CB   *Contributory Benefit(s):* pensions, survivors benefits and so on.

CCG   *Community Care Grant:* in the *Social Fund*, non-repayable grant available to *IS/JSA* recipients or potential recipients to meet one-off financial needs on re-entering the community after a period of institutional care and in certain cases of exceptional expenditure pressure – for example, disabled child, moving house.

CHB   *Child Benefit:* a universal non-taxable benefit payable for each child in a family from birth to age 19, or to a fixed *terminal date* related to the end of non-advanced secondary education if earlier. (Also, since 1988, for an extension period to school leavers awaiting a Youth Training place.) Phased in between April 1977 and April 1979 to replace the former dual system of Family Allowances (payable only for the second and subsequent children) and child tax allowances (age-related and payable for all children, but ineffective for lower-income families). Initially paid at the same rate for all children, but a new higher rate for the first or eldest child in a family introduced following a freeze in rates between 1987 and 1991. From April 1997, a third rate was payable for the first child in a lone-parent family, with the abolition of One Parent Benefit as a separate benefit.

CL   *Crisis Loan:* in the *SF*, replaced pre-1988 Urgent Needs Payment. Intended primarily to meet immediate financial needs arising from an emergency or a disaster for anyone (not just an income-related benefits claimant) without other recourse to funds whose health or safety would otherwise be affected. Some exceptions and easements.

Class 1   (Earnings-related) National Insurance contributions by employed earners (primary) and their employers (secondary).

Class 1a   National Insurance contributions paid by employers on the value of company cars and related perks.

Class 2   (Flat-rate) National Insurance contributions paid by self-employed earners.

Class 3   (Flat-rate) voluntary National Insurance contributions.

Class 4   (Profit-related) additional contributions payable by self-employed earners with profits above an annual threshold.

CP   *Community Programme:* job creation programme founded in 1982/83 that was replaced by Employment Training and, in 1993, by *Training for Work* (TfW).

CSA   *Child Support Agency:* established in April 1993 as an executive agency of the *DSS*. Responsible for administering a new system for the award, collection and enforcement of child maintenance.

CTB   *Council Tax Benefit*: income-related benefit designed to assist with costs of Council Tax: lineal successor of rates rebates.

CTC   *Child Tax Credit:* refundable tax credit to be introduced in 2001 to replace the married couples tax allowance.

DfEE   *Department for Education and Employment:* created in 1974 by combining the old Departments of Education and Employment.

DPTC   *Disabled Person's Tax Credit:* refundable tax credit introduced in 1999 to replace *Disability Working Allowance* in 1999 for people working 16 or more hours per week.

DSS   *Department of Social Security:* from June 1988, when the former Department of Health and Social Security (DHSS) split into its original components.

DWA   *Disability Working Allowance:* means-tested benefit introduced in April 1992 to supplement earnings for disabled people able to work at least 16 hours a week but with low earnings.

ETU   *Earnings Top-Up:* experimental income-related benefit.

FC   *Family Credit:* income-related benefit to top up low earnings for people with children, including self-employed people. Introduced in April 1988 as a more generous and streamlined replacement for Family Income Supplement.

GRB   *Graduated Retirement Benefit: State Earnings Related Pension Scheme* precursor 1961-75.

HB   *Housing Benefit:* income-related benefit introduced in its present form in 1988 to provide assistance with housing costs.

HBEP   *Housing Benefit Extended Payment:* since April 1996, a measure whereby rent and Council Tax is paid for a further four weeks after taking up work, irrespective of earnings, to unemployed people, lone parents, carers and government trainees who have been out of work for six months and are receiving income-related benefits.

HRP   *Home Responsibilities Protection (in pensions):* introduced by the Social Security Agency in 1975 to protect the retirement pension position of people precluded from regular employment because of caring responsibilities.

IB   *Incapacity Benefit:* taxable weekly National Insurance benefit introduced in April 1995 to replace previous Sickness and Invalidity Benefits (old cases being phased in) as maintenance benefit for people who do not qualify for Statutory Sick Pay.

ICA   *Invalid Care Allowance:* non-contributory, non-means-tested benefit introduced in 1976 to provide income maintenance for people who give up the opportunity of full-time work to provide care on a regular and substantial basis (at least 35 hours or more a week) to a severely disabled person.

ILF   *Independent Living Fund:* government-funded trusts set up in 1988 following the reform of the income-related benefits to help severely disabled people purchase care to enable them to live independently in the community.

ILO   *International Labour Organisation:* created as an international organisation of national governments in 1919 in the context of the postwar settlement and re-formulated in 1944 with the Declaration of Philadelphia. The International Labour Office, Geneva, is its executive agency.

ILO   Unemployment defined according to the ILO
unemployment definition based on self-reported unemployment as measured by responses to the Labour Force Survey.

IS   *Income Support:* income-related benefit introduced in 1988 as a successor to supplementary benefit to support people working less than 16 hours a week (24 hours a week until 1992).

JSA
Jobseeker's Allowance: benefit introduced in October 1996 to replace contributory unemployment benefit and income-related IS for all those aged 18 and over needing financial support because of unemployment.

LEL
Lower Earnings Limit: weekly earnings level below which there is no liability to pay Class 1 National Insurance contributions. Changes annually, set at the level of basic retirement pension rounded down to the nearest pound (sterling).

MoBA
Mobility Allowance: introduced from January 1976 (take-on phased by age from October 1995 to April 1997) to provide a cash benefit for the needs of disabled people under pension age with serious mobility problems.

MSC
Manpower Services Commission: organisation responsible for government training and job placement between 1974 and 1987.

NDDP
New Deal for Disabled People: pilots of a voluntary system of information and advice to assist lone parents on benefit to return to work.

NDLP
New Deal for Lone Parents: voluntary system of information and advice to assist lone parents on benefit to return to work extended nationwide in 1998.

NDLTU
New Deal for the Long-Term Unemployed: compulsory welfare to work scheme for people unemployed for more than two years, initially implemented in 1998.

NDYP
New Deal for Young People: compulsory welfare to work scheme for people aged 18-24 who have been unemployed for more than six months, introduced nationally in 1998.

NIF
National Insurance Fund: set up in 1948, into which National Insurance contributions and any Treasury Supplement are paid and from which expenditure on National Insurance benefits (and until 1989 Industrial Injuries benefits) is met.

PAYE
Pay-As-You-Earn: system for collecting Schedule E (employed earners') tax via employers. Class 1 National Insurance contributions also collected and Statutory Sick Pay and Statutory Maternity Pay reimbursed via the PAYE system.

PP   *Personal Pension:* an arrangement between an individual and a pensions provider, for example, an insurance company. Personal pensions are operated on a money purchase basis and can be taken out by anyone (whether employed or self-employed) aged between 16 and 74 who has some form of earnings.

PRG   *Pension Reform Group:* established by the *DSS* in 1997 under the chairpersonship of Tom Ross.

RA   *Rent Allowance:* HB paid to tenants in private (including housing association) accommodation, in cash rather than by way of rebates.

RP   *Retirement Pension:* taxable weekly contributory benefit payable to men and women who have reached state pension age.

RR   *Rent Rebate: HB* paid to tenants in local authority accommodation.

SDA   *Severe Disablement Allowance:* tax-free, non-contributory benefit for those incapable of work for at least 28 weeks who do not qualify for *IB* because of a deficient National Insurance record.

SERPS   *State Earnings Related Pension Scheme:* begun in 1978, the earnings-related additional pension in the state scheme on top of basic retirement pension. Originally based on the best 20 years of earnings.

SF   *Social Fund:* in two parts, a regulated Fund and a cash-limited discretionary Fund.

TECs   *Training and Enterprise Councils:* local organisations comprising employers, training providers, government agencies and others created in 1990 to provide, among other things, training for unemployed claimants.

TfW   *Training for Work:* training scheme for unemployed claimants created in 1993.

TOPS   *Training Opportunities Scheme:* a scheme providing specialist vocation training run by the MSC in the 1970s.

WFTC   *Working Families' Tax Credit:* refundable tax credit introduced in 1999 to replace *Family Credit*, payable through the wage packet (or to the principal carer if requested) to persons working 16 hours or more a week and who have dependent children.

YOP   *Youth Opportunities Programme:* a programme of job creation and training for young unemployed people that ran between 1978 and 1982/83.

YT   *Youth Training:* introduced in 1990 as the successor to *YTS*.

YTS   *Youth Training Scheme:* replaced *YOP* in 1982/83 as a scheme providing training for young unemployed people. It was replaced in 1990.

[1] DSS (1997e) is used heavily as the source of definitions.

Part 1
Setting the scene

ONE

The conundrum

Summary

More than half of the British population now receives some form of social security benefit and the number of claimants has been rising. This book begins to explain why this is the case by systematically collating existing evidence.

It is important to know why benefit caseloads are increasing in order to determine whether or not public money is being well spent. *Such knowledge should be used to guide the process of continual reform that characterises British social security policy.*

It is widely accepted that social security expenditure is too high, *and that the system of provision creates perverse incentives and varying forms of inappropriate dependency on the state.*

Some argue that the social security system fosters the growth of an underclass or welfare class *of people who are both economically and socially excluded.*

Whether either of the above beliefs can be substantiated by evidence is among the questions addressed in this book.

The volume is structured around a simplified model of *the four sets of factors that could affect the size of the benefit caseload: economic, demographic, institutional and ideological.*

Benefits for unemployed people, disabled people, children and families and retirement pensioners are considered separately, *before comparing and contrasting the different reasons why caseloads have grown.*

Why, 50 years after the flowering of the British welfare state, are increasing numbers of people seemingly dependent for their livelihood on cash benefits?

The pattern of growth is evident from Figure 1.1. It records the numbers of people receiving key benefits in 1949/50, close to the origin of the postwar welfare state, and in 1970/71 and 1998/99, the beginning and dates of the period covered by this review. In every case, the number of claimants in 1998/99 far exceeded that in 1949/50. Likewise, caseloads in 1998/99 were all higher than in 1970/71: the number of people receiving insurance-based Unemployment Benefit or Jobseeker's Allowance (JSA) grew by 50% and those receiving Income Support (IS) by 436%.

Figure 1.1: Estimated numbers receiving selected benefits (1949/50-1998/99)

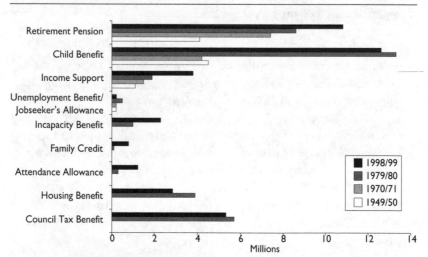

Source: DSS (1997b, 1999c)

The opening question is not simply rhetorical – it is unlikely that the architects of the welfare state would have contemplated that so many individuals and families would be 'living off the state' at the turn of the 21st century. Answering the question will help to clarify numerous issues that lie at the fulcrum of British politics. Politicians are divided in their support for spending on cash benefits. Some view social security as the touchstone of a civilised society. Others view it as wasteful, disproportionately claimed by the streetwise rather than being directed to those most in need. Others believe welfare spending to be corrupting, rewarding social and economic incompetence rather than promoting independence, enterprise and citizenship. Some even argue that social security has created a permanent, welfare class that is increasingly cut off from the shared values and norms of the wider society. For some, therefore, large and growing caseloads serve as evidence of the failure of the welfare state. For others, however, the same statistics demonstrate society's success in protecting large sections of the populace from the worst consequences of capitalism and individual misfortune.

Unfortunately there is no simple answer. The relevant literature is scattered across numerous disciplines and is generally not cumulative in the sense of being built on a constructive critique of earlier work. Indeed, while many sources pay cursory attention to the topic of rising claimant rolls, comparatively few address the question directly. Opinions differ as to the relative importance of the major motors of growth, but there appear to be no clearly demarcated schools of thought or theory that cross ideological boundaries. Few sociologists have paid the topic much attention, nor is there a strong econometric or other literature that has sought empirically to specify the relative importance of factors causing the number of benefit recipients to rise.

Substantial work has been undertaken within government, but much of this is not available for public scrutiny. Evidence of this work was provided by Peter Lilley, the last Conservative Secretary of State for Social Security, in the 1993 Mais Lecture, which is still regarded as one of the definitive statements on the topic (Lilley, 1993a). Internal civil service analysis also informed the fact sheets (DSS, 1997b) that accompanied the Labour government's review of social security which culminated in publication of a consultative Green Paper, *New ambitions for our country: A new contract for welfare* (DSS, 1998a). More recently, the government published an instructive account of the growth in social security expenditure (DSS, 2000a), which referred in passing to increased caseloads. Even so, there is no formal explanatory model in the public domain that has been subject to comprehensive peer review, nor even a widely accepted discursive account. It is intended that this book will lay the foundations of such an account, focusing on developments during the last three decades (1970s, 1980s, 1990s).

Social security in Britain

In 1908, the Liberal government under Lloyd George introduced the first national cash benefit scheme – old age pensions. This was accompanied by unemployment insurance in 1911, and by means-tested unemployment assistance from 1931 (which was developed from the transitional benefit that had come to be called the 'dole'). However, the basis of modern provision dates back to the Beveridge Report (Beveridge, 1942) and the subsequent 1944 National Insurance Act and 1948 National Assistance Act. The former created a comprehensive insurance scheme covering sickness, unemployment and retirement, while the latter established a national social assistance scheme to replace the local Poor Law system and unemployment assistance. Family Allowance, a tax relief for second and subsequent children, was introduced in 1946 (following legislation in 1945) and the National Health Service Act provided universal healthcare, free at the point of use.

In Britain today, the term 'social security' covers three kinds of cash benefits: contributory, means-tested and non-contributory. *Contributory benefits* are the descendants of insurance benefits, the receipt of which, as the name suggests, is conditional on a record of contributions that will typically have been made by both the recipient and his or her employer. These benefits are nominally paid for through contributions made to the National Insurance Fund (NIF), although the schemes are not funded in the strict actuarial sense. Instead, funding is 'Pay-As-You-Go' with current benefits being paid from current contributions to the NIF, which is topped up as necessary from direct taxation. The main contributory benefits are Retirement and Widows' Pensions, Incapacity Benefit (IB) and the first six months of JSA (a benefit for unemployed people). In the USA and many European countries, the term 'social security' is reserved exclusively for benefits that are contributory.

British contributory benefits are comparatively low by international standards. This can be traced back to Beveridge's major policy goal which was to alleviate poverty while ensuring perverse incentives not to work or save were contained. Hence, he provided for flat rate subsistence benefits rather than the earnings-related benefits favoured by European countries that followed the Bismarck model, designed to protect living standards and foster social cohesion. The low level of contributory benefits causes comparatively large numbers of recipients to rely on *means-testing*, the second kind of benefit, termed 'welfare' in the USA and 'social assistance' in Europe and elsewhere. About six million households – a little under one fifth – receive IS (or income-related JSA for unemployed claimants), the principal means-tested benefits. Income Support is universally available on the basis of need. Other means-tested benefits include Housing Benefit (HB), paid to low-income tenants, and Council Tax Benefit (CTB), a rebate on the local property tax, both of which are paid regardless of employment status.

The final category of social security comprises *non-contributory benefits* that are paid irrespective of income to individuals and families with particular characteristics. A number of non-contributory benefits are provided in respect of disability. They include Invalid Care Allowance (ICA) paid to carers in lieu of paid employment, Disability Living Allowance that is designed to meet the extra costs of disability, and Severe Disablement Allowance (SDA) which is provided for disabled people who do not qualify for IB. Child Benefit is a universal benefit payable for dependant children.

Under the Blair Labour government, two established means-tested benefits have been converted into tax credits and paid through the tax system – Family Credit (FC), for low-paid workers with child dependants, and Disability Working Allowance (DWA), for disabled people in work. Because of their origins, Working Families' Tax Credit and Disabled Person's Tax Credit are treated as social security benefits in this book.

Altogether 30 million people – more than half the population – receive some form of social security benefit, including 10 million retirement pensioners and almost 13 million children (DSS, 2000a). In 1998/99 benefit spending amounted to £95.6 million or 28.9% of all government expenditure. This equates to 11.2% of Gross Domestic Product (GDP).

Why the importance?

It is important to reiterate why it is vital to begin to explain the growing number of people reliant on cash benefits. In the context of political pressures to reduce public expenditure, a priori beliefs about factors driving the upward trend shape the broad thrust of welfare policy. Social security spending is considered to be too high and, to an extent, counterproductive, feeding welfare dependency and adding to social exclusion. Such views first became influential under Conservative governments, notably those led by Margaret Thatcher, but now inform Labour's approach to welfare reform.

Public expenditure

Social security, as already noted, is expensive, accounting for almost 30% of the tax bill. Moreover, expenditure has been rising rapidly and inexorably, more than doubling in real terms between 1970/71 and 1998/99 (Figure 1.2). A further slight rise is expected for 1999/2000. From a political perspective, high social security rolls necessitate high taxation and leave little scope for more popular forms of public expenditure.

Figure 1.2: Benefit expenditure as a % of GDP (1973/74-1998/99)

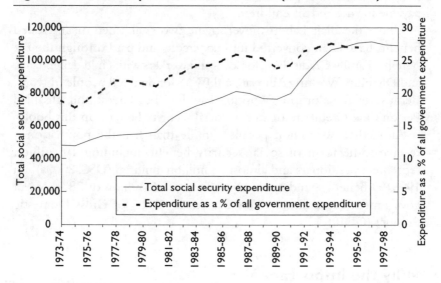

Source: DSS (2000a)

For much of the period from 1971 onwards, it was accepted that social security expenditure had a momentum of its own. It was demand-led, a product of adverse demographic and economic conditions. However, in his 1988 reforms, Norman Fowler, the then Secretary of State for Social Security, sought determinedly to put a brake on expenditure and, through changes to the State Earnings Related Pension Scheme (SERPS), did ensure that social security spending in the 2020s and 2030s would not increase to the extent previously anticipated. John Moore, Norman Fowler's successor as Secretary of State, unsuccessfully tried to argue that further expenditure was unnecessary since poverty, defined in absolute terms, had long since been eradicated. But it was Peter Lilley, who become Secretary of State in 1992, who succeeded in shifting the terms of the political debate by ensuring that all discussion of social security reform was set against a presumed consensus that expenditure was already excessive.

Tony Blair and the Labour government elected in 1997 implicitly accept that social security spending is too high, preferring instead to see rising expenditure on health and education rather than on paying people to be 'workless'. They are more explicit in stating that resources have been spent unwisely on social security and argue, in *The changing welfare state* (DSS, 2000a), that during the 1980s and early 1990s:

> ... the system became more of a problem than a solution. It concentrated on trying to deal with the consequences of social and economic change, with little attempt to address the causes of problems or the increasingly lax control of the routes onto benefit. (DSS, 2000a, p 13)

In the words of Tony Blair:

> Under the last government, social security spending went up, but poverty and social exclusion went up too. They cut away at the budget, sometimes creating problems along the way, for example, encouraging fraud in their cuts to Housing Benefit. But they failed to tackle the fundamental weaknesses of the welfare state. (Blair, 1999, pp 11-12)

The presumption is that social security is failing, and poverty remains widespread not so much because benefits are too low – although some benefit rates have recently been increased – but rather because too many people are dependent on benefits rather than in employment. Blair's view is that people have lost faith in welfare's ability to deliver, with the consequence that social security has become electorally unpopular.

Perverse incentives

Assuming, momentarily, that Blair is correct in his belief that cash benefits are unpopular, it is still important to establish why so many people claim social security benefits. Trends in demography, fluctuations in labour demand and changes in the availability and rules of entitlement are obviously all important, as will be documented throughout this book. However, political discourse has focused on the interaction between the incentive structure created by benefits, individual character and behaviour.

In the early 1980s, social security fostered Margaret Thatcher's generalised dislike of the 'nanny state': it mollycoddled individuals and sapped initiative. Later, more sophisticated arguments took root on the right of the political spectrum, many having their origins in the US. Charles Murray argued that the growing relative deprivation of the poor was a direct consequence of the US benefit system:

> The effect of the new rules was to make it profitable for the poor to behave in the short-term in ways that were destructive in the long-term.... We tried to provide more for the poor and produced more poor instead. We tried to remove the barriers to escape from poverty, and inadvertently built a trap. (Murray, 1984, p 9)

Murray argued that by providing better benefits for lone mothers, lone motherhood became more attractive and the pressure on fathers to provide was removed. He also postulated that the perverse incentives had a cumulative effect, changing behaviour and attitudes that were self-perpetuating and personally and socially destructive.

While Murray's ideas were disseminated by the political Right, their most influential adherent ironically proved to be Frank Field, briefly Labour's Minister for Welfare Reform in 1997-98. While Chair of the House of Commons Select Committee on Social Security, he wrote:

> Hard work is penalised by the loss of entitlement. Incentives reinforce welfare dependency. Honesty is punished by loss of income. It is in this sense that welfare is the enemy within. Its rules actively undermine the moral fibre of our characters. In so doing it eats into the public domain and so erodes the wider moral order of society. (Field, 1995, p 20)

Whereas Murray does not blame welfare recipients for acting rationally with respect to perverse incentives established by the welfare system, Lawrence Mead, another American commentator who has proved influential in the British debate, has focused on the character of welfare recipients. He has argued that the growth in poverty stemmed from the failure of the poor to work, either because they would not take jobs or could not keep them (Mead, 1986). As a consequence they were unable to fulfil their obligations to learn, work, and support their family and to respect the rights of others. In Mead's view, US welfare had to be made more authoritative through measures such as workfare – compulsory working for benefit in order to improve the conduct and character of the poor. Perhaps surprisingly, these views have also gained currency among the architects of the Labour government's welfare policy. Peter Mandelson, currently Secretary of State for Northern Ireland, but long-term confidant of Tony Blair, for example, is on record as saying that:

> ... a tough discipline is necessary to break the culture of hopelessness, idleness and cynicism which a concentration of hard core unemployment has bred on many estates throughout Britain where a generation has been brought up on the dole. (Mandelson and Liddle, 1996, p 87)

Welfare underclass and benefit dependency

The longer-term consequences that Murray believed followed from rational short-term actions included the undermining of family values and the work ethic, the fostering of a sub-culture of dependency and the creation of an underclass. He has recently argued of Britain that:

> What had been a nascent underclass in 1989 had by 1999 become one that increasingly resembled, in behaviour and proportional size, the underclass in America. My fundamental thesis is that large increases in the three indicators that I used in 1989 – dropout from the labour force among young males, violent crime and births to unmarried women – will be associated with the growth of a class of violent, unsocialised people who, if they become sufficiently numerous, will fundamentally degrade the life of society. (Murray, 2000, p 1)

While informed writers have not generally taken Murray's more provocative writings seriously, his core ideas closely resonate with the language used by Tony Blair in his analysis of current social malaise and the destructive role of cash benefits:

> The welfare state is encouraging dependency, lowering self-esteem and denying opportunity and responsibility in almost equal measure .... The more demands that are put upon it, the essentially passive

> nature of too much provision – especially benefits – is revealed. (Blair, 1997a)

> For a generation of young men, little has come to replace the third of all manufacturing jobs that have been lost. For a generation of young women early pregnancies and the absence of a reliable father almost, guarantee a life of poverty.... There is a case not just in moral terms but in enlightened self-interest to act to tackle what we all know exists – an underclass of people cut off from society's mainstream, without any sense of shared purpose. (Blair, 1997b)

Even very high levels of welfare recipiency do not necessarily prove the existence of an underclass or welfare class, nor help to determine whether individualistic tendencies or structural factors drive caseloads. Interestingly, few modern Marxist social theorists have even contemplated that the working class might be differentiated by benefit status. An exception is Mann (1986, 1992) who has suggested that a case could be made on the basis of agency: the respectable working class has always differentiated itself from the indolent and fraudulent, the undeserving claiming class. Likewise, Morris (1994) has proposed that the British welfare system perpetuated some of the stigma and moral condemnation that attached to the Victorian Poor Law – failing fully to deliver the social citizenship and rights to benefit to which T.H. Marshall aspired. As a consequence poor people in receipt of benefits can always expect to experience social exclusion.

However, it not clear that unemployed and non-employed people receiving state benefits differ in meaningful ways from the underemployed, those in part-time employment and those who suffer repeated spells outside the labour market. This reservation, expressed by Morris (1994), is increasingly justified by dynamic analyses of the labour market (Stewart, 1999) that reveal that large numbers of people appear to be trapped in the 'low pay no pay' cycle. Indeed, Gallie (1988) has concluded that, although the prevalence of long-term unemployment and insecure or non-standard forms of employment provide the structural foundation for an underclass, the cultural underpinnings do not exist. The membership of the potential underclass is so heterogeneous and lacks cohesion to such an extent that a collective self-awareness is most unlikely ever to emerge.

While neither the more dramatic of Murray's conclusions nor even the existence of an underclass are widely accepted among academics in Britain, many popular commentators have taken as gospel the existence of welfare dependency. The term was introduced into official parlance by John Moore in 1987, when he was Secretary of State for Social Security (Moore, 1987), and has been coupled with a long-standing anxiety in Britain about the abuse of social security and about fraud.

Dependency means different things to different commentators, but includes the notion that large, and probably increasing, numbers of people receive cash benefits for long periods (Walker and Ashworth, 1994). Rational dependency relates back to Murray's notion that the existence of high benefit levels relative to prevailing wages makes it rational for some people to claim benefits rather than to work (Trickey and Lødemel, 2000: forthcoming). Psychosocial dependency, on the other hand, reflects some people's unduly pessimistic expectations about what they are able to attain in the labour market which prevent them from seeking work or increasing their human capital. Cultural dependency refers to situations where people have come to accept a life-style without work, possibly because either they, their parents or significant others in their local community have become accustomed to living on benefit for long periods. Commonly, cultural dependency is believed to be under-written by illicit working while in receipt of benefits – and sometimes by drug peddling and other forms of crime. As employed in policy debates, the notions of cultural dependency and the underclass differ in degree rather than kind: the underclass being used to allude to a more widespread, more long-lasting and perhaps more threatening phenomenon.

Policy responses to concerns about dependency have taken a number of forms, including strengthening the conditionality of benefits, better enforcement of compliance and a move towards proactive benefit policies and active labour market measures that seek to facilitate the transition from benefits to work. These changes were begun under Conservative governments in the late 1980s and in the 1990s and have been taken substantially further since Labour was elected in 1997. Likewise, parallel policies to combat fraud were given extra impetus with the arrival of the Labour government. Policy responsibility was given to Frank Field, who fervently believed that the high level of means testing inherent in the British social security system encouraged dishonesty and that illicit working while on benefit was commonplace. As Minister for Welfare Reform, he sought, unsuccessfully as it turned out, to shift policies away from means testing, but he also commissioned a group of experts to help establish a counter-fraud strategy that has subsequently been pursued under new ministers.

Social exclusion

Although Blair might borrow the language of Murray, his policy response is very different. It is to 'modernise' social security and social assistance rather than to abandon welfare. While both might agree that benefit caseloads are too high, Blair – and certainly other architects of Labour's welfare reforms – gives somewhat more weight to structural determinants than Murray. Increased worklessness is seen as accommodating changes in the labour market and society that serve, in turn, to socially exclude people.

Labour's deployment of the term 'social exclusion' is complex, not to say confusing. Sometimes it is applied to geographical areas:

> ... particular communities have been hit by multiple disadvantages, such as unemployment, poor skills, low income, low-grade housing, high crime, bad health and family breakdown. We call this social exclusion because linked problems effectively shut people and areas out from participation in normal working and social life and access to public services that work. (DSS, 1998a, p 63)

On other occasions, as illustrated by the work of the Social Exclusion Unit, the focus is on marginalised groups such as school dropouts, teenage mothers, and people sleeping rough. The connecting explanatory motif is the existence of multiple deprivation and, in the absence of integrated planning and community commitment, the failure of multiple agencies effectively to work together to tackle causes rather than symptoms of social exclusion or to foster self-sufficiency. In such scenarios, large benefit caseloads are interpreted to be partly a product of the failure of other government policies.

The policy response currently being pursued is to increase the extent of 'joined-up' policy thinking and working across government departments. Improving education is seen as a means of enhancing the individual security and mobility that offers protection against poverty and social exclusion, while reducing social exclusion is considered to be essential if health inequalities are to be curtailed.

In developed welfare states, policy developments are frequently a reaction to the perceived inadequacies of the existing system as much as a direct response to prevailing and emergent social needs. In this context, the size of welfare caseloads can be interpreted as a measure of policy failure as well as a barometer of expressed need. Understanding why caseloads have reached the level that they have and the reasons for the direction of their movement is vital information in generating an appropriate policy response.

Guiding understanding

Reflecting the political debate that has surrounded social security and social assistance provision in Britain, the above discussion has emphasised the attitudinal and behavioural factors that may help to explain the growth in benefit receipt that has occurred over the last 30 years. However, most commentators would accept that other factors have played a part and may in, some cases, have been more important. In reviewing the evidence, it is important not to give undue weight to one set of factors over another. To achieve this a simple, heuristic model is employed to explore the interplay of different factors driving the increased caseloads (Figure 1.3).

Figure 1.3: Understanding the growth in the number of welfare recipients

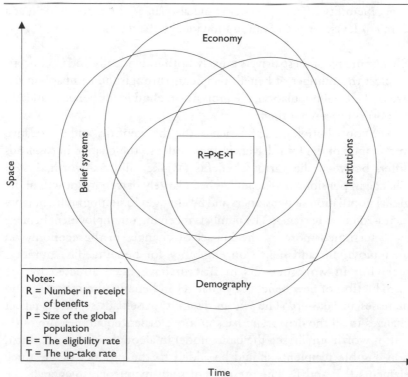

Economy

Space

Belief systems

$$R=P \times E \times T$$

Institutions

Notes:
R = Number in receipt
of benefits
P = Size of the global
population
E = The eligibility rate
T = The up-take rate

Demography

Time

The model recognises that the number of people in receipt of benefit (R) at a particular time is dependent on three entities:

- the number of people potentially eligible for benefit (the global population, P)
- the proportion of people eligible for benefit (the eligibility rate, E)
- the proportion of eligible people who receive benefit (the rate of up-take, T)

$$R = P \times E \times T$$

The three entities are in turn determined by an almost infinite set of influences. For reasons of simplicity, these influences are selected and grouped into four sub-sets that are termed 'drivers':

- the economy: especially factors influencing labour demand;
- demography;
- institutions that characterise the benefit system, notably those involved in the design and implementation of policy;
- belief systems that at the democratic level help to determine the acceptability of benefit systems and also shape them and which, at a micro level, serve to fashion individual behaviour.

Change in any of these drivers is likely, both individually and in concert, to affect the number of benefit recipients through their impact on the size of the total population, the proportion eligible for benefits, and the proportion receiving them.

The contribution made by each of the three entities and the relative importance of the four drivers in the model to the change in caseloads differs between the various benefits (Walker and Ashworth, 1998). Change in pensioner caseloads has been largely driven by growth in the global population of pensioners and by changes in demography, notably increased life expectancy. The numbers receiving unemployment benefits are determined more by the impact of changes in the economy on unemployment and hence on eligibility for benefit. The numbers receiving in-work benefits in Britain have been affected by the introduction of new benefits, by changes in benefit administration and increases in take-up. The rise in disability caseloads seems to reflect changes in all the drivers, perhaps in more or less equal measure.

It is worth amplifying the basic model in a couple of respects. First, non-eligible recipients should be added to the product of the three elements P, E and T. The presence of such recipients is generally the result of errors or fraud on the part of administrators and claimants. However, in certain cases such claimants are perfectly legitimate, as when a benefit is payable for a fixed period irrespective of changes in circumstances. In such a situation people will retain benefit even though they might no longer be eligible on the basis of their current characteristics. (In Britain this was the case for Family Credit [FC], an in-work means-tested benefit payable to families with dependant children that existed between 1988 and 1999.) This phenomenon of 'benefit drag' impinges on the apparently straightforward task of defining eligibility for benefit and benefit take-up (Walker, 1980).

Second, it is important to recognise that the above processes operate over time and space. The temporal dynamic is very important. The population at one point in time is a function of the number of births and deaths and net migration in a previous period. Likewise, the change in the number of people eligible for benefit over a given period is determined by the difference between the numbers who become eligible and those who cease to be eligible during that period. Moreover, the characteristics that govern people's current eligibility for benefit are much influenced by their past experiences and decisions. Change in the number of recipients in any period is therefore determined by the change in the population, the change in the eligibility and take-up rates, and the change in the number of non-eligible claimants.

Another way to think about change in the number of recipients is to focus on the dynamics of benefits (see Walker and Ashworth, 1994; Leisering and Walker, 1998). The rise or fall in recipient numbers is a function of changes in flows on and off benefit, the latter being a consequence of the time that people spend on benefit. In Britain, information on these elements is only gradually becoming available, as policy moves from being essentially passive, simply paying out benefit to those people who are eligible, to proactive, aimed to influence claimant attitudes and behaviour in ways that affect the number receiving benefit. (Indeed, a new variant of the old 'chicken and egg' dilemma is to consider whether policy objectives in Britain have changed in response to this new information, or whether new information is being collected in the light of new policy objectives.) The drivers identified above can affect flows on and off benefit in different ways under varying circumstances.

Some account needs also to be taken of spatial processes. The economy can no longer be defined by the boundaries of a nation state. Influences on domestic labour demand are global. Equally there may be regional and local variations in the demand for benefits. Certainly labour demand varies spatially within nation states and there is evidence of cultural differences in the consumption of social security provisions that differ between different geographical areas (Walker and Huby, 1989; Huby and Walker, 1989).

For ease of exposition, housing policy is taken to be an additional driver located within the 'institutions domain'. In Britain, changes in housing policy, notably the shift in the subsidy system, from one based on subsidising the cost of construction ('bricks and mortar' subsidies) to one based on individual financial need, has had a notable impact on the expenditure on welfare benefits and some effect on recipient numbers.

The strategy

The remainder of this volume is devoted to trying better to understand why large and increasing numbers of people in Britain need to claim cash benefits. The explanation is sometimes complex and so the book is organised to guide readers through the various arguments and to enable them easily to make use of the material for different purposes.

Chapter 2 introduces the reader to the British social security system and provides a brief overview of recent economic and demographic developments. Thereafter the book is divided into four substantive parts, each devoted to one of four groups of benefit recipients: unemployed people; disabled people; families and children; and retirement pensioners. Obviously there is some overlap between these groups but for many years the British policy debate has been couched in terms of the benefits received by these groups, which means that appropriate statistical data are available. The final part of the book presents an overview of the findings and compares and contrasts the factors responsible for the growth in the size of the four claimant groups.

Each of the four substantive parts of the book contains six chapters, beginning with a chapter that summarises trends in claimant numbers and ending with one that provides a summary of findings. The remaining chapters cover the four drivers, the economy, demography, institutions and beliefs. The order of the central four chapters varies according to the relative importance of the four drivers in explaining growth in claimant numbers.

Therefore the reader who wants a reasoned account of the overall increase in claimant numbers might begin with the final chapter (Chapter 27). Someone interested in the unemployed might turn to Part 2. To get an overview of trends they should read the first chapter in Part 2 (Chapter 3) while the last (Chapter 8) provides a synoptic overview of factors driving the rise and fall in claimant caseloads. The detail is presented in Chapters 4 to 7.

The period covered by the analysis commences in 1971 and ends in 1999, although the most recent information sometimes applies only to 1998. Reflecting the jurisdiction of the Department of Social Security (DSS), from which most official data emanate, statistics apply to Great Britain (that is England, Scotland and Wales), unless otherwise indicated. Two generic terms, 'cash benefits' and 'social security', are used interchangeably to refer to the benefit system as a whole.

TWO

Taking an overview

Summary

The British economy has altered radically in the last three decades. While international trade in goods still exceeds that in services, employment in manufacturing has halved to just 15% of the total.

After eight years of economic growth, *unemployment has fallen back markedly from the historic highs experienced in the early 1990s.* Male employment remains at comparatively low levels, part-time employment has risen to 25% of the total and women now account for 45% of the workforce.

There is an increased financial premium on education and a polarisation in wage levels and between employment-rich households, with more than one worker, *and employment-poor households,* with none.

Population growth has been sluggish for 30 years but demands on the social security system have been increased by growth in the retired population, an almost threefold rise in the number of lone parents and a growing recognition of the needs of disabled people.

Spending on cash benefits has more than doubled in real terms since the early 1970s and now accounts for 30% of total public expenditure. Coverage is comprehensive and nationally uniform and comprises a mix of insurance, means-tested and other non-contributory schemes. Retirement pension is the most expensive element, accounting for 37% of the total, but means-tested schemes, which together absorb 32% of total expenditure, are more important than in continental Europe.

> *Public support for the cash benefit system remains strong* but, echoing political rhetoric, there is also concern about its possible disincentive effects and the existence of fraud. Benefit recipients themselves report financial hardship and a sense of shame associated with being a claimant.
>
> *A degree of consensus that employment is the principal defence against poverty has replaced outright ideological hostility towards the benefit system,* evident among some politicians during the 1980s. Policies are currently being 'modernised' and made proactive so as to promote work for those who can and support for those who cannot.

The simple model introduced in the last chapter groups the myriad influences driving social security and social assistance caseloads into four: those relating to the economy, demography, institutions, and beliefs. The intention in this chapter is to provide an initial account of these four sets of drivers as they apply in Britain, leaving it to later chapters to explore how they might interact to explain the growth in the number of benefit recipients. As a byproduct the reader is offered an introductory overview of the British economy and system of cash benefits.

The British economy

Britain is a medium-sized, advanced, trading, economy. Ranked fifth among OECD (Organisation of Economic Co-operation and Development) countries in terms of the size of its economy (as indicated by Gross Domestic Product, GDP), its population is the 14th most prosperous within the OECD and is placed 23rd in the world as measured by per capita GDP (OECD, 1999; Walton, 2000).

Manufacturing generates about 18% of the country's GDP. By 1990 it had been overtaken by financial intermediation which, in 1997, accounted for 23% of the total value of the economy. In the same year, transportation contributed 8% to GDP and construction 5%. Services, defined to include both the public and private sectors, together with financial intermediation noted above, accounted for almost exactly 50% of the total economy. Wholesale and retailing added another 13%, while, in contrast, agriculture contributed little more than 1% to the total.

Turning to international trade, that in goods exceeds trade in services by a ratio of 3.2 to 1. However, whereas the balance of trade in goods is invariably negative, this tends to be offset by a positive balance of the trade in services. In 1998, the last full year for which statistics are available, imports of goods exceeded exports by £20.5 billion (12.5%), whereas the export of services exceeded imports by £12.1 billion (25%).

The UK is now in its eighth year of economic recovery and continuing growth has assuaged doubts, apparent in 1998, that the economy might tip into recession. Since coming to power in 1997 the Labour government has adopted a tight fiscal policy, adopting the expenditure constraints set by the previous government while aiming for sustainable economic growth. One of the new Chancellor of the Exchequer's first moves was to make the Bank of England independent, and to give it responsibility for meeting an inflation target (largely through its control of interest rates). The government's current fiscal stance is broadly neutral and, in the view of the OECD, plans for extra spending on priority areas can be accommodated while maintaining a balanced budget and achieving a fall in the ratio of public debt to GDP (OECD, 1999).

Faced with a tightening labour market and hints that the economy might be at risk of overheating, the Bank of England began raising interest rates in September 1999 after reducing them seven times in the previous year. Exporters argue that the pound is already overvalued on the foreign exchanges and that economic conditions vary nationally such that the risk of the economy overheating is restricted to the South East. Even so, the combination of this strong and comparatively lengthy period of recovery, together with structural reform, has helped employment to rise and unemployment to fall. Seventy-four per cent of the population of working age is in employment compared with an EU average of around 60%, and the latest figures (November 1999) show total unemployment to be at 5.9%, much below the average for the European Union (Figure 2.1; ILO definition; DfEE, 2000). Unemployment defined in terms of people claiming benefit is even lower, at 4%.

However, taking the 30-year perspective that is the focus of this book, it is apparent that the current buoyant economy is not typical. Britain has experienced major recessions in the early part of each of the last three decades and every recession has brought a higher level of unemployment. Unemployment in 1994 was 360% higher than the corresponding point in the economic cycle (Evans, 1998).

Over this period there has also been a marked trend towards de-industrialisation, with the proportion of manufacturing employment falling from around one third of the total in the 1960s to about 15% today (HM Treasury, 1997). Growth on the service sector has been

`Figure 2.1: Standardised unemployment rates (1980-98)

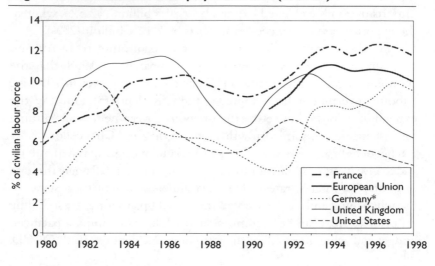

*West Germany prior to unification.
Source: OECD (1999)

strong, but employment levels in the economy as a whole have only in the last five years begun to rise above the levels of the late 1960s. Many, but by no means all, of the jobs created have been low-skilled, and part-time employment is increasing as a proportion of the total. As a consequence, whereas only 15% of the workforce was employed part-time in 1971, this figure had risen to 25% in 1999.

Even now, the employment rate for men (79%) is not much above its lowest level (75%) for 50 years: there are currently 1.5 million men aged between 25 and 49 who are not in paid work. In contrast, employment rates for women have risen and now stand at 69%. With the labour force as a whole projected to increase from 29.7 million in 1996 to over 31 million by 2001, demand for female labour is expected to continue to rise in contrast to that for men (IER, 1998; HM Treasury, 1997). Women already account for 45% of all those in employment.

The rise in the female participation rates has led to a polarisation between 'employment-rich' households, with more than one adult in paid work, and 'employment-poor' ones that contain no earner. In fact, the number of workless households more than doubled between 1979 and 1995/96 to comprise about 20% of all working-age families (DfEE, 1998). These numbers will have fallen with the decline in unemployment (and possibly as a result of new policy initiatives) although not in direct proportion. This is because the growing number of employment-poor households was partly a consequence of the rise in the number of people having no contact with the labour market. Between 1995 and 1999, the number of lone parents not in work and receiving state benefits fell from 1.05 million to 940,000, and the number of people (the majority of them men) claiming incapacity or long-term sickness benefit declined from over 1.77 million to 1.46 million.

Although unemployment was more widespread, both geographically and industrially in the 1990s recession than in earlier periods, it remained concentrated among particular 'at risk' groups, who also find more difficulty returning to work: older people, single people, those without skills or with a health problem (Trickey et al, 1998). Unemployed young people tend to obtain work more quickly than other groups, but a subset suffers long spells without work.

Within the labour market, the dispersion of wages has increased markedly and the financial return to education has risen. The highest decile for male wages rose 80% in real terms in the 20 years to 1996, while the lowest decile increased by only 12% (HM Treasury, 1997). There is a substantial 'gap' between the level of skills demanded by the economy and those possessed by people who are not currently participating in the labour market. Indeed, 20% of the adult population have poor literacy and numeracy skills. A phenomenon of a 'low pay, no pay' cycle is also evident, with comparatively unskilled people moving in and out of work (Gregg and Wadsworth, 1997a; Trickey et al, 1998).

In summary, the British economy has undergone major restructuring over the last three decades that has left a legacy with both positive and negative attributes. In recent years the labour market has certainly adjusted better to the competitive demands of the global economy than most of those in continental Europe. This has required the introduction of policies to encourage the development of a flexible labour market and a willingness to accept the consequences in terms of less stable employment and more non-standard forms of work. However, much of this change has been facilitated by the increased labour market participation of women. Men have fared less well. They face a higher risk of unemployment and levels of economic inactivity are close to an historic high. This, in turn, has implications for benefit caseloads.

Demography

Demographic influences on the number of people claiming cash benefits are inevitably complex. Between 1971 and 1998 the UK's population grew comparatively slowly, from 55.6 million to 59.2 million. The population of Great Britain (the UK less Northern Ireland), rose to a similar extent, from 54.1 million to 57.5 million over the same period. (Great Britain is the jurisdiction covered by the DSS in London and therefore the geographical unit to which almost all official statistics on cash benefits relate.) The growth was mainly due to the ageing of the population. Births fluctuated in line with the number of women of child-bearing age, but fertility was low and falling. Net migration, negative in the 1970s, became positive in the 1980s, and grew again in the 1990s. However, the annual excess of births over deaths (112,000) still exceeded net migration between 1981 and 1998 (93,000).

While there has been little change in the size of the total population, other demographic developments have increased the number of people whose circumstances place them at risk of requiring help from social security. The number of people of pensionable age has increased (Figure 2.2) and, while the number of children has fallen, changes in the nature of family life have helped increase the chances of them being poor.

Figure 2.2: Demographic changes, Great Britain (1971-99)

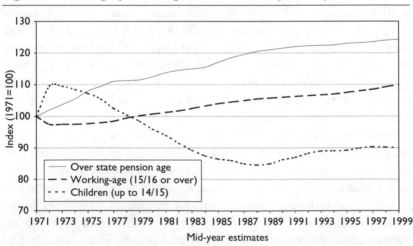

Note: School leaving age revised from 15 to 16 in 1972.
Source: DSS (2000a)

Families and children

Perhaps the most striking change has been in the nature of the family, with an increase in cohabitation – which rose between 1979-95 from

3% to 10% among women aged 18-49 – and a decline in marriage (DSS, 1997a). Divorce rates increased annually during the 1970s, although the rate of increase slowed after 1980 and has fallen slightly since 1996.

Total period fertility rates – which record the number of live children that a woman can expect to give birth to over her lifetime – have fallen (from 2.37 per woman in 1971 to 1.70 in 1998), and so has total family size (The Stationery Office, 2000a). On average each couple now has 1.7 children. Reflecting changes in the prevalence of marriage, an increasing proportion of births – currently 36%, which is more than three times the proportion 30 years ago – occur outside of marriage. Most of these births are to cohabiting couples.

The number of lone parents has grown, and the composition of the lone parent population has changed. Between 1971 and 1996 the number of lone parents rose by over one million, from 600,000 to 1.7 million and by 1998/99 they accounted for 22% of all families with children compared to just 7% in 1971 (The Stationery Office, 2000b). Most lone mothers are either separated or divorced, but increasing numbers are never-married mothers, of which a small though growing minority have never cohabited or had a steady relationship.

It is partly as a result of these changes that children now face a greater risk of experiencing poverty. (Another important factor has been the rise in unemployment.) The proportion of children living in a household without an adult worker increased threefold, from 7% in 1979 to a peak of 21% in 1994/95, falling back to about 18% in 1999. The number and proportion of children living in households with less than median income has also risen. In 1979 just over 1.5 million children (10%) fell into this category compared with 2.6 million in 1994/95 and almost 2.7 million in 1997/98 (33%) (Howarth et al, 1999).

Sick and disabled people

Estimates of the extent of disability are sensitive to the definitions used, but one large-scale survey recently indicated that one in five of the adult population (8.5 million) is disabled (Grundy et al, 1999). The number of people of working age reporting a health problem or disability has increased since the mid-1980s (Cousins et al, 1998). Whether this is due to increasing prevalence, changing attitudes towards disability, or the reporting of impairments is unclear. Nevertheless, for over a decade disabled people have been the fastest growing category of workless households. The number of men in this category has grown particularly quickly.

The level of disability increases noticeably with age. About one in ten people aged under 45 have a long-standing illness or disability. This ratio rises to around one in four for people aged between 45 and retirement age. Rates of disability are very high among the oldest age groups in the population, and the number of disabled elderly people has been increasing rapidly on account of rising longevity. Women constitute a large majority of the 'very old'.

Pensioners

The number of pensioners increased by 44% between 1971 and 1998. Declines in the size of successive birth cohorts for much of this period were more than offset by increases in longevity. While the incomes of pensioners are generally considerably less than those of people of working age, pensioners as a group have enjoyed the fastest income growth of all over the last three decades. This reflects the maturing of successive state pension schemes introduced during the course of the century, returns to the State Earnings Related Pension Scheme (SERPS) introduced in 1978, and the acquisition of private, occupational pensions which became particularly important for people whose working life began in the early 1950s (DSS, 1999c). However, the elderly population itself has aged on account of the increased longevity, exposing a larger proportion of pensioners to the risks of capital depreciation and the onset of disability and its attendant expenses.

To summarise, while changes in population size have been small, the ageing of the population, the erosion of the traditional family and the increased prevalence of disability can all be expected to have placed additional demands on the British system of cash benefits.

Institutions

As noted already in Chapter 1, Britain's system of cash benefits is quite distinctive, reflecting its origins primarily as a system of poverty relief rather than as a mechanism to facilitate social cohesion (McKay and Rowlingson, 1999). It relies more on the provision of a comprehensive, means-tested safety net and less on social insurance than most countries in continental Europe, which tend to follow Bismarck's legacy rather than that of Beveridge. Figures for the early 1990s show that, whereas means-tested benefits in Britain accounted for 31% of total social security expenditure, the corresponding figures for Germany, France and Italy were 12%, 10% and 9% respectively (Eardley et al, 1996). In 1998/99, just under 50% of expenditure was met from the National Insurance Fund (NIF), the rest from general taxation (DSS, 1999i).

By providing general assistance based on financial need, rather than categorical support related to prescribed contingencies, the British system should be better able than most to respond to rapid and unforeseen social and economic change. On the other hand, this strategy emphasises the demand-led nature of welfare expenditure and provides little scope for financial control. Figures 2.3a and b show that, while total social security expenditure rose by 127% in real terms between 1973/74 and 1998/99, expenditure on means-tested benefit, excluding those relating to housing costs, increased by 528%. Central government expenditure on means-tested housing support rose from nothing in 1972/73 to £11.1 billion in 1998/99, or 12% of the total.

The British system is also highly centralised. Most contributory, non-contributory and means-tested benefits are administered by one organisation, the Benefits Agency, which is itself an executive agency of the national DSS that has policy responsibility for all benefits. There are just two benefits – namely, Housing Benefit (HB), a means-tested payment to tenants, and Council Tax Benefit (CTB), a rebate on the local property tax – that are administered by local government, on an agency basis. In addition, since October 1999, in-work benefits for low-income families (Working Families'Tax Credit) and disabled people (Disabled Person'sTax Credit) have been delivered through the tax system and are now the policy responsibility of the Inland Revenue, the tax authority.

Benefit rates are uniform nationally and generally take no account of local conditions. The one exception is the Social Fund (SF), a system of loans and grants for people in exceptional need, which, although administered by the Benefits Agency (BA), allows for local priorities through the mechanism of devolving a budget to district offices (Walker and Lawton, 1989). Because local government has no policy control over benefit levels, social security is seldom an issue in local political elections. Again this is different from many continental European countries. In the 1970s and 1980s local authorities did provide welfare advice services on a large scale, but this is now largely the responsibility of not-for-profit organisations.

Figure 2.3a: Expenditure on contributory, non-contributory and means-tested benefits (1973/74-1997/99)

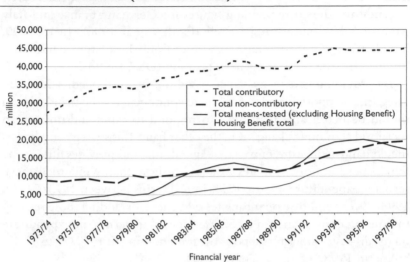

Figure 2.3b: Expenditure of contributory, non-contributory and means-tested benefits as a % of all social security spending

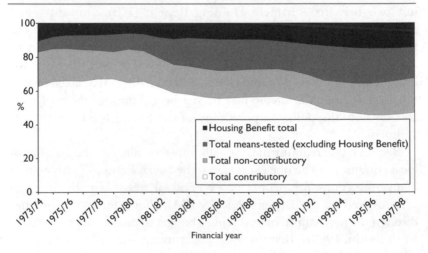

Source: Calculated from Evans (1998); DSS (2000a)

Benefit levels are not generally fixed on the basis of systematic analyses of adequacy, although they can be affected by them (as with an increase in Child Benefit announced in 1998). Most independent studies suggest that the benefit safety net does not enable benefit recipients to attain a socially acceptable minimum standard of living (Oldfield and Yu, 1993; Middleton and Thomas, 1994). Upratings tend to follow cost of living indices rather than wages growth.

Although the coverage of state social security provision is extensive, the comparatively low level of benefit has stimulated private provision in the area of retirement pensions. (Beveridge himself was keen not to squeeze out alternative forms of provision.) In 1997, 65% of pensioners had income from occupational pensions (PRG, 1998). Personal insurance-based pensions have also been heavily promoted since 1998, but very few pensioners receive significant amounts of income from this source.

Coverage

While the British benefit system is comprehensive in its coverage, it is also complex. There are around 30 different separate benefits, including 14 schemes that currently apply to disabled people, eight to elderly people, and 10 paid to families with children. The system is also in a state of perpetual development in response to changing social needs, financial constraints and ideological fashion. Table 2.1 documents its recent history.

The basic safety net is provided by Income Support (IS) and income-based Jobseeker's Allowance (JSA), which together are universally available to anybody working less than 16 hours per week on the basis of a means test[1]. People who work for 16 or more hours each week can apply for means-tested assistance to help cover their rent and local property-based tax (HB and CTB respectively), and those with children can receive Working Families' Tax Credit.

In addition to benefits available on grounds of lack of income, there is a large range of cash benefits payable to categories of claimants in particular circumstances or facing certain contingencies. For example, the basic state retirement pension is an income replacement benefit available to pensioners on the basis of their contribution record, while both contributory and non-contributory income replacement benefits are provided for disabled people. Benefits also exist to meet the additional costs of disability, maternity and child rearing, and to offer compensation in, for example, the event of industrial injury.

Table 2.1: A recent history of social security provisions in Britain

	Major changes	New benefits
Unemployed		
1980	Supplementary benefit recast to provide legal entitlement to extra need additions	
1988	Supplementary benefit replaced by:	Income Support Social Fund
1988	Income-related benefits restructured to simplify system	
1996	Unemployment Benefit replaced by:	Jobseeker's Allowance National Insurance Contribution holiday
1997/98	New Deal Welfare to Work schemes	
Sick and disabled		
1971		Attendance Allowance Invalidity Benefit
1973	Attendance Allowance extended	
1975		Invalid Care Allowance Non-Contributory Invalidity Pension
1976		Mobility Allowance
1977	Extension to Non-Contributory Invalidity Pension	Housewives Non-Contributory Pension
1983		Statutory Sick Pay
1984	Non-Contributory Invalidity Pension and Housewives Non-contributory Pension replaced by:	Severe Disablement Allowance
1986	Invalid Carers' allowance extended to married woman	
1992		Disability Living Allowance and Disability Working Allowance
1995	Sickness and Invalidity Benefits replaced by:	Incapacity Benefit
1999	Disability Working Allowance replaced by:	Disabled Person's Tax Credit

Table 2.1 cont.../

Pensioners

1978		Earnings-related retirement, widows' and invalidity pensions (SERPS)
1980	Supplementary Benefit and pensions recast to provide legal entitlement to extra need additions	
1988	Supplementary pensions replaced by:	Income Support
1988	Personal pensions introduced with state contribution	
1989	Pensions paid at pensionable age irrespective of working	
1995	State pension age equalised	

Families and children

1971		Family Income Supplement
1976		One Parent Benefit
1979	Family Allowance replaced by:	Child Benefit
1987		Statutory Maternity Pay
1988	Family Income Supplement replaced by:	Family Credit
1993		Child Support
1996		Back to Work Bonus
1997		Child Maintenance Bonus

Housing cost benefits

1973/74	National scheme of Rent Rebates and Rent Allowances for all in and out of work	
1974/75	Rate Rebate remodelled on Rent Rebates	
1982/83	Rent Rebates and Rent Allowances replaced by:	Housing Benefit
1989	Rate Rebates replaced by:	Community Charge Benefit
1993	Community Charge Benefit replaced by:	Council Tax Benefit

The extensive coverage of the social security system means that a large percentage of the population is likely to be receiving benefit at any given time. Almost everybody above pensionable age (65 for men and 60 for women) will be in receipt of a state pension and/or means-tested IS[2]. Benefit is also paid on behalf of every child under the age of 16 and to young people between the ages of 16 and 18 who remain in full-time education. In 1998, 17% of people of working age were also receiving benefit in their own right or as a dependant.

As would be expected, the proportion of people in receipt of benefit varies geographically according to local economic conditions and demographic factors (Figure 2.4). In the more buoyant South East and East of England, between 11% and 12% of people of working age themselves receive benefits, but this figure rises to 21% in Scotland, to 22% in the North East of England and to 24% in the North West and in Wales (DSS, 1999c). It follows from these regional variations in the prevalence of benefit receipt, that the social security system not only helps to meet individual needs and provides a corrective to the unequal distribution of primary income, it also provides a partial antidote to regional economic imbalances (Walker and Huby, 1989).

Expenditure

A total of £95.6 billion was spent on cash benefits in the financial year 1998/99. This represents about 30% of all public expenditure and 11.2% of GDP (Figure 2.5). Although this sum is large, expenditure is currently on a downward trend: spending in 1993/94 was equal to 12.7% of GDP. Moreover, this level of expenditure is modest in comparison with that of several countries in continental Europe, even allowing for the fact that Britain's economy is at a more buoyant phase in the economic cycle (Figure 2.6).

Figure 2.4: Proportion of working-age population receiving cash benefits, Government Office for the Regions (1998)

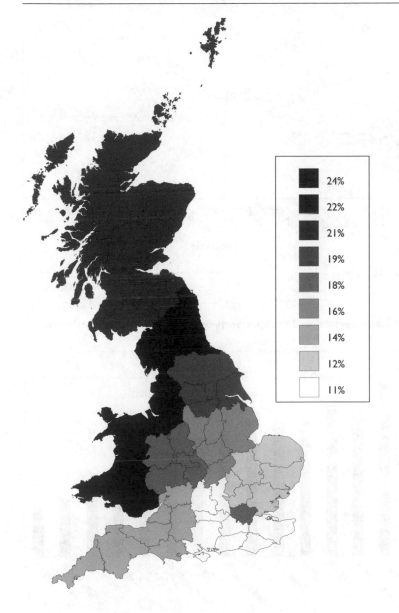

■	24%
■	22%
■	21%
■	19%
■	18%
■	16%
■	14%
■	12%
□	11%

Source: DSS (1999c)

Figure 2.5: Benefit expenditure as a % of GDP (1948/49-1996/99)

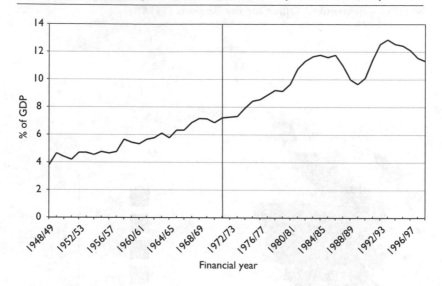

Source: DSS (2000a)

Figure 2.6: International comparisons of social security expenditure (1995)

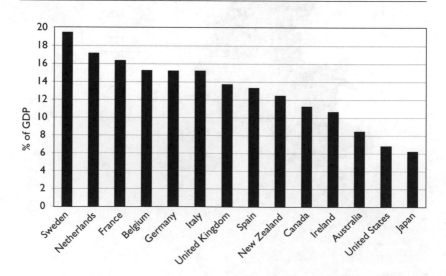

Source: DSS (2000a)

Around two thirds of the rise in real expenditure on cash benefits since 1948 (that is, after taking account of inflation) has occurred since 1971. Annual real growth averaged 4.9% in the 1970s, 3% in the 1980s and 5% in the 1990s until 1996/97. The growth in the 1970s was partly attributable to the downturn in the economy associated with the 1972 hike in oil prices and subsequent high levels of inflation. However, it was also caused by the introduction of new benefits, such as those to cover rent and property taxes and those for disabled people and low-paid workers with child dependants (Table 2.1). Rising unemployment was accompanied by some slackening in the enforcement of the actively seeking work obligations (benefit and employment services were separated and not reunited until the introduction of JSA in 1996).

Under the Thatcher governments of the 1980s, the growth in expenditure was severely constrained. Upward pressures on costs triggered by the deepening recession in the early years of the decade were partly offset by tightening eligibility criteria and reducing the value of some benefits. By the end of the decade tacit encouragement given to the unemployed to leave the labour force in order to claim Incapacity Benefits had ceased, at least at national level.

The upturn in the rate of growth of benefit expenditure in the first half of the 1990s was again triggered by recession. However, it was exacerbated by changes in housing policy that increased rents and expenditure on HB. Also, the introduction of the Disability Living Allowance precipitated an unexpectedly large increase in spending on disabled people. Overall spending subsequently fell by 1% in real terms between 1996/97 and 1998/99, led by the decline in unemployment. The fall was assisted by the maturation of policies that had triggered increases early in the decade and perhaps by the implementation of policies, such as the introduction of JSA in 1996 and the New Deal Welfare to Work programmes provided by the 1997 Labour government. (The latter link advice, training and employment experience to benefit receipt for people of working age – DSS, 1998a.) However, expenditure is projected to begin increasing again, rising by 5.3% by 2001/02. This is the result of extra help being given to families with children (as part of the commitment to end child poverty by 2019), as well as low-income pensioners (Walker, 1999a; DSS, 1999i, DSS, 2000a).

Despite the existence of large numbers of benefits, over three quarters of the total expenditure is accounted for by just five: Retirement Pension (37%); Income Support (12%); Housing Benefit (12%); Child Benefit (8%); and Incapacity Benefit (8%). While the precise balance between these benefits is clearly affected by the prevailing state of the economy, people over retirement age always receive the largest portion of expenditure. In 1998/99, 46% of total spending was accounted for by payments to elderly people above retirement age (Figure 2.7). Younger people with a long-term illness or disability accounted for 24%, while spending specifically directed to families and children made up another 19% of the total. Benefits to unemployed people absorbed just 6% of total social security expenditure.

Figure 2.7: Distribution of benefit expenditure, by type of beneficiary, Great Britain (1998/99)

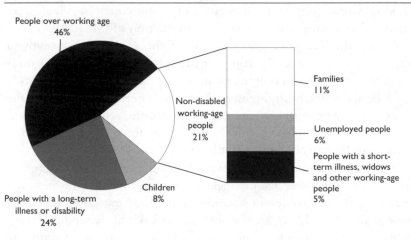

Note: Percentages may not add up to 100% due to rounding.

Since 1978/79, the earliest date for which figures are available, the strong growth in expenditures on elderly people – caused by predominately demographic factors – has been exceeded by rising spending on disabled people. The latter has been due in part to the greater recognition accorded to the costs of disability in the form of new benefits and reflected in higher uptake (Figure 2.8).

Belief systems

While the legacy of Beveridge still permeates the British benefit system, it has never fully reflected his aspirations for a comprehensive social insurance system complemented by supplementary provision provided by mutual organisations and only residual means testing.

Moreover, it is important, of course, to acknowledge the diversity of beliefs among policy makers and the public and to recognise that they change over time. In this brief synopsis a distinction is made between the ideas informing the language of policy discourse in Britain, the views of the 'general public' as revealed by opinion polling, and the attitudes and perspectives of claimants.

Figure 2.8: Trends in benefit spending by type of beneficiary (1978/79-1998/99)

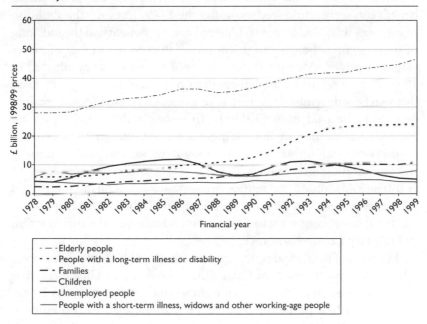

Source: DSS (2000a)

Welfare ideologies

For the first 25 years of postwar history, the perspectives of policy makers were strongly influenced by the Beveridge legacy and the ideas of Titmuss. The latter emphasised, among much else, the role of altruism in the modern welfare state, the aspiration for greater equality, the importance of social rights and the expansion of welfare to address new social needs and injustices created by the economy and changes in social values. However, the expansion of provision in the 1970s, which involved the creation of more means-tested and non-contributory benefits, further eroded the pre-eminent role that Beveridge had foreseen for universal social insurance as opposed to selective provision. It was further accompanied by the growth of an active welfare rights lobby, partly a reaction to the low take-up of benefit associated with means testing, and also the emergence of an emphasis on claimants' right to benefit.

With the election of the Thatcher government in 1979, the rhetoric changed to one of retrenchment. Margaret Thatcher had a profound distaste for a welfare state dominated by government, which she believed eroded individual responsibility, and a commitment to reduce public expenditure so as to cut taxation and free up private enterprise. Some benefit cuts were introduced soon after the 1979 election – the abolition of earnings-related additions to Unemployment Benefit and the indexing of social security benefits to prices rather than to the higher of either wages or prices. A major review of social security was conducted in 1984/85 leading to the implementation of substantial changes in 1988 that significantly reduced future state retirement provision (down-grading benefits to be paid from SERPS). In response to continuing rising expenditure, further ad hoc changes were introduced by successive Conservative administrations that sought in various ways, often by tightening eligibility criteria and increasing anti-fraud measures, to constrain expenditure and reduce benefit caseloads. During this period local government spending on welfare rights also fell. An exception to the trend of seeking ways to reduce expenditure was the introduction of Disability Living Allowance.

The ideas of the radical right, especially those of US thinkers including Charles Murray, Larry Mead and others discussed in Chapter 1, first became influential in British policy circles in the late 1980s and 1990s. They were often promoted by US foundations such as the Hudson Institute (Walker, 1998a, 1999a). As already noted, the concept of benefit dependency was first used by a British minister in 1987 and a debate about the emergence and consequences of an underclass linked with benefit use became apparent around the same time.

A political consensus also began to develop in the early to mid-1990s around three premises: that social security had to be adapted to meet the needs of a flexible labour market; that employment provided the best defence against poverty; and that social security policies should be active rather than passive. The conditionality inherent in benefit receipt was made explicit by the replacement of Unemployment Benefit with the introduction of JSA. The bureaucratic language changed symbolically so that an unemployed claimant was now called a 'jobseeker' and benefit receipt was made conditional on jobseekers signing a Jobseeker's Agreement. Piloting of workfare-like schemes was also commenced.

The new Labour government led by Tony Blair has carried forward the same emphasis on employment and personal responsibility, but changed the symbolism of language yet again. It is now engaged on a campaign to 'modernise' welfare and to make it 'proactive' rather than 'passive', thereby making it part of the solution to poverty and social exclusion rather than part of the problem. Through a series of welfare to work schemes (New Deal), the introduction of a minimum wage and benefit reforms (Chapter 1), Labour aims 'to make work pay', to offer 'work to those who can and security to those who can't', and to promote partnerships in the delivery of welfare. In March 1999, Blair added the objective of eradicating child poverty within 20 years (Blair, 1999).

While the political consensus on welfare reform remains largely intact and Labour's broad approach, the so-called 'third way' (Giddens, 1998), continues to attract support, there are grass-root concerns that Labour has not moved quickly enough or even in the right direction (Coddington and Perryman, 1998; Richards, 2000). Moreover, throughout the last 30 years there have been commentators advocating 'a return to Beveridge', with a greater attachment to social insurance and universality and reduced reliance on selectivity (Atkinson, 1970; Judge, 1980; Commission on Social Justice, 1994). Their voices are still heard (Field, 1996a, 1996b; Deacon, 1999; Lister, 1999).

Public attitudes

During this 30-year period of extensive policy change, public support for social security waxed and waned although perhaps not quite to an extent comparable with the changes in political rhetoric (Bryson, 1997; Taylor-Gooby, 1998; Williams et al, 1999). Support for welfare spending, even at the expense of higher taxation has, if anything, increased since the early 1980s and there is persistent support for reducing the income gap between rich and poor (Table 2.2). Negative attitudes towards unemployment have tended to lessen, although they may have increased recently with falling unemployment (Bryson, 1997; Golding, 1998). Support for social insurance, although not well informed and based more on individual self-interest than social solidarity, is strong, if not as high as in mainland Europe (Taylor Gooby, 1997; Stafford, 1998). However, opinion polls reveal more enthusiasm for expenditure on health and education than on social security, a factor which Labour took account of in framing its pre-election strategy (Anderson and Mann, 1997).

Public opinion is sensitive to the possible behavioural effects of welfare benefits that have so exercised the ideologues, and is also concerned about the possibility of fraud. In 1998, 50% of the public felt that the welfare state made people less willing to look after themselves, 47% said that benefits for the unemployed were too high and discouraged people from working, and 80% believed that large numbers of people falsely claimed benefits. Overall, therefore, Hills and Lelkes (1999) conclude that there is public support for many of the policies that the Labour government has introduced which promote greater social justice while insisting on the exercise of personal responsibility. This is not altogether surprising since the development of Labour's policies has been much influenced by the results of polling. However, it remains to be seen whether the marked shift in public attitudes evident in Table 2.2 between 1996 and 1998 is a statistical aberration, the consequence of a buoyant economy and a declining risk of unemployment, or the reinforcement of attitudes by the rhetoric used by new Labour.

Benefit recipients

The perspectives of benefit recipients are not necessarily at one with those of the general public. Until 1998, however, a large proportion of the public accepted that benefit levels were low and caused hardship, the complaint of large numbers of claimants who report foregoing basic essentials and being forced into indebtedness (Kempson, 1996). There is also evidence that the margin for financial error in budgeting is so small that families seek to avoid risk which, in some cases, may cause them to remain on benefit rather than gamble with a job (McKay et al, 1997). Families with children appear to suffer most deprivation and in response the Labour government has increased some benefits payable in respect of children.

Attitudes to the receipt of benefit vary between different groups of claimants and possibly between different categories of benefit. Pensioners are more satisfied with the level of benefits than are younger people, but tend to find the system more intrusive and stigmatising and value such confidentiality as the administration can offer. Claimants of means-tested and unemployment-related benefit also emphasise feelings of worthlessness and futility that accompany the receipt of benefit and the loss of social status that it confers. These factors have been associated with the comparatively low take-up of means-tested benefits (Oorschot, 1991).

Table 2.2: Public attitudes towards welfare benefits and benefits recipients (1983-98) (%)

	1983	1984	1987	1989	1990	1991	1993	1994	1995	1996	1998
Social welfare											
Wanting 'increased taxes and spending on health, education and social benefits'	32		50			65			61		63
Agreeing that 'the welfare state makes people nowadays less willing to look after themselves'			52	39		33	41	44	47	44	50
Saying 'when thinking of income levels generally in Britain today, the gap between those with high incomes and those with low incomes is too large	72	75	79	90	81	80	85	85	87		80
Benefits for the unemployed											
Agreeing that 'benefits for the unemployed are too low and cause hardship'		49	51		50		55			48	29
Agreeing that 'benefits for the unemployed are too high and discourage them from working		28	29		29		24			32	47
Unemployed benefit recipients											
Agreeing that 'around here, most unemployed people could find a job if they wanted one'			41	52		38	27	32	38	39	54
Fraud											
Agreeing that 'most people on the dole are fiddling in one way or another'			32	33		28	31	34	33	35	39
Agreeing that 'large numbers falsely claim benefits these days'	65			65							80
Take-up											
Agreeing that 'large numbers of people who are eligible for benefits these days fail to claim them'											79

Source: Hills and Lelkes (1999)

There have been significant improvements in the delivery of benefits in the 1990s that are reflected in increasing levels of consumer satisfaction. Even so, significant minorities of claimants complain about the quality of service, the complexity of the benefit system – a factor that has been associated with the low take-up of certain benefits – the duplication in making claims and the general hassle involved in moving on and off benefit. Indeed, claimants have identified hassle as a factor that might actually inhibit movement off benefit (Shaw et al, 1996b).

Finally, recent research has indicated that unemployed claimants recognise the obligations inherent in the receipt of benefit: the requirement to be available for work, to seek it actively and to abide by the terms of their Jobseeker's Agreement (McKay et al, 1999). There is also evidence that the vast majority of claimants to actively seek work as required to do, and continue to do so over long periods. Rather than learning to be dependant on benefit, the people with the least skills, education and experience remain on benefit for longer periods because of the barriers that confront them in finding work (Shaw et al, 1996b; McKay et al, 1997, 1999).

main body

Post script

The substance of the four 'drivers', the economy, demography, institutions and belief systems, introduced in the heuristic model presented in Chapter 1 has been sketched out in the context of Britain in the three decades from 1971. Armed with this brief description of Britain's economy and the structure of its cash benefit system, together with an appreciation of recent demographic trends and the values that serve to mediate claims on the public purse, it is time to investigate the reasons for the rise in claimant caseloads.

Notes

[1] Eligibility for benefit is conditional on an habitual residency requirement and, since November 1999, asylum seekers are only eligible for a package of £10 in cash and vouchers worth 90% of IS.

[2] A small number will defer pension receipt for up to five years.

Part 2
Benefits for unemployed people

THREE

Trends in claimant unemployment

Summary

Unemployment in 1999 was higher than in 1971 despite eight years of economic growth. Claimant unemployment fell to 1.14 million (4%) in 1999 compared with 690,000 (3.3%) in 1971.

Fluctuations in economic conditions and secular changes in the labour force are the main explanations for rising unemployment caseloads, but demographic changes have occasionally exacerbated upward trends.

A key debating issue is the relative importance of individual behaviour and work disincentives created by the benefit system itself in explaining the trends in benefit receipt. The various possibilities are examined in Chapters 4 through to Chapter 8.

The trends

Despite eight years of uninterrupted economic growth, the rate of unemployment in December 1999, as measured by the number of people registering and claiming benefit, was higher than it had been in January 1971 (Figure 3.1). Moreover, the comparison – 3.3% in 1971 and 4.0% in 1999 – is hardly fair, since the earlier figure includes many people (for example, people aged under 18 and men aged over 60) who are no longer considered to be part of the labour market. Furthermore, at the turn of 1971, unemployment had been rising steadily for 18 months from a low point of 498,600 in June 1969, and had reached 690,000. In December 1999, unemployment had fallen to 1.14 million, from a high of 2.96 million in 1993.

Virtually all the changes that have been made in the method of counting unemployment since 1971 have reduced the year-on-year count

Figure 3.1a: Claimant unemployment (1971-99)

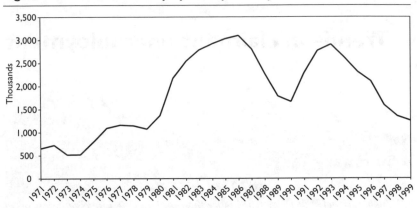

Figure 3.1b: Claimant and ILO unemployment rate (1971-99)

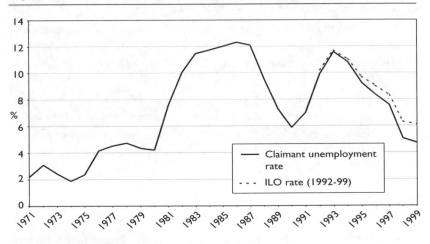

Source: DfEE (2000) and earlier years

of unemployment. This means that the official series presented in Figure 3.1a, while accurate as a record of the number of people claiming benefit on account of unemployment, does not truly compare like with like. For this reason, the new Labour government has begun to make more use of the unemployment measure deployed by the International Labour Organisation (ILO). This is based, not on a count of people receiving unemployment-related benefit, but on the reports of respondents to the Labour Force Survey as to whether they consider themselves to be unemployed and seeking work. As is apparent from Figure 3.1b, the

ILO measure reveals higher levels of unemployment than are indicated by the unemployment count.

Between the relatively low levels of unemployment recorded in 1971 and 1999, claimant unemployment rose to an unprecedented postwar peak of 12% in 1986, and reached a secondary high of 11% in 1993, but never fell below the 1971 value. Moreover, the troughs in unemployment associated with high points in the economic cycle increased from 515,000 in 1973 to 1.07 million in 1979, and to 1.66 in 1990, a trend that has only been reversed since 1997.

Figure 3.2 records the number of people claiming benefits specifically on the grounds of unemployment for the period 1971 to 1999. Unfortunately, it is not possible to plot the total number of people receiving financial support from the government on account of unemployment, since claimants can receive a number of benefits simultaneously in addition to, or occasionally instead of, specific unemployment benefits. It is known that Housing Benefit (HB) was received by 494,000 people in 1998 who also received unemployment-related benefits, and by 489,000 people of working age who were neither disabled nor lone parents and who therefore might have also been unemployed. Council Tax Benefit (CTB) was received by similar numbers of working-age claimants.

Figure 3.2: Unemployment Benefit and Income Support recipients

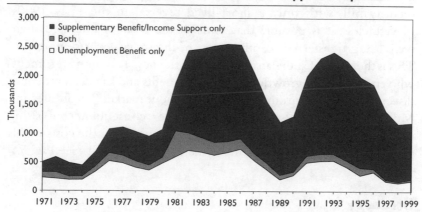

Source: DSS (1999c) and earlier years

As would be expected, the numbers claiming the two kinds of unemployment, specific benefits included in Figure 3.2 track the pattern of unemployment, although with varying sensitivity. Until September

1996, when contributory Unemployment Benefit was merged with means-tested Income Support (IS) to create Jobseeker's Allowance (JSA), it was payable for one year on the basis of a person's National Insurance contributions. Reflecting the short-term nature of Unemployment Benefit, the caseload followed the rise and fall of unemployment closely, but did not increase in a sustained way because long-term unemployed claimants did not accumulate in the system. Instead, long-term unemployed people claimed IS which was paid indefinitely while a person remained without work. Consequently, the Income Support (or Supplementary Benefit as it was called prior to 1988) caseload increased six-fold from 273,000 in 1971 to 1.88 million in 1993, falling back to 1.42 million by 1996. Over this entire period, the proportion of unemployed people receiving means-tested benefit rose from 54% to 82%. Unemployment fell noticeably after the introduction of JSA, a phenomenon that is discussed later in Chapter 6.

Rising unemployment caused a significant rise in social security spending on unemployed people – it increased by 161% between 1979 and 1982, and only began falling in 1989 (Figure 3.3). Since the level of benefit payable to individual claimants rose by only 3% in real terms over this period, the growth in expenditure was almost entirely driven by the increase in the claimant count. Real expenditure rose again after 1991, reaching a peak in the financial year 1995/96, but spending on unemployed people continued to fall as a proportion of the total social security bill, with only a short-lived reversal in the early 1990s. Nevertheless, it is possible that some of the costs of unemployment were being transferred to other parts of the social security portfolio. This is the view of some analysts close to the new Labour government, who emphasise the growth in disability benefits and the detachment of discouraged workers from the legitimate labour market (Leadbeater and Mulgan, 1997; see also Part 3). (Another consequence of rising unemployment was an increase in early retirement, but the costs of this were largely met through unemployment-related benefits; see Part 5.)

Strategy

The challenge in the remainder of this section is to begin to understand the reasons for the fluctuations in the number of people receiving unemployment-related benefits, and especially the sustained increase. The obvious starting point is developments in the economy, the changing nature of the labour market and the impact of cyclical variations in

Figure 3.3: Expenditure on state benefits for unemployed people

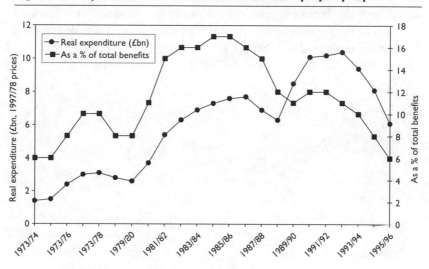

Note: Benefits for unemployed people include: Unemployment Benefit, Income Support (formerly Supplementary Benefit) and Housing Benefit.

Source: Barr and Coulter (1991); Evans (1998)

aggregate demand. These are discussed first, in Chapter 4, since they constitute the principal drivers. However, at times during the last 30 years demographic change, considered in Chapter 5, was not benign but exacerbated already difficult economic conditions.

Institutional factors were also important in the British context, as is revealed in Chapter 6. For the most part policy was reactive, and often developed rapidly in an attempt to curtail the actual or apparent growth in caseloads. However, it is also necessary to consider government training and labour market measures, which have changed in number, scope and purpose over this period and, within the social security sphere, the development of in-work benefits to compensate for low wages and to sustain work incentives.

This last point touches on the fourth of the drivers introduced in Chapter 1: beliefs and their manifestation in behaviour. Much of the political concern about benefit caseloads, and especially about the possibility that the benefit system was distorting behaviour and promoting benefit dependency, was aired in the context of high levels of unemployment and the increasingly evident phenomenon of long-term unemployment. Whether ideology or fact drove the political debates of the 1980s and 1990s is a moot point. Either way, evidence on the impact of individual beliefs and behaviour on benefit receipt is presented in Chapter 6. Tentative conclusions about the relative importance of the various factors driving the numbers of unemployed people claiming benefit are rehearsed in Chapter 7.

FOUR

The economy and unemployment

Summary

High inflation, triggered by the oil crises of the 1970s, led to tighter control of public spending and, with the election of the Thatcher government in 1979, an explicit belief that the control of inflation was more important than full employment. The unemployment rate rose to unprecedented levels and did not return to the levels of the early 1970s until 1999. Caseload numbers remain 65% above their 1971 level.

Rising unemployment coexisted with increasing employment over most of the 30-year period. A decline in manufacturing was more than offset by increased employment in the service sector, providing a mix of low and high paid jobs that have been increasingly of a part-time and/or short-term nature. Educational standards have risen, financial returns to qualifications have increased and wage dispersal has grown.

People who become unemployed are disproportionately male, young, poorly qualified, with little experience or with a poor work record. The same groups predominate among the stock of unemployed, although older people and members of ethnic minority groups, who find it more difficult to return to work, are also over-represented.

An increase in the average duration of unemployment was the major determinant of rising caseloads. Older workers, those with health problems, tenants (often an index of material deprivation) and people with dependant children were most at risk of long-term unemployment.

The prevalence of people experiencing repeated spells of unemployment while trapped in a 'no pay low pay' cycle may have increased.

The election-winning motif 'It's the economy, stupid', coined on behalf of President Clinton, is equally valuable in understanding Britain's increase in unemployed claimants. It is necessary to consider how the economy has changed, and how this might influence the characteristics of unemployed people and the time that they remain without work. However, it is first necessary to take account of the marked change in the approach to economic policy that has occurred over the last three decades.

Changed policy goals

Hindsight suggests that the immediate postwar pattern of full employment, interrupted by comparatively brief economic downturns, ended with the oil crises of the early 1970s. Traditional Keynsian methods of demand management appeared to lose their effectiveness. Economic policy errors in the early 1970s contributed to rapidly rising inflation which, combined with low growth, triggered 'stagflation', and the need for tough action by the incoming Labour government in 1974. An increasingly tight rein was imposed on public spending from 1976 onwards, which involved a change in financial planning from a volume to a cash basis. This meant that instead of planners deciding on, for example, the number of hospitals to build, and then determining their cost as had been the usual practice, the cash sum was to be fixed ahead of deciding the number of units to be built. Central government also took greater powers to control the spending of local government.

This tightening of fiscal and monetary planning reflected a shift in priorities, with the control of inflation, rather than the maintenance of full employment, as the prime economic goal. These changes were compounded by the election of a Conservative government, headed by Margaret Thatcher and much influenced by monetarist advisers. From the perspective of left of centre economists writing a decade or more after the event, "Britain had become the laboratory for an extraordinary experiment in economic theory" (Hutton, 1995, p 68). Faced with the second rise in oil prices, the new government set on the path of the 'Free Market'. Policies were aimed at reducing government borrowing and setting interest rates at an attractive level for savers to finance the deficit (Hutton, 1995). Full employment was rejected as a realistic goal (Meacher, 1989; Hutton, 1995) and, instead, the government explicitly chose unemployment as a means of controlling wage pressures, thereby easing inflation with a view to creating economic stability (Hutton,

1995). Economic stability became the government's prime concern (White, 1991), and employment became a secondary issue.

The outcome of the experiment was dramatic. Inflation, which had touched almost 25% in the mid-1970s, fell below 10% in 1982, and remained below this level, with a minor peak in the early 1990s (Figure 4.1). High interest rates boosted the value of the pound, stemming inflation, but imposed major constraints on Britain's exporters. Unemployment rose dramatically, not peaking until 1986, and, as noted above, has never returned to levels that existed in 1976, let alone those of the 1960s.

Figure 4.1a: UK claimant unemployment and GDP

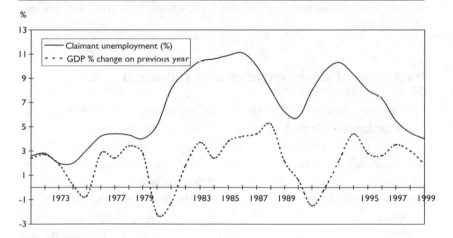

Figure 4.1b: Inflation and interest rates

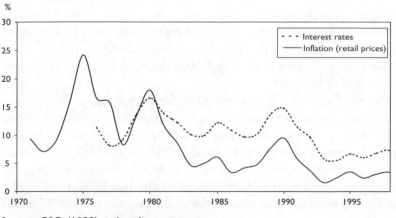

Source: CSO (1999) and earlier years

The policy focus on inflation rather than unemployment has been maintained through to, and including, the current Labour government, with its emphasis on 'prudent public finance'. The policies that were implemented in response to rising unemployment, which were multifarious and changed over time, are discussed in Chapters 6 and 7. Suffice to say here that policies adopted in the early part of the period included ones that modified the method of measuring unemployment, sought to reduce labour supply, and changed work incentives by cutting benefit levels and increasing work incomes. Latterly, policies have focused on making unemployed people more effective at seeking work, and more flexible in the work that they would accept. The new Labour government has carried forward these policies but, in addition, is seeking to offer high quality training and work experience (Bennett and Walker, 1998).

Patterns of employment and labour demand

The rise in unemployment that occurred in the early 1980s was the more or less anticipated outcome of policy. It took place, however, against a secular growth in the number of people in employment – a trend that only faltered briefly between 1990 and 1993 – and a changing pattern of world trade. The latter, in particular, was associated with a marked decline in manufacturing – the number of manufacturing jobs in Britain fell by 52% between 1971 and 1999, with the greatest rate of decline occurring between the years 1974 and 1975. Because the manufacturing industry was geographically concentrated, especially the traditional sectors of transport, machinery and chemicals, rises in unemployment in the 1980s were most marked in the North West. The recession of the early 1990s was more widespread, with high spots of unemployment occurring in parts of London and the South East. Even so, unemployment rates in the North West far exceeded those in London and the South East.

The employment that was created in this period was predominantly in the service sector and, particularly during the later 1980s and 1990s, comprised increasing numbers of part-time and temporary jobs that typify the new labour market. Total employment rose by 21% from 22.9 million in 1974, to 27.8 million in 1999, while employment in the service sector rose from 47% in 1971, to as much as 67% in 1997. The number of jobs in non-marketed services and business services increased by 71% and 40% respectively over the same period. In 1998, the service sector accounted for 70% of all employment.

A disproportionate number of the new jobs created were filled by women, who, by 1999, accounted for 47% of the employees compared with only 38% in 1971. In 1999 of the total workforce, 45% were women. A significant number of the newly created jobs were part-time, although the overall increase in the number of women in the labour market meant that between 1984 and 1999, the proportion of women in part-time work actually fell from 53% to 44%. Over the same period the proportion of men in part-time jobs increased from 7 to 11%.

More importantly, from the perspective of unemployment, significant numbers of the new jobs are thought to have been temporary. Unfortunately, official statistics series tend to improve over time and to focus on issues that are germane when the data are compiled. Hence, it is impossible to determine the proportion of jobs that were casual or short-term prior to 1992. However, even in the brief period between 1992 and 1997, the proportion of employees in temporary jobs increased from 5.9 to 7.7%. It has since fallen back a little to 7.2%, perhaps reflecting the increasingly buoyant economy and the pressures on employers to retain staff in a tightening labour market. While more women than men hold temporary jobs – 7.8% in 1999, compared with 6.5% of men – the differentials have narrowed considerably. In 1992, a woman was 45% more likely than a man to hold a temporary job, but only 20% more likely to do so in 1999 (DfEE, 2000).

The skills required by industry have also changed quite radically since the 1970s, placing a premium on some skills and making others redundant. The proportion of employees classified as skilled manual workers fell from 40% in 1971 to 33% in 1996, while the number of managers and employers increased from 15% to 21%. Because the proportion of semi-skilled and unskilled remained constant, this led to a polarisation in demand and a mismatch between demand and supply. Very high skilled and low skilled workers were in demand, but not the large group in the middle that had formerly provided the bedrock of British industry. The same trends were evident among women.

The number of people with qualifications, and the premium placed on qualifications by employers, has also increased. By 1996, 69% of people aged 16-69 (and not in full time education) had some form of qualification, compared with only 41% in 1975. Thirteen per cent had a degree and 25% some form of higher education compared with 6% and 12% respectively 21 years earlier (ONS, 1998). Changes among women were equally marked, with the quadrupling in the number acquiring degrees during this period being especially dramatic. Since qualifications have generally been acquired early in life, these developments conspired to put older people at further disadvantage in the labour market. So, in 1996, whereas 87% of people aged 20-29 had some form of qualification, this was only true of 69% of those aged 40-49 and 55% of people aged 50-59.

The impact of these developments on the employment prospects of low skilled workers is clear, and particularly marked for men. Between 1979 and 1990, employment levels fell among all groups of men, but dropped twice as fast for men with the lowest level of education as for those with even intermediate qualifications (Gregg and Wadsworth, 1996a). As an inevitable consequence of these processes, men without qualifications are disproportionately represented among the unemployed. In 1996, 29% of unemployed people had no qualifications at all, compared with 14% of those in employment (DSS, 1997b) while, at any one time, between one third and one half of unemployed male claimants will be unskilled, compared with less than a tenth of the working population.

Women fared better than men in the period up to 1990 and have continued to do so. However, the importance of education also appears to affect women's employment prospects, with employment rates rising fastest among the best educated.

These labour market changes were accompanied by a marked increase in the dispersal of wages (Figure 4.2). Real wage growth occurred throughout the wage distribution in the early 1970s, with some contraction in wage differentials happening between 1972 and 1975 (Gosling et al, 1996). Between 1975 and 1977, the effect of Labour's social contract with the trade unions was to lessen wage inequality, but thereafter median and high earnings entered a period of sustained growth, while low earnings, those in the bottom decile, stagnated. The result was that, by 1990, the dispersal in wages was greater than at any time since at least 1886.

Further analysis reveals that the return to skills and education increased over the same period. This reflects the growing demand for skills, driven by changes in productivity or product markets that was not matched by an equally rapid increase in the supply of skilled labour (Gosling et al, 1996). But it does not explain all the increase in wage dispersal that occurred. Wage inequalities increased markedly between workers with low levels of skill and education; the wages of later cohorts of young workers fell markedly in relation to earlier ones, and the growth in wage dispersal was great among young workers with limited skills. It would

Figure 4.2: Indexed male hourly earnings by percentile (1972-92)

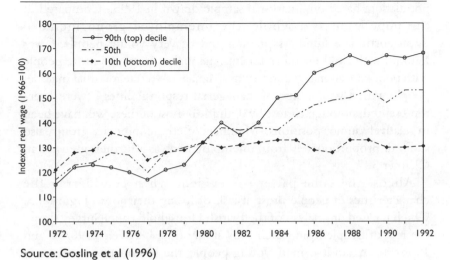

Source: Gosling et al (1996)

appear that the pattern of opportunities and constraints facing young people changed differentially with new possibilities opening for the best qualified at the same time as routes for the least academically gifted, such as traditional apprenticeships, disappeared.

The net result of all these developments has been to make the unskilled, poorly educated and inexperienced relatively more vulnerable to unemployment. The stagnation in real wages at the bottom of the labour market will also have served to erode the financial attractions of work versus benefits. But at the same time, an increasing number of low waged workers will have been denied the opportunity to acquire the assets that might have protected them from the worst financial consequences of unemployment.

Characteristics of unemployed people

The differentially changing risk of unemployment experienced over the last three decades is likely to have altered the composition of the unemployed population, which may in turn have altered the social significance of unemployment and the dynamics of the unemployed population. Unfortunately, information on the changed composition of unemployment caseloads is surprisingly limited, and this section therefore focuses on the age profile.

First, however, Table 4.1 lists characteristics of the unemployed claimant population, based on a national sample drawn in 1995. Compared to the population as a whole, the unemployed group included disproportionate numbers of men and of very young people, fewer families with children, more tenants, manual workers and more people with poor educational qualifications. Managers – a category that includes people with a wide range of managerial responsibilities – were over-represented, although almost by definition most of these will have been in relatively junior positions. Members of ethnic minority groups also suffer disproportionately from unemployment, as is further discussed in Chapter 5.

Almost the same pattern is evident when considering the characteristics of people most at risk of losing their jobs. Figure 4.3, which is based on analysis of the British Household Panel Survey, shows the risk of people losing their jobs at any time between 1990/91 and 1995/96. Again it is men, young people, the less qualified and those with limited job tenure who appear to have been most disadvantaged.

Turning to changes in the composition of the claimant population, Figure 4.4 indicates that the proportion of unemployment accounted for by both the youngest and oldest age groups has increased over time. Correspondingly, the employment rates of older workers, notably men in their fifties, have fallen, suggesting a secular trend, with successive generations each more disadvantaged than earlier ones (Campbell, 1999b). The proportion of men aged between 55 and 64 without a job doubled to about 40% between 1979 and 1997. However, with the very buoyant economy of the late 1990s, it is possible that employment rates may have stabilised and even reversed. Directly comparable data are not available, but it is known that the number of men aged 50-64 who were economically inactive fell slightly, from 31.6% to 30.7% between 1997 and 1999.

Table 4.1: Characteristics of the whole population and the unemployed population (1995) (%)

	General Household Survey (whole population)	Jobseeker's Allowance Survey (unemployed population)
Gender		
Male	49	74
Female	51	26
Age		
16-24	16	24
25-34	24	31
35-44	22	20
45-54	21	16
55+	17	9
Ethnic group		
White	93	89
Indian	2	2
Pakistani/Bangladeshi	1	3
Black	2	4
Other	2	2
Household type*		
Single person	28	37
Partner and children	24	35
Partner, no children	36	23
Lone parent	9	4
Other	3	0
Tenure		
Owner-occupier	67	37
Renting	33	63
Socio-economic group		
Professional	4	2
Managerial	15	24
Skilled non-manual	34	16
Skilled manual	21	26
Semi-skilled manual	19	22
Unskilled	6	10
Qualifications		
Higher education	22	8
A level or equivalent	11	8
GCSE grades A-C or equivalent	23	24
GCSE grades D-G or equivalent	11	12
Other	2	2
None	31	46

Note *From the Jobseeker's Allowance Survey, only heads of household are included in this figure (those living with their parents are excluded).
Source: ONS (1997) and McKay et al (1997)

Figure 4.3: Risk of unemployment

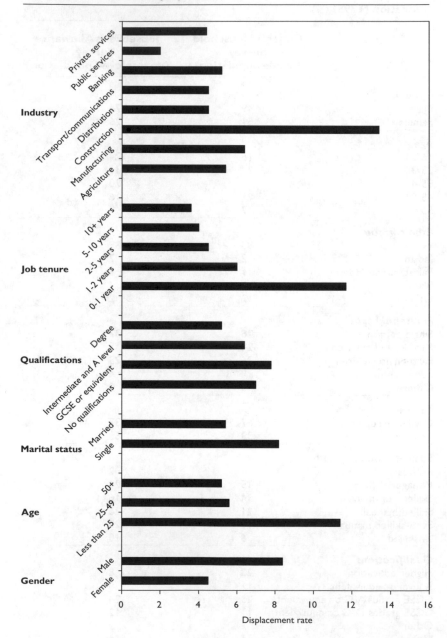

Source: Institute of Fiscal Studies

Figure 4.4: The age of unemployed claimants

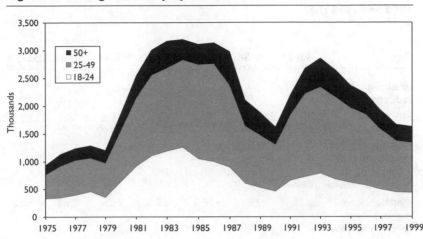

Source: ONS (2000) and earlier years

It is not easy to account for these changes. Certainly, as noted above, older workers have arguably become more disadvantaged as a group with the rising importance of qualifications. However, the risk of losing a job increased steadily with age even among the better paid (Table 4.2). It is also higher among people with an occupational pension and this raises the possibility that rising unemployment among older workers was voluntary rather than structural. However, the following facts, when taken together, suggest that this was not the case (Campbell, 1999a):

- the risk of older people losing a job between 1990 and 1996 was higher among the least well paid;
- the same risk was highest in declining industries in which older people were over-represented;
- the higher risk of displacement occurred across sectors – within the private sector, civil service, local authorities and health service – after controlling for gender, wages, pension provision and change in employment;
- the risk of losing a job increased with age;
- wage rates among older workers fell relative to prime age workers over the last 20 years;
- only about a tenth of people over 55 ever returned to work;
- the scale of the increase in joblessness among older workers was too large to be attributable solely to personal choice.

Table 4.2: Probability of people involuntarily losing their jobs between 1990 and 1996 (%)

Age	Men				Women		
	45-49	50-54	55-59	60-64	45-49	50-54	55-59
In non-declining industries							
Member of an occupational pension scheme and in the top quartile of the wage distribution	19.6	28.9	39.6	65.6	25.6	36.1	52.5
Member of an occupational pension scheme	12.1	19.3	28.2	53.6	16.6	25.2	40.2
In declining industries							
Member of an occupational pension scheme and in top quartile of the wage distribution	29.3	40.4	51.9	76.2	36.5	48.2	64.6
Member of an occupational pension scheme	19.6	28.9	39.6	65.6	25.6	36.1	52.5

Source: Campbell (1999a)

As is further discussed in Chapter 5, the deteriorating labour market position of young people can be explained partly by demographic influences. The large birth cohorts of the 1950s and early 1960s entered the labour market during the recessionary years of the 1970s and early 1980s. Furthermore, later cohorts of young people had to compete with older, more experienced people for basic entry jobs that would, in previous periods, have been the almost exclusive preserve of labour market entrants. Unemployment rates for 18-24 year olds (11.7%) in 1999 were almost three times those for people of prime working age (4.5%), and almost two-and-a-half those of people aged over 50 (4.6%) (ONS, 2000). Unemployment among 16 and 17 year olds was even greater, at 20%.

Figure 4.5a: Duration of unemployment spells to date (1975-98) (000s)

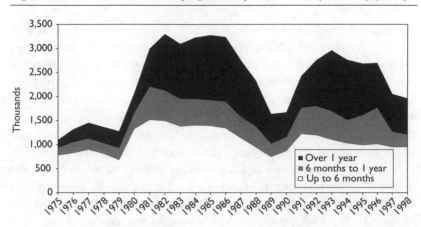

Figure 4.5b: Duration of unemployment spells to date (1975-98) (%)

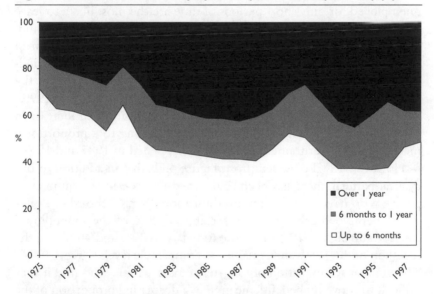

Source: ONS (1999) and earlier years

The high levels of unemployment encountered in the 1980s and 1990s will have expanded the kinds of people who experience unemployment – around 10 million people suffered a spell of poverty sometime between 1991 and 1995 (HM Treasury, 1997). However, it remains the case that the unemployed caseload comprises large numbers of people who were disadvantaged in the labour market even before becoming unemployed.

Duration of unemployment

There are a number of reasons why policy attention has increasingly come to be focused on the duration of unemployment. First, long-term unemployment is not only associated with severe deprivation but also serves as a priori evidence of the existence of welfare dependency. Second, and more important in the immediate context, it is now recognised that the size of the claimant caseload is affected more by variation in the time that it takes people to find work than by fluctuations in the number of people becoming unemployed (HM Treasury, 1997).

The proportion of unemployment that is long term has increased since 1971, although the rate of increase has fluctuated with the economic cycle (Figure 4.5a and b). A recession typically starts with a slowdown in the rate at which people find jobs, causing the average duration of unemployment to rise, rather than with a substantial increase in the number of employees losing their jobs. Since people who have been unemployed for only short periods of time are the most likely to leave benefit, they are most affected by the slackening of labour demand. This initially results in an increase in the number and proportion of claimants in official statistics who have been unemployed for short periods (ie less than six months). This was evident in 1980 and 1989, in the preludes to the corresponding recessions of the early 1980s and 1990s. The newly unemployed are also the first to benefit from an increase in labour demand, and their number falls first, leading to a proportional increase in long-term unemployment as happened in 1987 and 1997.

However, it is also evident from Figure 4.5b, that in addition to this cyclical pattern, there has been a sustained increase in the number of people who have been unemployed for more than 12 months. Long-term unemployment accounted for around 20% of the unemployed caseload during the 1970s but rose to between 30% and 40% after the recession of the 1980s and remained at comparable levels (Gregg, 1997). The gradual accumulation of long-term cases, people who find it very difficult to move off benefit[1], means that a decreasing proportion of the unemployed stock is likely to be floated off the caseload with each economic recovery. This is one reason why the new Labour government targeted a New Deal programme specifically on the long-term unemployed.

Analysis of the factors associated with long-term unemployment echoes the risk factors associated with becoming unemployed. In the mid-1990s men, people aged over 55, those with children – especially pre-school-aged children, tenants and people with health problems –

were all destined to remain unemployed for longer than other groups (McKay et al, 1997). In contrast, the factors associated with more rapid moves off unemployment-related benefits included being married, having academic qualifications, possessing a car and having recent work experience. Young people were also found to be more likely to move off benefit quickly, but a significant minority rapidly returned to unemployment; an eighth of those who found work in 1995/96 reclaimed unemployment benefits within a month, and two fifths within six months (Trickey et al, 1998).

The rapid movement in and out of employment that is characteristic of young people is thought to be becoming increasingly prevalent among other groups. Indeed, in 1998, 60% of unemployed claimants had already had two or more spells of unemployment before their current one began. Apart from age, the factors that have been found to be statistically associated with such instability include being single, male, not having children, suffering a health condition and lacking qualifications (Trickey et al, 1998). Previous experience of employment is also a good predictor of whether a person will continue to suffer unstable employment. In fact, econometric analysis suggests that unemployment itself accounts for two thirds of the significantly increased risk of employment that young people experience as a result of being unemployed at some point during their late teens and early 20s (Gregg, 1999).

To the extent that 'churning' in and out of unemployment has increased, this may signal that the social and personal cost of unemployment is being borne more widely – an objective of policy in the late 1980s and 1990s. As such, it may not add to the caseload at any point in time. It will, however, increase the number of people who receive benefit over a longer period. Over the period 1990 to 1992 three times as many people claimed Unemployment Benefit as were receiving it in any month (Walker and Ashworth, 1998). This may, in turn, increase the transaction costs associated with administering unemployment-related benefits.

What has been learned

Changes in the economy over the last 30 years have made the labour market much more risky, especially for those with limited skills or education. Job opportunities have remained most abundant for those with high level skills, although low waged openings also exist for the unskilled. Spells of unemployment have, on average, lengthened, even allowing for variations in the economic cycle, which has largely driven the claimant count. Repeated spells of unemployment may also have become more prevalent.

Note

[1] The probability of someone who had been unemployed for more than a year moving off benefit in any month was less than one in 100 in 1996/97 (Trickey et al, 1998).

FIVE

Demography and unemployment

Summary

Large cohorts of young people exacerbated already high unemployment in the late 1970s and early 1980s. Numbers have also been boosted by the increased employment participation of women, notably by mothers of young children.

In contrast, male employment rates fell substantially as, to a lesser extent, did those of lone parents. Older men were the worst affected. The economic inactivity rates for men aged 50-59 quadrupled, and rose to 57% among 60 to 64 year olds.

Even so, *unemployment rates remained highest among young people* and fell much less quickly than among other groups during periods of economic recovery. Unemployment among ethnic minority groups also fell comparatively slowly.

Whereas Chapter 4 was primarily concerned with changes in labour demand that have contributed to variations in the unemployed caseload, the focus in this chapter is on labour supply. It appears that, at certain points over the last 30 years, simple changes in demography have conspired to exacerbate the mismatch between the demand for and supply of labour.

Table 5.1 reveals that the working-age population grew by 13% between 1971 and 1998. Moreover, the growth in the number of people in the early part of their prime working years (namely between 30 and 44 years of age) was, at 36%, very much greater. The passage of this cohort through the labour market exacerbated the problems created by the downturn of the 1980s, since a subset of this cohort would have been aged 15-19 in 1981 when the recession began to bite. Table 5.1 confirms this, showing that the number of people in this age range

Table 5.1: Age distribution of resident population (000s)

Age	1971	1981	1991	1998	Growth to 1998 (1971=100)
15-19	3,736	4,589	3,611	3,543	95
20-29	7,745	7,886	9,045	7,663	99
30-44	9,544	10,683	11,906	12,985	136
45-59	9,559	9,313	9,259	10,545	110
60-64	3,147	2,885	2,818	2,747	87
15-64	33,051	35,356	36,639	37,483	111

Source: CSO (1998)

increased by 23% between 1971 and 1981, while the number aged 20–29 increased by just 2%. Clearly a large cohort of new labour market entrants is likely to be much at risk of unemployment, even in the absence of a downturn in the economy, such as that which occurred in the 1980s.

Large cohorts also tend to pose significant constraints on the chances of career progression and wage growth through promotion for members of the cohort and those cohorts that follow later. This labour market cohort has, therefore, been doubly disadvantaged, and may face further difficulties in the immediate future, as large numbers of people approach the labour market vulnerability associated with late working life.

Demography is also implicated in the recent decline in the numbers of young unemployed people, evident in Figure 4.4. The number of people aged 15 to 29 fell by 11% between 1991 and 1998.

Gender differences

The basic demographic arithmetic that precipitated change in the labour market was compounded by changes in the propensity of people to work. The changing patterns of employment among women have attracted most popular comment, although more dramatic changes occurred among men in the period up to 1991. Taken together, they mean that the total labour force has increased from 25.2 million in 1971 to 28.5 million 1999.

Female participation

To begin with female economic participation rates, Figure 5.1 shows that the proportion of women who were economically active rose from about 47% in 1983 to about 54% in 1991, only to fall back somewhat after that. But the major change in economic behaviour was really confined to women aged between 25 and 34. In the early 1980s only 55% of this group were economically active whereas by, 1996, 72% were either in work or looking for work.

The underlying reason was the increased propensity of women to work while still having dependant children. Only 52% of mothers with dependant children were working in 1977/79, of whom 29% were employed full-time. By 1998, 63% were doing so, and 40% of these were engaged in full-time employment (Thair and Risdon, 2000). Moreover, the number of mothers with a pre-school-aged child who worked more than doubled from 25% to 55% over the slightly longer period 1973 to 1998, while the proportion of mothers with children aged 10 and over in paid work increased from 67% to 77%. Interestingly, there was virtually no change in economic activity of women with children aged 5 to 10 during this later period. One interpretation of these figures is that attitudes to working changed among women with pre-school-aged children, and also that more women went back to work or took up a career when their children reached secondary school than had happened in earlier generations.

Figure 5.1: Economic activity of selected women (1979-96)

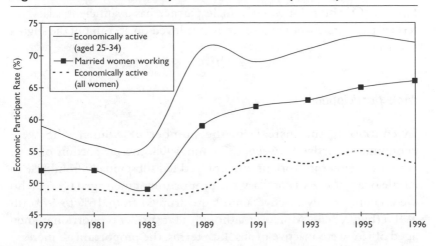

Source: ONS (1998a)

At the same time that more married women mixed motherhood and employment, the reverse trend was apparent among lone parents (see Part 5). That said, it is important not to exaggerate this trend. The proportion of all single, widowed, divorced and separated women, including those without children, who were economically active, only dropped from 74% in 1973 to 67% in 1996.

Between 1974 and 1997, the number of women in the labour force increased from 9 million to 11 million. Given that, overall, economic participation increased by 9% during this period, it would appear that 30% of the increase in the female labour force was due to the growth in the number of women of working age. The remainder can be attributed variously to changes in attitude and perhaps new opportunities as the kind of skills demanded by employers have shifted in favour of women.

The level of female unemployment fluctuated over the period 1971 to 1997, in line with macro-economic conditions, but was at no time greater than for men (Figure 5.2). However, it is important to recognise that women may be more prone to move out of the labour market entirely during periods of recession, and not claim benefit, creating a form of hidden unemployment. This can occur when women earn less than the minimum earnings threshold and are not eligible for contributory Jobseeker's Allowance (formerly Unemployment Benefit), and when they are partnered. Sometimes, if the man is also unemployed, he claims benefit on behalf of the whole family, and his partner ceases to be visible in the unemployment statistics. (This may change as the result of plans to place an obligation to look for work on the partners of unemployed claimants when there are no dependant children in the family.) Occasionally, where a male partner has a sufficient salary, his female partner may not register as unemployed on account of the stigma involved.

Male participation

In contrast to the increase in the number of women who were economically active between 1975 and 1998, the proportion of men who were either in work or unemployed fell substantially from 82% to a little over 70%. As a corollary, the proportion of men aged 60-64 who were economically inactive almost quadrupled from 16% to 57% (in 1996) (Figure 5.3). Moreover, although a far smaller proportion of men aged 50-59 were inactive in absolute terms, the proportionate increase was even greater – a rise from 4% to 19%. Changes of this order warrant

Figure 5.2: Unemployment rates for men and women (1975-99)

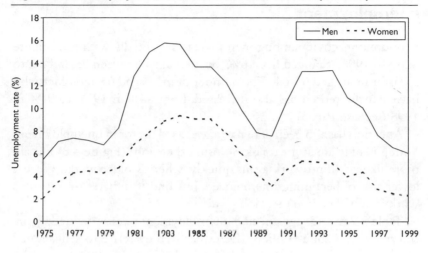

Source: ONS (2000) and earlier years

Figure 5.3: Male economic inactivity (1975-98)

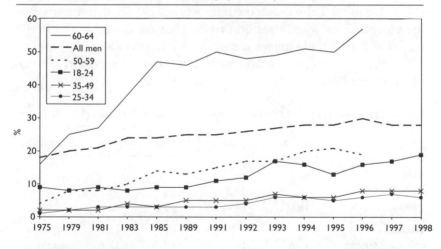

Source: ONS (2000) and earlier years

the description 'dramatic' and, while they do not help explain the growth in claims for unemployment-related benefits, the evidence already presented above suggests that much of this increased inactivity among older men was involuntary, and perhaps part of the same social phenomenon.

Age differences in economic participation and unemployment

Economic inactivity among men increases markedly with age (Figure 5.3). In 1996, it ranged from 6%, for men aged between 25 and 34, to 57%, for men aged 60-64. The number of men aged 65 and older who have actually retired has also increased, from 84% in 1971, to 94% in 1998 (see also Part 5).

Attention has also been drawn to age as a risk factor in unemployment. Young people are at great risk of losing their jobs (Figure 4.3) but are more likely to find work again quickly, whereas older workers face a lower risk of becoming unemployed, but find it difficult to return to work if ever they lose their job.

Table 5.2 records age-specific unemployment rates as defined by the International Labour Office (ILO), that is, they relate to self-defined unemployment rather than to claims for benefit. In 1998, the risk of unemployment fell rapidly with increasing age during the first half of working life, but after the age of 49 rose for men, although not for women. Unemployment was disturbingly high among school leavers (19.5%). Table 5.2 also shows the proportional change that occurred in the preceding six years, a period that covered the depths of the 1990s recession and the subsequent recovery. While overall unemployment fell markedly during this period, unemployment among 16 to 17 year olds remained high.

Table 5.2: Age-specific ILO unemployment rates (1992-98) (%)

	16-17	18-24	25-34	35-49	50-60/64
Men					
Change 1992-98	0	-30.3	-43.3	-44.7	-44.7
1998	19.5	13.4	6.7	4.7	5.7
Women					
Change 1992-98	+3.0	-12.0	-29.2	-31.1	-32.0
1998	17.3	10.3	5.9	4.0	3.4
Total					
Change 1992-98	+1.6	-24.1	-39.4	-39.7	-42.2
1998	18.5	12.0	6.3	4.4	4.8

Source: ONS (1999)

It is also worth noting that the economic recovery appeared to benefit men more than women. Although unemployment remained lower for women than for men at all ages, the proportionate fall in male unemployment was somewhat greater.

Unemployment among ethnic minority groups

Net migration did not add substantially to the potential labour force during the period 1971 to 1998, and at the end of the period all ethnic minority groups taken together made up just 6% of the population of working age.

However, minority groups were disproportionately affected by unemployment. Figure 5.4 plots the unemployment rate for various ethnic groups over the period 1984 to 1998, during which time unemployment as a whole fell from 11.2% to 8%. Unemployment was clearly much higher among minority groups than among the white population. Twenty-seven per cent of Pakistanis and Bangladeshis were unemployed in 1995, as were 24% of Afro-Caribbean descent and 12% of people of Indian origin. The first two figures are more than three times the corresponding value for whites.

Furthermore, it is apparent that differentials widened over the last decade and more. As the economy improved, unemployment among whites fell twice as quickly as it did among ethnic minorities considered as a group. Moreover, economic participation rates among the male members of ethnic minority communities are lower than for whites and fell faster in the decade to 1995: they declined from 80% to 76% while those of white males fell from 88% to 86%. Whereas economic participation by white women increased over this period, no clear trend was evident among women from minority groups.

What has been learned

The 11% growth in the working population between 1971 and 1998, together with increased economic participation among women, added to the excess of labour supply over demand. This was particularly marked during the economic downturn of the early 1980s, when unemployment soared, especially among young people, and, to a lesser extent, among older workers. The effects were long lasting, for, until very recently, unemployment among young people had not fallen as fast as for other

Figure 5.4: ILO unemployment rates among ethnic groups (1979-98)

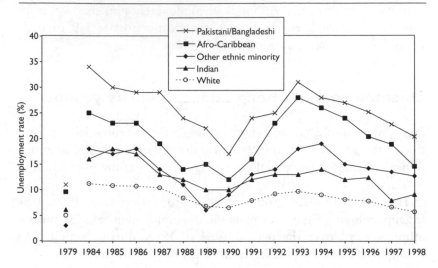

Source: Sly (1996); Nickell (1999)

groups, while lower participation rates among older men persist. Taking the period 1971 to 1999 as a whole, compositional changes were conducive to a falling unemployment rate, with decreases in the numbers of young people and those in their pre-retirement years (groups at high risk of unemployment) and some increase in the proportion of female workers. While economic recovery in the 1990s resulted in unemployment rates closer to 1971 levels than before, the larger labour force meant that the unemployment caseload still exceeded one million in 1999.

SIX

Unemployment institutions

Summary

Labour market and social security policies changed radically between 1971 and 1999, in ways that were often explicitly designed to influence the size of the unemployed caseload. *Small-scale training and work experience schemes introduced in the 1970s were massively expanded in the 1980s, to provide surrogate employment and reduce the claimant count.* For a period, some unemployed claimants were financially encouraged to leave the labour market.

Resources devoted to training were then reduced, while new measures to tighten the eligibility conditions for benefit helped to support the emphasis on flexible job search while also reducing expenditure and claimant numbers. In 1996, with the introduction of Jobseeker's Allowance (JSA), benefit receipt was made conditional on signing and following an agreement. This strategy is now complemented by the Labour government's commitment to offer quality training and work experience, obligatory for some groups, through New Deal welfare to work programmes. These policies appear to have reduced claimant unemployment in the context of a growing economy.

A radical shift in the ratio of means-tested to insurance-based support for unemployed claimants occurred as a result of policy changes and lengthening unemployment. This process was also fuelled by policies to increase rents for tenants in social housing, thereby increasing the Housing Benefit (HB) caseload.

Increased means testing focused policy attention on work incentives which, together with evidence of low pay, led to the introduction of in-work benefits for families in order to adopt the rhetoric of the current government, 'to make work pay'.

Labour market and social security policies, and the institutions to design and implement them, altered radically between 1971 and 1999. The process of change was inevitably shaped by a combination of factors in the policy domains – with new perceptions, policy goals and policy models – as well as developments in the labour market, discussed in Chapter 4. An understanding of these changes is important to any assessment of the impact of policy on the numbers of unemployed claimants. For a blow by blow account, the reader is directed to Clasen (1994); here a brief sketch has to suffice.

Government job creation and training

A Conservative government was in power in the early 1970s. Unemployment was still low although, at the time, half a million unemployed seemed high. Trade unions appeared powerful, and it was a time of industrial unrest that precipitated the election of a Labour government in October 1974 with the barest of majorities. Nominally still committed to full employment, Labour was confronted with high and rising inflation, and chose the route of wage restraint, through a social contract with the trade unions, and constraints on public spending. Unemployment hit one million in 1975, and although never publicly recognised, it was apparent that Labour had abandoned its commitment to full employment (Deacon, 1981).

One response to the unemployment was to expand existing training and job creation programmes and to add new ones. However, members of the government have since admitted that in doing so ministers primarily wanted to demonstrate that "something was being done about unemployment" (Deacon, 1981, p 78; Barnett, 1982). Labour used institutions established by the preceding government, notably the Manpower Services Commission (MSC), with its two executive agencies, the Employment Service Agency and the Training Services Agency, which were established in 1974. Significantly, the strategy document *People and jobs* that led to the establishment of the MSC also resulted in the separation of employment assistance from the benefit provision, both physically and administratively, a strategy that was reversed in 1996 with the introduction of Jobseeker's Allowance (MSC, 1975).

From the beginning, the MSC gave its attention to making contingency plans 'should unemployment reach a high level'. A programme of opening new Jobcentres providing 'self-service' and upgraded advisory support was initiated. In addition to the Training

Opportunities Scheme (TOPS), providing for specialist vocational training, a Special Programmes Division was created. In 1978, this launched the Youth Opportunities Programme (YOP) that provided training and work experience for young people and paid them an income just above benefit levels. A key objective was always to remove as many young people as possible from the unemployment register (Maguire, 1993). But, while in the initial stages it appeared to benefit the disadvantaged people it served, its success rate – measured in terms of progression into employment – fell, and it was discredited by its reputation as a source of 'cheap labour' for employers (Roberts, 1995). By 1982/ 83, when YOP was replaced by the Youth Training Scheme (YTS), it was recruiting 543,000 people per year who would otherwise have appeared in the unemployment count (Table 6.1).

Table 6.1: Characteristics of entrants to the Youth Opportunities Programme

	1978/79	1979/80	1980/81	1981/82	1982/83	1985/86
Total number of entrants	162,000	216,000	360,000	553,000	543,000	390,000
% of entrants who were:						
Male	50	52	51	53	54	56
Female	50	48	49	47	46	44
Current year school leaver	70	60	65	66	71	92
Other young people	30	40	35	34	29	8
Aged 16-17	90	91	91	92	92	99
Aged 18 years	10	9	9	8	8	1

Source: TC (1988)

The Special Programmes Division also established the Special Temporary Employment Programme to create temporary work for the long-term unemployed; this was to evolve into the Community Enterprise Programme and, then, into the Community Programme in 1982/83. The Community Programme, which had the same effect on the unemployment count, filled 243,444 places in its most successful year, 1985/86 (Table 6.2). The Community Programme then became Employment Training and later, in 1993, Training for Work. In the process, a failure adequately to impose quality control meant that the

Table 6.2: Characteristics of entrants to the Community Programme (%)

	1983/84	1984/85	1985/86	1986/87	1987/88
Male	77	77	78	76	74
Female	23	23	22	24	26
Aged 18-24	55	62	66	61	54
Aged 25+	45	38	34	39	46

Source: MSC (1986)

quality of training was highly variable, and the concept of training devalued in the minds of Employment Service clients.

When the Thatcher government came to power in 1979, they cut the budget of the MSC by 16%, but initially they did not radically change the objective of providing a practical response to high unemployment. Perhaps inevitably, however, the quality of placements deteriorated and the support for trainees or workers declined (Alcock, 1999).

However, by 1982/83, the tone of the MSC annual reports was changing, with the objective 'to safeguard the creation of skilled manpower for industry's present and future needs' placed first. And by the time that the MSC was replaced, briefly by the Training Commission in 1987, and then its responsibilities devolved to local Training and Enterprise Councils (TECs), policy objectives had been entirely reformulated. Rather than creating work and, through such schemes as the Job Release Scheme, encouraging older people to actually leave the labour market, the aim was, "to encourage the development of a skilled and adaptable labour force" (TC, 1988). This meant cutting back on the use of training schemes as a form of job creation and imposing direct pressure on the unemployed to find work. This took the form of the imposition of regular 'Restart' interviews with employment advisers, an initiative credited with reducing the time spent claiming benefit by 5%, and more or less compulsory attendance at 'Jobclubs' designed to inculcate positive attitudes towards work and job search (Alcock, 1999). Indirect pressure was also applied to take any employment on offer, with the threat of benefit sanction. The next development, with the introduction of JSA in 1996, was to reintegrate job search and job placement with benefit provisions for the unemployed.

The YTS, influenced in its design by the German dual system of apprenticeships, briefly marked an explicit recognition of the need to provide all young people with good quality basic training. Extended from a one to two year programme in 1986 as unemployment peaked, in 1988 all 16 and 17 year olds not in education were guaranteed a place on YTS, but entitlement to Income Support was withdrawn (in all but the most exceptional circumstances). Reduced funding made it impossible to guarantee quality training for all, and YTS and Youth Training (YT), its successor, introduced in 1990 when responsibility was passed to local TECs, came to offer stratified provision. Modern Apprenticeships, introduced in 1994 and National Traineeships, which replaced YT, perpetuate the differentiated provision.

From the early 1970s onwards, training schemes have served to reduce the claimant count. Recently, the numbers on training schemes have fallen, notably among the young, with the proportion of 16 year olds entering training programmes falling from over 50% in 1982 to 23% in 1989, and just 9.1% in 1998 (Maguire, 2000) (Table 6.3). In the latter period, young people who might have been at risk of unemployment have been increasingly held in the post-compulsory education system.

Table 6.3: Participation rates in education

Age	Participation rate (%)		
	1989	1997	1998
16	51.5	69.3	70.5
17	35.5	57.2	58.2
18	18.7	37.6	37.3

Source: Maguire (2000)

Unemployment benefit regimes

Despite major reforms of the benefit system in 1980 and 1988, the system of benefits for the unemployed remained structurally unchanged from 1971 to 1996. There were, however, minor changes that reflected longstanding concerns to maintain work incentives, while the changing structure of unemployment effected changes in the pattern of benefit provision.

The proportion of unemployed people receiving contributory Unemployment Benefit fell markedly between 1971 and 1996, with the proportion being dependent on mean-tested benefit correspondingly increasing from 35% in 1971 to 79% in 1996 (Figure 3.2). The major shift in the balance between insurance and means-tested benefits occurred between 1980 and 1982, coinciding with the commencement of the 1980s recession, a differential that has subsequently been maintained. The recession, it will be remembered, coincided with a large cohort of young people commencing work, many of whom did not have the record of contributions to qualify them for receipt of Unemployment Benefit. The recession also initiated the secular rise in the number of long-term unemployed claimants who would have exhausted entitlement to benefit after 12 months.

However, the abolition of an earnings-related supplement to Unemployment Benefit, which took place in 1982, must be added to these structural changes. The real value of the supplement had been allowed to decline from 1972 onwards, and by the time of its abolition it was only paid to 10-15% of unemployed claimants at any one time (Clasen, 1994).

The shift away from insurance towards means-testing accompanied the rise in unemployment in other countries (Eardley et al, 1995), but was perhaps more marked in Britain on account of the low level of insurance benefits relative to means-tested ones. This stemmed from the postwar origins of the National Insurance system, which aimed to provide flat rate subsistence benefits, to encourage people to take advantage of alternative systems of provision that, in the case of unemployment insurance, unlike retirement pensions, never developed (Walker et al, 1995). As a result, slight changes in the relative values of benefits resulted in large shifts in the balance of provision.

One factor influencing this balance was housing costs. These rose ahead of the rate of inflation for much of the period under consideration. From the early 1980s onwards, public sector rents were allowed to rise, with the unemployed protected, initially through the then main social assistance scheme (Supplementary Benefit) and, after 1982, by means of a separate Housing Benefit. Until 1995, owner-occupiers could claim all the interest paid on outstanding mortgages and the number of people doing so increased, partly on account of a policy of council house sales that extended home ownership to groups at greater risk of unemployment. Because most people with more than minimal housing costs would have needed to supplement their contributory Unemployment Benefit with means-tested assistance, changes in the relative level of housing cost translated directly into greater benefit expenditure and, less directly, into increases in the size of the means-tested caseload.

Throughout the 18 years of Conservative rule, policy with regard to Unemployment Benefits was driven by the twin concerns of minimising, and if possible reducing, expenditure and enhancing work incentives, monetary and otherwise. Many of the policy changes reduced the value of insurance benefits, thereby increasing claims for means-tested benefits. (Between 1983 and 1996 the value of Unemployment Benefit fell from 36% to 28% of average incomes – Hills, 1998.) In 1980 Unemployment Benefit was made taxable, benefits were increased by 5% less than other benefits in the annual uprating, and payments to strikers and people with occupational pensions were reduced. In 1988 contribution conditions were tightened, removing 350,000 from Unemployment Benefit; 300,000 of these transferred to Income Support, the new means-tested benefit that replaced Supplementary Benefit. The penalty for voluntary unemployment was increased from 13 to 26 weeks. In 1989 eligibility to insurance benefits was again restricted by legislation that required unemployed people to prove that they were looking for work.

Jobseeker's Allowance and Welfare to Work

The stricter benefit and work enforcement regimes were brought together with the introduction of Jobseeker's Allowance, which also furthered the trend towards means testing. Jobseeker's Allowance merged Unemployment Benefit and Income Support. Eligibility was based on contributions and lasted for six months (reduced from 12 under Unemployment Benefit) after which jobseekers were subject to means testing. Benefit was to be assessed by social security staff located in Jobcentres, with eligibility made conditional on signing a Jobseeker's Agreement. In addition, the introduction of a new computer system enabled staff to monitor jobseekers' job search on a fortnightly basis.

The explicit aim of introducing JSA was to encourage people to move off benefit more quickly, and thereby to reduce the size of the claimant population. It was also anticipated that greater outflows from benefit might lessen wage pressures and indirectly stimulate labour demand (Walker, 1999a). The introduction of JSA is thought to have reduced registered unemployment by between 100,000 and 200,000 between summer 1996 and spring 1997 (Sweeney and McMahon, 1998). However, this positive impact seems to have been limited to those areas where labour demand was high (Smith et al, 2000).

Jobseeker's Allowance remains the bedrock of the British system of benefits for unemployed people under the new Labour government. Indeed, it is argued, Labour would have needed to introduce such a scheme had the Conservatives not done so earlier; the reason is that it embodies the social contract between government and beneficiary which emphasises the promotion of personal responsibility that underlines much of Labour's rhetoric. What has been added is a suite of proactive labour market policies (New Deal), focused on particular disadvantaged groups that blend increased compulsion with the aspiration to offer accredited training and quality work experience (see Table 6.4).

A key objective is to reduce the number of people claiming benefit by encouraging a more rapid move into work. The schemes for young people and the long-term unemployed are both compulsory, sustained by the possibility of denying benefit to sanctioned claimants. By far the largest of the New Deals, in terms of funding, is that aimed at young people, which was introduced nationally in April 1998. This is compulsory to all people aged 18-25, after six months of unemployment. It comprises a Gateway of intensive jobsearch followed by, for people who do not find work, a set of 'Options' lasting for six months, all of which comprise an element of accredited training. Those completing an option without securing employment enter a Follow-through phase of more intensive help with jobsearch. Participants in New Deal are not included in the claimant unemployment count.

By the end of October 1999, a total of 379,500 young people had joined New Deal, of whom about 135,000 were still actively involved. Most (47%) were in the Gateway phase but the second largest group (18%) comprised young people who had already reached the Follow-through phase. Inflows have stabilised at around 15,000 per month and it is predicted that the size of the programme will eventually fall to 90,000 (Hasluck, 2000). Based on the first year of the programme it is estimated that the number of unemployed young people fell by about 30,000 as a direct result of New Deal. This represents a fall of around 40% in youth long-term unemployment (Anderton et al, 1999).

Development of in-work benefits

The Beveridge reforms of the 1940s instigated family allowances within the tax system in recognition of the costs imposed by children and to limit the financial disincentives to work created by the introduction of National Assistance, the forerunner of Income Support. These were converted into non-contributory, non-means-tested, cash benefits in 1979.

Table 6.4: New Deal 'Welfare to Work' programmes in Britain

Target group	Duration of worklessness	Funding £m	Com-pulsion	Content	Remuneration	Subsidy to employer*	Implementation
Young people aged 18-24	More than six months	2,620	Yes	*Gateway:* Intensive help, advice and guidance *Options:* Subsidised employment Voluntary work Environmental Task Force Self-employment Full-time education/ training *Follow-through:* Renewed Intensive help	 Rate for job Wage or £15.83/wk grant Wage or £15.83/wk grant Wage or £15.83/wk grant	£60/wk for six months Training contribution of £750	Pathfinder areas: January 1998 Nationwide: April 1998 All options to include accredited training of one day/wk
Long-term unemployed aged 24+	More than two years	450	Yes	*Gateway:* As above *Options:* Subsidised employment Full-time education/training *Follow-through:* As above	Rate for job	£75/wk for six months	June 1998
Partners of the unemployed	Duration of partner's unemployment	60	Yes	Likely to be similar to New Deals for young people and long-term unemployed above			April 1999
Lone parents	No restriction by duration	190	No	Advice Access to programs Follow-up			Pilots: July 1997 Nationwide: October 1998
People with disabilities	28 weeks in receipt of benefits on grounds of incapacity	200	No	Test schemes			September/October 1998

Note: In September 1998, UK£1 = US$1.66.

* Participants who do not receive a wage continue to receive an allowance equal to the Jobseeker's Allowance. Travel grants may be made.

However, in the early 1970s the Conservative government recognised that family allowances did not fully resolve the work disincentives faced by low skilled parents, and sought to introduce a variant of a negative income tax scheme. Finding the problems of implementation insurmountable, they introduced Family Income Supplement (FIS) in 1971, a cash benefit for parents working 30 hours or more a week, payable on the basis of a household means-test. Take-up remained notoriously low and the caseload did not rise above 100,000 until the early 1980s.

In 1988, however, the Thatcher government introduced a more generous version, called Family Credit (FC), which again, it had been hoped, might be paid by employers through the Pay-As-You-Earn (PAYE) income tax system. The new benefit had a simpler structure (Figure 6.1), with the same multiple objectives as FIS, namely: to provide extra support for families; to ensure that they were better off in work than not; and to reduce marginal tax (deduction) rates (DHSS, 1985). Ideologically averse to job creation and other measures designed to boost labour demand 'artificially', the Conservatives used in-work benefits to boost in-work incomes.

Family Credit was originally restricted to people working at least 24 hours per week. The hours threshold for FC was reduced to 16 hours in April 1992 and, as an incentive to work longer hours, higher benefit was introduced for people working 30 hours or more in July 1995. Disregards on maintenance and childcare costs were added in April 1992 and October 1994 respectively. Partly as a result of these changes, the FC caseload rose markedly, to 733,000 in February 1997, 12% of all working families with children (Walker and Wiseman, 1997). Although FC was designed to facilitate a transition from welfare to work, much of the expenditure was used sustaining a growing proportion of the caseload who remained in receipt for long periods (Ashworth and Walker, 1993; Walker and Ashworth, 1994). However, the benefit served as a 'parachute' for two earner households when one person lost a job (Marsh and McKay, 1993).

The Labour government is also committed to the need to subsidise low paid work and, in October 1999, replaced FC with an even more generous scheme, Working Families' Tax Credit, which it is expected will be received by 1.4 million households, 500,000 more than received FC. From April 2000 Working Families' Tax Credit is to be paid through the tax system (HM Treasury, 1998; Walker and Wiseman, 1997).

While in-work benefits serve to provide an effective set of financial inducements to move into work, in Britain they add complexity and

Figure 6.1: Net income after housing costs for a couple with two children on Family Credit, and Working Families' Tax Credit

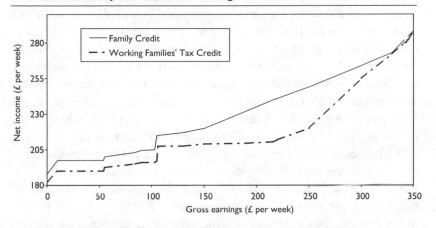

Note: Assuming an average rent and council tax; earnings of £3.50 an hour; and no other income or capital
Source: HM Treasury (1998)

uncertainty to the transition, creating two different benefit systems defined in terms of the hours that a person works. This may impede movement out of unemployment. They also create a 'poverty trap', through the interaction of the tax system with the withdrawal of benefit as income rises. In 1996, an average family might gain as little as £10 per week in net income from a wage rise £165 once account had been taken of income tax and the withdrawal of FC and HB. Such disincentives might help to explain the accumulation of long-term recipients within the caseload. Under Working Families' Tax Credit the marginal benefit deduction rate is reduced, but more people are brought within scope of the poverty trap.

Private insurance

Finally, it is worth noting briefly that the decline in the coverage of contributory Unemployment Benefit has been accompanied by a limited growth in the provision of private insurance (Walker et al, 1995). However, while there are free-standing policies available that offer income maintenance during unemployment, most policies are thought to be sold through creditors (insurance companies, building societies, credit card companies and so on) keen to ensure that borrowers will always be able to meet their repayments.

There are no publicly available estimates of the number of workers who have taken out private insurance against unemployment. Informed sources suggest that the market penetration of policies linked to mortgages may vary between 10% and 25%, depending on the lender. What is clear is that a significant expansion occurred in 1991/92 as the last recession took hold, but that sales have fallen with unemployment.

There are severe limitations on the cover that is commercially available at affordable cost. Unemployment insurance is most often packaged with other insurance for accidents or sickness, and typically, when linked to a bank or credit card loan, life assurance. Although some companies will offer insurance against insolvency, others restrict cover to redundancy and so exclude the self-employed (already excluded from the state scheme). Also, insurance can often only be obtained at the time of negotiating the loan or shortly afterwards. But most important are invariably specific exclusions, of which the following are fairly typical:

- the first 30 days of unemployment or financial insolvency;
- unemployment occurring during the first 90 days of the plan (with a new mortgage) or 180 days (for a further advance or re-mortgage);
- unemployment lasting for more than 12 months;
- those without regular and continuous work for at least 12 months;
- voluntary unemployment or insolvency;
- unemployment that is a recurrent, regular or seasonal feature of the job;
- unemployment at the end of a fixed-term contract;
- periods when a payment is taken instead of notice;
- unemployment occurring outside the UK.

The net result is to exclude many of those whose circumstances result from the trends towards a more flexible labour market: the long-term unemployed and those in precarious forms of employment. Moreover, these are the very same people who are not well served by social insurance.

The last Conservative government expected further expansion of private insurance when it excluded mortgage interest payments for the first six months of a claims, but the evidence is that expansion of the sector has been limited. It would seem, therefore, that the new realities have done little to change the arithmetic of unemployment insurance. Risk remains highly differentiated, with those most at risk being least able to afford higher premiums. Indeed, in some respects the arithmetic has worsened, for the socially necessary expenditures of the unemployed have increased while state support has lessened and the availability of permanent well paid jobs has declined.

What has been learned

To conclude, policy has shifted from schemes in the 1970s to provide alternative work for the unemployed towards, in the 1990s, proactive measures to encourage them to find employment. Both approaches have sought to reduce unemployment directly, rather than to use demand management policies to stimulate the economy. Tony Blair concludes, as did his predecessors, that any prospect of full employment has "been completely broken down" (Blair, 1999). Nevertheless, by the end of 1999, the number of job vacancies and the number of people recorded as looking for work were approaching equilibrium.

Most of the individual policies that were introduced aimed to reduce the numbers claiming Unemployment Benefit. In the 1970s and early 1980s, claimants were defined out of unemployment by placing them on work experience and training courses, or by explicitly encouraging them to move to other benefits. Table 6.5 lists the schemes introduced between October 1979 and January 1987, and their effect on the level of claimant unemployment. Latterly, benefit eligibility criteria have been tightened, and active labour market policies introduced, including the extension of in-work benefits. It was estimated that, in 1996, unemployment was 5.5 million (including those who want to work but were 'inactive', those on government training programmes and those working part-time who wanted full-time work) compared to the official claimant count figure of two million (Convery, 1997).

New policies, notably JSA and Labour's New Deal Welfare to Work initiatives, seem also to have reduced claimant unemployment in the context of a buoyant economy.

Table 6.5: The effect of legislative changes on claimant unemployment (1979-87)

Date	Change	Estimated effect on monthly count*
Oct 1979	Change to fortnightly payment of benefits	+20,000
Oct 1979	Compensating downward adjustment to published seasonally adjusted totals	-20,000
Feb 1981	First published estimate of effect on unemployment register of special employment and training measures (coverage increased from 250,000 participants at start of 1979 to 668,000 by Jan 1986	370,000 (-495,000 - Jan 1986)
July to Oct 1981	Seasonally adjusted figures for these months reduced by 20,000 to compensate for effect on count of emergency procedures to deal with DHSS industrial action	-20,000
July 1981	Unemployed men aged 60 and above, drawing Supplementary Benefit for a year or more given option of long-term rate in return for not registering for work	-30,000 by May 1982
July 1982	Taxation of Unemployment Benefit. Suggested that this might have reduced count by encouraging single parents to switch to (untaxed) supplementary benefit	No estimate available
Oct 1982	Change in definition and compilation of monthly unemployment figures from a clerical count of people registered for work at Jobcentres and careers offices to a computer count covering only benefit claimants *(In addition, the estimated effect on the number of school leavers recorded:*	-170,000 to -190,000 -26,000†)
Oct 1982	Monthly publication of number of unemployed people seeking part-time work (less than 30 hours a week) discontinued. Final figure for September 1982	-52,000
April 1983	Men aged 60 and over and not entitled to benefit no longer required to sign on at benefit offices in order to get NI credits	-107,400 by June 1983
June 1983	All men aged 60 and over allowed long-term rate Supplementary Benefit rate as soon as they come onto Supplementary Benefit. As a result of provision introduced in November 1980 barring school leavers from claiming benefit until September each year, together with change in monthly count to claimants only in October 1982 unemployed school leavers are missed from the monthly figures for June, July and August each year	-54,000 by Aug 1983 -100,000 to -200,000

Table 6.5: cont.../

Date	Change	Estimated effect on monthly count*
Oct 1984	Change in Community Programme eligibility rules. Entry now limited to unemployed benefit claimants only	-29,000 by Jan 1986[†]
July 1985	Reconciliation of Northern Ireland DHSS records with computer records	-5,000
July 1985	Payment of Unemployment Benefit in arrears	No estimate available
March 1986	Introduction of a two-week delay in publication of the monthly unemployment count to 'improve accuracy'	-40,000 to -90,000 (average -50,000)
June 1986	New method of calculating unemployment rate, using a larger denominator. Initially this was published alongside rate calculated on old basis but from September 1986 the new count has not replaced it	Between -1% and -1.5% (typically -1.4%)
Oct 1986	Abolition of right to half and three quarter rate Unemployment Benefit for people with insufficient NI contributions to qualify for full rate (decision announced on 15 January 1986)	-24,000 after 1 year -30,000 after 2[†]
Oct 1986	Abolition of right to half and three quarter rate Unemployment Benefit for people with insufficient NI contribution to qualify for full rate (decision announced on 15 January 1986)	-2,000 to -3,000
Oct 1986 to Jan 1987	Introduction of tighter availability for work test	-95,000 after one year -120,000 after 2 years[†]

* Estimated effects are those published by the Department of Employment, except where marked.

[†] Estimated effect derived from Department of Employment. DHSS or Treasury data by the Unemployment Unit.

Source: UU (1987)

SEVEN

Beliefs, behaviour and unemployment

Summary

Since the late 1980s many policies have been premised on the assumption that people need to be coerced to find work, and there is much concern about the financial disincentives to work created by the benefit system.

The empirical evidence is that very few claimants prefer not to work or fail actively to engage in job search. Most people who become long-term unemployed appear to do so not as a result of receiving benefits, but because they do not have the attributes that would help them secure employment.

The evidence on disincentive effects is equivocal. Financial disincentives may be less important than uncertainty, risk aversion and the practical constraints imposed by complex systems and poor administration. Partners of unemployed claimants receiving benefits are less likely to work than those with employed partners, but only a fifth of the difference is due to financial disincentives created by the benefit system. On the other hand, there is some evidence of people on in-work benefits not seeking better paid work.

The largest portion of fraud relates to people working while claiming benefit. The work is typically casual and of short duration.

The change in policy thrust described in Chapter 6 reflects a sustained shift in ideology away from a belief in the possibility of full employment towards a commitment to evolve modern supply-side policies that are thought better to support a flexible labour market. The focus in this chapter is less on the 'big ideas' that guide policy, and more about the prevalent beliefs about how policy works. The correspondence between beliefs and empirical reality provides further qualitative insight into the likely effectiveness of policies in reducing unemployment levels.

Attachment to the labour market

There has been a growing acceptance that some people remain unemployed because they want to (Deacon and Mann, 1997). Some have argued that people are feckless, others that there has been a breakdown of community norms such that "the messages of responsibility, striving, self-help and self-improvement have been progressively weakened" (Dennis, 1997, p 89). Yet others suggest that means-testing sets up incentives to cheat and mix illicit work with benefit receipt (Field, 1996a). The growth in long-term unemployment and the fact that chances of leaving unemployment decline with its duration (Figure 7.1) have fed such beliefs.

Whatever the reasoning, the British research evidence generally does not support the basic contention that benefit dependency is widespread;

Figure 7.1: The chance of leaving unemployment (mid-1990s)

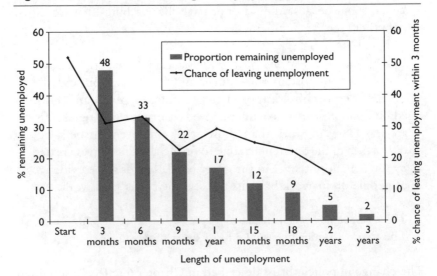

Source: Author's calculations from information made available by the DfEE

certainly not in the sense of people choosing to remain on benefit rather than needing to spend long spells as claimants. While two thirds of claimants believe that people have to work illicitly if they are 'to make ends meet', very few people appear to do so (Shaw et al, 1996b). Of course, it might be that illicit work is ubiquitous and that respondents were simply too coy to admit it. While possible, such coyness fits uneasily with the hypothesis that a welfare class exists in which the norm is to defraud the system. It is perhaps more likely that, in many areas, casual work is not readily available to people without the appropriate skills or the necessary access to suitable contacts. Many people also acknowledge a fear of getting caught. If abuse of the system exists on a large scale it is probably confined to comparatively small localities (Jordan et al, 1992).

Similarly there is little to suggest that the discouraged worker syndrome is widespread in Britain or that people find life on benefits congenial, quite the contrary. Words such as 'stigma', 'outcast' and 'second class citizen' are used frequently by claimants to describe their lives on benefit (Clasen et al, 1997; Shaw, 1998). Over half of claimants – three quarters of those with children – are in debt, and fewer than half claim to be managing satisfactorily.

All the British research evidence suggests that unemployed claimants are and remain active in the pursuit of work (Kempson, 1996). Half typically spend the equivalent of a day a week seeking work and make an average of one formal application every week (Bottomley et al, 1997). Many do much more even though they often recognise that their chances of securing work in the short term are limited. People do become disheartened and reduce their job search for periods, but there is no evidence of sustained withdrawal among the long-term unemployed. Indeed, as many people increase the intensity of their job search as reduce it. Likewise, it would be wrong to presume that claimants either are, or become, inflexible as to the kind of job that they are prepared to take, although most respondents have limits beyond which they will not go (Table 7.1). For example, in 1995, half of unemployed claimants in Britain said that they would not move home in order to find work, sometimes because of the financial and practical costs of moving but also because of the loss of support networks that helped in the challenge of making ends meet. However, more than four out of five unemployed people did say that they would accept a temporary job or shift work, or – if it paid sufficient – part-time employment (Bottomley et al, 1997).

Table 7.1: Type of work said to be acceptable by unemployed jobseekers in Britain (1995)

Condition	Number accepting	% accepting
Status		
Employee	3,470	78
Self-employed	116	3
Employee or self-employed	848	19
Can't say	6	*
Full-time	3,045	68
Part-time	200	5
Full or part-time	1,226	27
Part-time if full-time not available		
Yes	1,506	49
Possibly	837	28
Short-term/temporary work		
Yes	3,150	71
Possibly	568	13
Specificity of job sought		
Particular type of job	1,262	29
Range of jobs	1,378	31
Any job	1,759	40
Can't say	25	1
Shift work		
Yes	3,309	74
Possibly	252	6
Night work		
Yes	2,772	62
Possibly	285	6
Weekend work		
Yes	3,320	74
Possibly	391	9
Work with variable hours		
Yes	3,731	84
Possibly	291	7
Work more than 40 hours per week	3,704	88
Living away from home		
Yes	1,724	39
Possibly	538	12
Move away from area		
Yes	1,578	35
Possibly	777	17

* less than 0.5%, more than zero.

Source: Bottomley et al (1997)

To summarise, the evidence is clear that very few unemployed claimants prefer welfare benefits to a job or consistently flout benefit regulations. It is true that the chances of finding a job are much less for long-term recipients than for new claimants and that some people remain on benefit for long periods. However, statistical modelling suggests that particular individuals are destined to become long-term recipients on account of their prior characteristics, not that people become dependent as a consequence of receiving benefits.

The impact of disincentives

Policy makers have wrestled over the years with the financial disincentives inherent in the provision of out-of-work benefits. They lay behind the introduction of Family Income Supplement and the 1980 and 1988 reforms, and have influenced the detailed design of policy. When Family Credit was introduced, the means-test was based on net rather than gross income to prevent marginal benefit withdrawal rates in excess of 100% that were possible under FIS. Labour's Working Families' Tax Credit also has a lower rate of withdrawal designed to lessen disincentives.

Moreover, changes in the structure of the labour market, notably the increased wage dispersal (Figure 4.2), have conspired to worsen the problem of disincentives, since wages at the bottom of the distribution have not increased in real terms for 20 years. Moreover, there is evidence that the wage received on re-entry to the labour market has fallen steadily in real terms, from £107 per week in 1984 to £99 in 1997 (Gregg, 1999).

The thinking behind disincentive effects frequently presumes that people seeking work set a 'reservation wage' – the lowest amount that they would be prepared to work for (but see Dawes, 1994). In late 1995 the median reservation wage set by British jobseekers claiming benefit was £135; median manual earnings were then £272 (Bottomley et al, 1997). While the reservation wage was typically between £20 and £30 less than people hoped to get, the latter was still only about three fifths of the national median wage. This should not generally have been a major impediment to securing work, even though return to work jobs tend to offer much below average wages. Moreover, there is little evidence that it is benefits that set the floor to the wages that people are prepared to accept. Only 20% of jobseekers said that they took account of benefit levels when fixing their reservation wage; the overwhelming majority (87%) reported that they determined their minimum in light of the amount that they needed to live on; almost half (47%) took account of nothing else.

What people say, of course, is not necessarily what they do. However, multivariate analysis using objective measures revealed two sets of independent determinants; one was needs-driven while the other reflected prior work experience – former professionals and managers set the highest thresholds (Bottomley et al, 1997). More importantly, the same research showed little difference in the reservation wages of claimants who found work and those who did not, and that 44% of claimants leaving benefit took jobs paying less than their reservation wage. In the early 1990s, the average unemployed person took a job paying 9% less than they had previously earned or 14% less than they would have been receiving had they not been made unemployed (Gregg, 1999).

The evidence of powerful practical disincentive effects is not strong. This is understandable in that people do not work only for money, while the stigma of unemployment may itself create a powerful incentive to work. However, this is not to say that structural disincentives are not important at the margin. For example, a recent study following up people returning to work after a spell of unemployment found that 15% of those receiving in-work benefits had turned down the prospect of a better paid job or more hours for fear of the effect on their benefit income (Trickey et al, 1998).

Indeed, there is evidence that fear and uncertainty may be as important a brake on people returning to work as high reservation wages. People living on low incomes need necessarily to be risk averse and taking a job is necessarily a risky enterprise (Jenkins and Millar, 1989; Dobson et al, 1994). Not only might the job not last, but take home pay is difficult to calculate. People moving off Income Support in 1994 (mostly into work) were asked about any worries that they had prior to leaving benefit and the problems that they had actually encountered when doing so (Shaw et al, 1996). Over a fifth had concerns about whether the job would last. Just under a quarter foresaw the difficulty of managing financially until the first pay-day, and almost as many actually found this to be a real problem.

The design of the benefit system exacerbates uncertainty. Like Jobseeker's Allowance today, Income Support acted as a passport to other benefits, for instance, free medical prescriptions and eye-tests, only some of which were available to people in work. In one study only 2% of unemployed claimants knew which of nine passport benefits applied in which circumstances (Shaw et al, 1996).

The administration as well as the design of benefits can also conspire to deter people from taking employment. Seventy-three per cent of claimants receiving Income Support in 1994 agreed that applying for benefits could be 'a big hassle' and there is evidence that this concern was sufficient to deter people from taking potentially insecure jobs in order not to risk having to reapply for benefit (Shaw et al, 1996b). Twelve per cent of claimants receiving Income Support in 1994 had to wait at least a month for their first benefit payment and this caused them problems with the payment of rent, meeting general expenses and even paying for food (Shaw et al, 1996a). Then again, 7% of all the people who moved off Income Support in the same year experienced problems resulting from delays in the payment of Housing Benefit and 6% waiting for Family Credit. Given that only a small minority of former Income Support claimants applied for these benefits, processing delays were clearly prevalent and must have contributed to the uncertainty and insecurity associated with the process of returning to work.

It would appear, therefore, that claimants in Britain were generally unable to make informed choices about the financial utility of taking a job versus remaining on benefit. Any disincentive effects that are created by the British benefit system must therefore be a matter of hunch and impression rather than calculation and precision.

Employment participation by the partners of unemployed people

The heavy and increasing emphasis on means-testing in the British system of unemployment-related benefits has focused concern that the household means-test might deter partners from working. Indeed, in 1995/96 the employment rate for partners of unemployed people was around 31% below the corresponding rate for the partners of people in work (McKay et al, 1997). However, it appears that in reality little of this overall shortfall can be directly attributed to perverse incentives created by the benefits system.

The fact that the partners of unemployed claimants are less likely than other partners to be employed, even before the claimants became unemployed, has two important implications. First, it suggests that two-earner couples are less prone to the need to claim unemployment-related benefits, either because they are less at risk of unemployment, or because they decide not to claim but to live on the wages of the partner remaining in work. Second, claimants whose partners are still employed may find it easier to return to work, since they need only to supplement an existing wage rather than to provide for an entire household. In addition, claimants in couples where both partners usually worked were also typically better educated, older and less likely to have children (especially pre-school aged children) than claimants from couples with one breadwinner. These factors may well also contribute to claimants being better able rapidly to return to work.

The majority of people (73% at least) who were working when their partner became unemployed continued to do so. Some did cease work, notably in situations where the partner was female and/or had no formal qualifications, and where the couple was dependent on a means-tested, unemployment-related benefit. Any resultant fall in the proportion of partners working generally seemed to be short-lived once partners were back at work. More surprisingly, it appears that almost as many people begin working following the unemployment of their partner as ceased to do so.

Statistical modelling, undertaken before the introduction of JSA (Elias, 1997) suggested that slightly under two fifths of the shortfall in the employment of the partners of claimants was due to the unemployment of their claimant partner. This includes a fifth that was possibly attributable to the ending of entitlement to Unemployment Benefit after 12 months of unemployment.

Benefit fraud and dependency

It is important to juxtapose research evidence, which strongly indicates that most unemployed claimants have a strong attachment to the labour market and that few abuse the system, with official concerns about the extent of illicit working while claiming benefit. For example, a recent official review, chaired by Lord Grabiner (2000, p 3), suggests that "at any one time, 120,000 people are fraudulently working and claiming" and that £465 million is lost each year through claimants' failure to declare earnings. Because the measurement of fraud is notoriously difficult – measures include 'confirmed' and 'strongly suspected' fraud – these figures must be treated with caution. Also it is impossible to secure reliable estimates of whether the extent of fraud has changed over time given repeated changes in the energy and methods used to detect fraud. In the mid-1990s, 40% of the fraud associated with Unemployment Benefit and Income Support was linked to working and claiming, 32% to living together and 13% to the use of false identities or addresses.

On the basis of this official evidence, between 7% and 11% of claimants would appear to be engaged in fraud at any one time. While these figures are not insignificant they nevertheless suggest that the vast majority of benefit recipients, even long-term recipients, are not found to be engaged in fraud. Those who are appear to be motivated by perceived necessity and opportunity. Most say they need the work to make ends meet. Working on benefit comes long down the list of financial coping strategies – after delaying payment of bills but above pawning valuables, selling essential possessions, seeking charity and 'petty crime' (Kempson et al, 1994).

It would appear that most of the people working illicitly on benefit accept work offered to them rather than deliberately soliciting it. The work undertaken is mostly casual and short-term – a day's work paying £40 £50 in cash. High nominal tax rates (given the earnings disregard of only £5 per day), together with the administrative hassle entailed, are reasons that are typically given for not reporting the earnings. With tighter eligibility criteria and more conditionality, more people are likely to be sanctioned unless they are deterred from claiming. Many of those who are sanctioned feel unfairly treated, often believing themselves to have had no alternative but to do as they did (Vincent, 1998).

In the public's view, benefit fraud is less serious than crimes against the person or burglary, although more serious than petty shoplifting (Rowlingson et al, 1997). There is also sympathy for 'deserving' poor people who commit fraud out of neccesity in order to make ends meet. Among claimants not committing fraud, the reasons given are generally practical – lack of opportunity and fear of getting caught rather than for reasons of principle.

Fraud boosts caseloads to an unknown extent. Reducing fraud would cut benefit expenditure but not necessarily caseloads – those prevented from working might simply remain on benefit but enjoy a lower standard of living. Theoretically, fraud could raise living standards, erode the financial incentive to leave benefit and thereby add to the average time that people remain in receipt of benefit. However, given the comparatively small number of people thought to engage in fraud, the effect of this is likely to be marginal.

What has been learned

The empirical basis for a shift towards more coercive policies or the concern with the financial incentives created by benefits is not strong. Nevertheless, these concerns continue to exercise policy makers.

Most unemployed people, even those who have been out of work for long periods, maintain a strong attachment to the labour market. They also appear relatively flexible in the kind of jobs they will consider taking, match expected wages against their perceived needs rather than fixing them in relation to benefit levels, and take jobs paying less than their expectations. While people appear to be put off working when their partner is unemployed, because of the effect of means testing, even this effect is not as strong as previously thought. What appears to be more important in keeping people on benefit, and hence determining caseloads, is a lack of appropriate skills and uncertainty about the risks involved in moving from benefit to work.

Fraud undoubtedly adds to caseload size but it is impossible to say by how much. However, it does not appear sufficiently widespread to justify viewing unemployed benefit recipients as belonging to a culturally dependent welfare class.

EIGHT

Understanding trends in unemployment-related benefits

Summary

Unemployment caseloads have been driven upwards by de-industrialisation and by the priority given to the control of inflation over full employment as a policy goal.

Social security and labour market polices have sought to contain the growth in caseloads, initially by diverting people out of the labour market or into training in large numbers.

Subsequent tightening of the benefit regulations may have reduced the total claimant count by, perhaps, 350,000. It also shifted the balance of provision radically towards means-testing.

Concern about work incentives has led to the provision of in-work benefits that have created a new category of benefit recipient. In 1999 the number of employed people receiving means-tested benefits fell only a little short of the number receiving unemployment-related benefits.

Most recently, proactive welfare to work policies have been developed to reduce the unemployment caseload by providing assistance, training and work experience. Their long-term effectiveness remains to be established. In the short term they are reducing the claimant count by about 215,000.

Having reviewed the literature, what story can be told about the increased number of claims for unemployment-related benefits?

The growth in the number of claimants of unemployment-related benefits between 1971 and 1999 was the direct result of the de-industrialisation of the British economy, a process that changed forever the nature of the labour market, added a new dynamic, and radically restructured the set of employment opportunities available (Figure 8.1). The impact of labour market changes was mediated by labour market and social security policies that themselves evolved in response to the new economic environment, and were guided by a varying mix of ideology and pragmatism. A shared understanding developed between successive governments that the goal of full employment had become unrealistic, and that high inflation was a worse evil than high unemployment. From the late 1980s onwards the common belief emerged that policies needed to accommodate the new needs of the flexible labour market.

Although throughout most of the period total employment continued to grow, jobs were lost in large numbers from the traditional manufacturing sectors and 'replaced' by service sector jobs, many of which were low paid and latterly part-time and short-term. Claimant unemployment rose to at least three million in 1986, accelerated by an influx into the labour market of a large cohort of young people. Unemployment had approximately halved by 1990, only to rise again to over 1.5 million in 1993, from which point it has fallen consistently. The proportion of long-term unemployment rose to over 45% in 1993 and it is probable that 'churning', the process by which people move in and out of short-term employment, increased.

By December 1999 the *rate* of claimant unemployment was approaching that in 1971, but the number unemployed and claiming benefit was 65% higher on account of a sustained growth in the labour force. Moreover, the coverage of social security has been considerably reduced and eligibility criteria have been tightened, which means that like is not being compared with like.

In reality, unemployment in the 1980s was much higher than recorded. It was reduced by the expansion of work experience and training courses begun in the 1970s that, by the first half of the 1980s, were absorbing upward of half a million people at any one time. In 1999 New Deal for Young People similarly served to reduce visible claimant unemployment by about 43,000 and New Deal for the Long-term Unemployed by 15,000.

A series of changes were introduced in the eligibility criteria for contributory Unemployment Benefit (later to become Jobseeker's Allowance). These, together with lengthening spells of unemployment, changed the ratio of contributory to means-tested benefits from 2:1 in 1971 to closer to 1:2 in 1999.

Figure 8.1: Understanding unemployment-related benefit caseloads

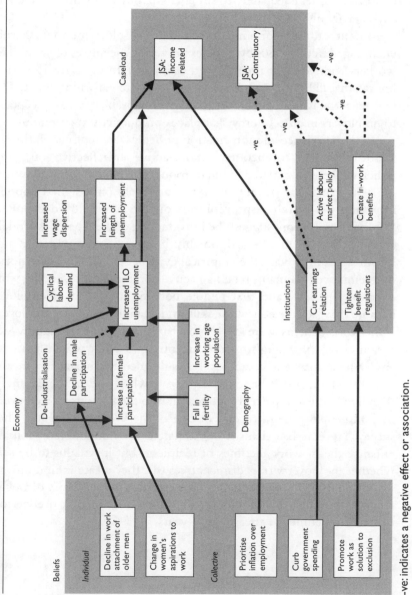

-ve: indicates a negative effect or association.

Female activity rates, notably those of mothers with young children, also rose between 1971 and 1999, adding between 2% and 3% to the labour force and a disproportionate number of the newly created jobs were taken by women. The higher female employment rates reflected the changing aspirations and priorities of women. In addition, however, women may also have been under increased economic and social pressure to work in order adequately to support a family in a world where jobs paying a 'family wage' have become scarcer.

In contrast, the economic activity rates of older men fell sharply, encouraged in the 1980s by policies providing incentives to swap older workers with younger unemployed claimants. In the early 1990s it is known that ill health was a key factor in de facto early retirement. This may reflect an increase in the threshold of employability that is acceptable to employers in an economy that places productivity at a premium.

Work experience and job creation policies were replaced in the late 1980s by policies to encourage more active and effective job search policies. These culminated in the introduction of Jobseeker's Allowance in 1996 that made benefit receipt conditional on a signed contract imposing job search responsibilities on the unemployed claimant. Published evaluations suggest the introduction of these policies brought about reductions in caseload, notably in areas of comparatively high labour demand. In fact, the empirical evidence is that the vast majority of unemployed claimants retain an active commitment to finding work over long periods, and that people become long-term unemployed because they lack the education, skills and qualities sought by employers.

In-work benefits were developed to complement the supply-side measures by enhancing financial incentives to work which had been eroded by stagnant entry wage levels and the increased reliance on means-tested unemployment benefits. By 1999, when one of these benefits (Family Credit) was partially integrated into the tax system, well over a million people were in receipt of one of the in-work benefits. Their success has yet to be exhaustively evaluated. They undoubtedly initially enhance the in-work incomes of recipients but it remains to be seen whether the 'poverty trap' disincentives that they create inhibit upward income mobility. Either way, they have created a new category of welfare recipient drawing a mix of labour market and benefit income over periods that can sometimes be measured in years.

(Chapters in this part of the book were largely written by Marilyn Howard)

NINE

Trends in benefits for disabled people

Summary

In Britain, specialised disability benefits were largely a creation of the 1970s, and now fall into four distinct groups: income maintenance benefits, extra costs benefits, wage supplements and compensation benefits.

Caseloads for the income maintenance and extra costs benefits have increased markedly since their introduction, with much of the growth occurring in the late 1980s and during the 1990s.

The take-up of wage supplements has been below expectations and the growth in compensation benefits has been only moderate.

By 1999 disabled people had become the second largest group of social security recipients, and the number of disabled people of working age receiving disability and incapacity benefits exceeded the number claiming benefits because of unemployment.

This chapter first introduces the reader to the main cash benefits for disabled people, before summarising the patterns of benefit receipt and, finally, outlining the strategy to be adopted in this part of the book.

First, we should note that 'disability' is a complex and sometimes contentious concept. The traditional 'medical model' emphasises the person's impairments and inability to perform tasks as the main reason for their disadvantage. Alternatively, the 'social model' emphasises the role of social structures in creating this disadvantage. Each model carries a set of assumptions and vocabulary, using the term 'disability' in different ways (see Berthoud et al, 1993, for a fuller discussion). Here we refer to 'disabled people' as people with an impairment who are disadvantaged in society, and 'disability benefits' as those payable once some kind of impairment test (often as well as other eligibility conditions) has been satisfied.

An introduction to disability benefits in Britain

Welfare benefits for disabled people in Britain divide into four sets (Table 9.1): benefits to provide income maintenance, to cover the additional costs of disability, to supplement wages, and to provide compensation for loss of faculty.

- The three *income maintenance benefits* (Incapacity Benefit, Severe Disablement Allowance, Income Support) are payable on the basis of an assessment of incapacity for work. Entitlement to Incapacity Benefit also requires sufficient National Insurance contributions, Severe Disablement Allowance involves a disablement test, and Income Support necessitates a means test. People who are considered incapable of work but who fail the National Insurance conditions for benefit receipt are entitled to receive National Insurance Credits (meaning that they can continue to build up entitlement to a state pension).
- The benefits to meet the *extra costs of disability* (Disability Living Allowance care component for people who become disabled before the age of 65 and Attendance Allowance for older people) are based on demonstrable need for care or supervision. The mobility component of Disability Living Allowance requires that a person is unable or virtually unable to walk, and is only payable for people claiming before the age of 65. The benefits are non-contributory and not subject to a means test.
  Payments to enable people to purchase their own personal assistance, such as the Independent Living Fund and Direct Payments from their local authority, are not social security payments and so are not considered further.
- Disabled Person's Tax Credit, a *wage supplement*, is aimed at people who are disadvantaged in the labour market because of disability and who work for more than 16 hours a week. The intention is to help people make the transition into work and so help them to move off Incapacity Benefit. The scheme is means-tested, partially integrated into the tax system and paid via the employer in the wage packet.

- *Compensation benefits* (Industrial Injuries and War Pensions) are contingency based and dependent on the degree of disability, measured in terms of loss of physical or mental faculty.

People can receive more than one benefit at a time. In 1999:

- 17% of people who received Incapacity Benefit also received Income Support;
- 70% of those receiving Severe Disablement Allowance also received Income Support;
- 42% of those receiving the Disability Living Allowance also received Income Support;
- 31% of those receiving the Disability Living Allowance mobility component also received Income Support (DSS, 2000e).

People with identical impairments may qualify for different benefits on account of the cause of impairment or differences in work history, and the level of payment may vary by a factor of almost three. In 1999/2000, someone might have received £417.65 per week from the war pensions scheme or £145.95 from Severe Disablement Allowance and Disability Living Allowance (Paterson, 2000).

Taken overall, the numbers of people claiming disability benefits have increased dramatically since the early 1970s when most benefits for disabled people were introduced. There has been a three-fold increase in people receiving the main income maintenance benefit (now Incapacity Benefit), and a ten-fold increase over the numbers originally expected to claim benefits for attendance and mobility (Berthoud, 1998a). The explanation for these developments is complex. Perhaps most important has been a change in the public conception of disability, which resulted in the introduction of a number of benefit schemes in the 1970s which may, in turn, have changed the self-perceptions, attitudes and behaviour of disabled people themselves. Demographic changes, notably the ageing of the population, have undoubtedly increased the prevalence of disability among the retired population. The increase in the receipt of disability benefits by people of working age will have been affected by a mix of all of these factors but also by changes in the labour market. Before considering each of these factors in turn, it is appropriate to detail the growth in benefit receipt since 1971.

Table 9.1: Sickness and disability benefits

Benefit	Description	Disability tests
Income maintenance		
Incapacity Benefit	Taxable NI benefit. Maintenance benefit for people unable to work because of sickness or disability including those who do not qualify for Statutory Sick Pay. Paid at three rates depending on duration of incapacity. Individual assessed on ability to do any work (rather than usual occupation) after 28 weeks	Largely assessed by the personal capability assessment, including the former 'all work test'. This is based on inability to perform a variety of physical and mental functions, from which a score is derived to establish if the individual has reached a threshold above which he or she is not expected to look for work in order to receive benefit
Severe Disablement Allowance (SDA)	Tax-free, non-contributory benefit for those incapable of work for at least 28 weeks who do not qualify for Incapacity Benefit	Most SDA claimants must also be at least 80 % disabled
Income Support	Means-tested safety net; includes additional payment for disabled people (the 'disability premium')	

Table 9.1: Sickness and disability benefits

Benefit	Description	Disability tests
Extra costs		
Disability Living Allowance	Non-contributory, tax-free, non-means-tested benefit to meet extra costs of care and mobility needs of people aged under 65 when their claim starts	Need for care or supervision from another person for the care component; Unable or virtually unable to walk used for the mobility component
Attendance Allowance	Non-contributory, tax-free, non-means-tested benefit to help meet the extra costs which arise from the care needs of people aged 65 and over	Need for care or supervision from another person
Wage supplements		
Disabled Person's Tax Credit	Formerly Disability Working Allowance, now a means-tested tax credit to be payable via the wage packet	Prior receipt of specified disability benefits
Compensation benefits		
War pensions *Industrial Injuries Scheme*		Degree of disablement, where a loss of physical or mental faculty is assessed as causing disablement amounting to a particular percentage (includes additional allowances for extra costs)

Trends in benefit receipt

In 1999, the last year for which statistics are available, 2.88 million people of working age were claiming benefits on grounds of sickness or incapacity. Accounting for 48% of all working-age claimants, they constituted the largest group of welfare beneficiaries after retirement pensioners. In addition 1,267,000 people over retirement age received Attendance Allowance (DSS, 2000d).

There are substantial flows of people onto sickness and disability benefits from other kinds of social security benefits. About half of claimants who change the type of benefit that they are claiming enter the 'sick and disabled' category, but comparatively few disabled people move to other benefits or into work. Of the 2,760,000 people of working age who were claiming sickness or disability benefits in August 1996, 66% were still doing so three years later (DSS, 2000e). Indeed, the evidence is that most sick or disabled people claiming benefits do so more or less permanently and that, if anything, the length of time spent on benefit has been increasing. In 1999 almost three quarters of claims from sick and disabled people of working age had lasted for two years or more, irrespective of the benefit claimed (DSS, 2000e).

Income maintenance

The number of people receiving income maintenance benefits on the grounds of long-term incapacity (lasting over six months) grew by 363% between 1973-74 and 1994-95 (Evans, 1998). Awards of Incapacity Benefit have since fallen, but the number receiving Severe Disablement Allowance has risen, although stabilising during 1999. However, numbers of people receiving Income Support with a disability premium have continued to increase steadily.

Incapacity Benefits

The number of people receiving the former Invalidity Benefit increased more than three-fold from 500,000 to 1.77 million between 1975 and 1995, the year that it was replaced by Incapacity Benefit (Berthoud, 1998a). The proportion of women receiving this benefit grew at almost twice the rate of men over this period, and the average time spent on benefit went up from three to five years between 1985 and 1995 (DSS,

1998e). This growth took place despite changes to benefit entitlement, which included the tightening of the medical controls prior to the 1995 reforms.

The introduction of Incapacity Benefit was intended to reduce the number of claimants, and this has been achieved, although not to the extent that was originally anticipated. It had been expected that, over the first three years, more than half a million people would lose benefit as a result of the new incapacity test. This was anticipated to consist of 240,000 existing Incapacity Benefit and 85,000 Income Support claimants, together with 160,000 new Incapacity Benefit and 35,000 Income Support claimants (*Hansard*, 29 March 1995, col 556w, House of Commons). In fact, only 160,000 people left Incapacity Benefit during the following two years, and a quarter had their benefit reinstated on appeal (Berthoud, 1998a). By 1999 there were 1.5 million beneficiaries, compared with 1.8 million four years earlier (DSS, 2000f).

While the 1995 changes to the incapacity test did not increase flows off Incapacity Benefit to the extent anticipated, they do seem to have reduced the number of people starting a new spell on long-term benefit, from 350,000 per year under Invalidity Benefit to only 130,000 under Incapacity Benefit (Berthoud, 1998a). Moreover the decline has continued. Figures for new spells on all rates of Incapacity Benefit (and including those receiving National Insurance Credits) dropped from 242,000 in the quarter ending May 1995 (that is, just after its introduction) to 181,000 in the quarter ending November 1999 (DSS, 2000f).

The All Work Test was replaced on 3 April 2000 by the Personal Capability Assessment (PCA). The threshold of incapacity that had to be met to qualify for benefit and the method of assessment has not changed as a result of the PCA. The assessment process was enhanced so that it focuses on what people can do despite their illness or disability, as well as determining whether they satisfy the benefit incapacity threshold.

Incapacity 'credits only'

People who are considered incapable of work but who fail the National Insurance conditions for benefit receipt are entitled to receive National Insurance Credits (enabling them to continue to build up entitlement to a state pension). Some of this group may also be entitled to Income Support (see below), but the statistics do not tell us precisely how many. The numbers of people receiving Credits rose steadily from 45,000 in

June 1977 to 78,000 in 1987 (DSS, 1996a). The following year, numbers jumped to 110,000, and by 1995, the last year of Invalidity Benefit, had reached 512,000. Statistics for the quarters ending between May 1995 and November 1999 show the numbers increasing still further, from 556,480 to 746,500 (DSS, 2000f). This suggests that the introduction of Incapacity Benefit has had little impact on the steady growth of this group. We would expect that the more stringent functional tests of capacity would apply equally to recipients and Credits-only cases. That the numbers of Credits-only cases continues to rise would seem to indicate a trend in the opposite direction for Incapacity Benefit recipients, which may reflect other changed conditions of entitlement. Rules which could have a bearing on declining numbers claiming this contributory benefit include the removal of payment of benefit for five years past retirement age, and changes to the rules allowing different periods out of work to be linked together.

Income Support

Overall, the number of people receiving means-tested benefits for sickness or disability has risen by 150% since 1973, the growth since 1989 being particularly marked (Evans, 1998).

The numbers claiming Income Support with disability premium has increased at the same time as the rate of growth of Incapacity Benefit claims has stalled (Berthoud 1998a). People can qualify for the disability premium if they receive one of the other Incapacity Benefits, or are assessed as being incapable of work, or if they receive a benefit to meet extra costs, such as Disability Living Allowance. However, it is impossible on the basis of current statistics to determine which one of these factors is the most important, or whether changes in Incapacity Benefit have directly increased demand for Income Support. Certainly, claims made by disabled people for Income Support were increasing before the introduction of Incapacity Benefit in 1995. The number of disabled people receiving Income Support increased from 330,000 in May 1990 to 699,000 in 1995, and to 940,000 in November 1999 (DSS, 2000b). Numbers of people receiving the Severe Disability Premium at the lower rate (for single people) also increased from 323,000 to 464,000 (DSS, 2000b).

Figure 9.1: Trends in receipt of income maintenance benefits for disabled people (1972-98)

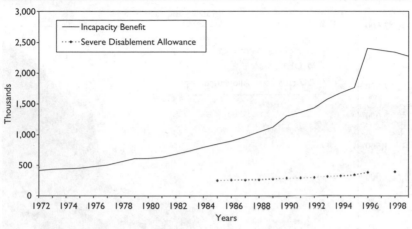

Source: DSS (1999c)

Severe Disablement Allowance

This is a smaller-scale benefit, received by 368,000 people by the end of November 1999 (DSS, 2000f)). Numbers claiming this allowance have increased only slightly since its inception in 1984. Between 1995 and 1999 the number of beneficiaries grew from 324,500 to 370,00. The peak year for new claims was 1994/95, when 34,000 new spells were recorded, but the numbers have since tailed off to 25,000 in 1997/98, and 15,000 in 1998/99 (DSS, 1999b).

Benefits for extra costs

At the time of its introduction, Attendance Allowance was expected to reach 250,000 people, while Mobility Allowance had an estimated target population of 150,000 (Berthoud, 1998a). By 1997/98 both caseloads had increased to more than ten times the original estimates, to 2.4 million and 1.3 million respectively. Disability Living Allowance was formed in 1992, from the merger of Attendance Allowance and Mobility Allowance, and the introduction of two new lower rates of benefit. The combined caseload grew by one million within five years (Social Security Select Committee, 1998), but the rate of increase has since begun to slow down, falling from an average annual increase between 1993 and 1996 of 14%, to 5% between 1997 and 1999 (DSS, 1999a). Although,

Figure 9.2: Trends in receipt of extra costs benefits for disabled people (1972-99)

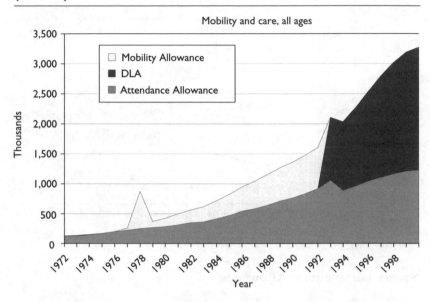

Source: DSS (1999c)

since 1992, Attendance Allowance has been restricted to people aged over 65 who are so severely disabled that they need a great deal of help with personal care or supervision, the caseload nevertheless grew from 890,000 in 1993 to 1.23 million in early 1999. Recipients are mainly women, and more than half are aged over 80 (DSS, 1999c). The overall trends in 'costs' benefits are shown in Figure 9.2 above.

Compensation schemes

Trends in the receipt of compensation benefits have been much less dramatic. There were 253,000 war pensioners in 1998, compared to 229,000 in 1984 and 514,000 in 1970 (Brown, 1984). However, the growth in numbers claiming industrial injuries benefits has been noticeably greater. Between 1984 and 1998, numbers receiving industrial injuries disablement benefit increased from 189,000 to 276,000 (DSS, 1999c). Both programmes together fail to account for more than 7% of total benefit expenditure on sick and disabled people, and will not be further considered in this chapter.

Figure 9.3: Trends in receipt of earning supplement benefits for disabled people (1993-98)

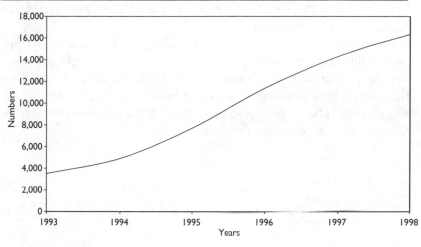

Source: DSS (1999c)

Earnings supplementation

Disability Working Allowance, the main wage top-up for disabled people in work, enjoyed only limited take-up. It started with a lower than anticipated caseload and increased only slowly, to 16,453 awards on 31 January 1999, less than a third of the 50,000 initially anticipated recipients (Figure 9.3; DSS, 1999c). Disability Working Allowance was replaced by Disabled Person's Tax Credit in October 1999, payable by the Inland Revenue, and up-take is expected to be twice that of Disability Working Allowance. As of January 2000, 20,992 people were receiving the Disabled Person's Tax Credit (Inland Revenue, 2000).

Strategy

The number of people receiving benefits on grounds of disability increased very markedly between 1971 and 1999. In the first year there were few specialist benefits for disabled people; those of working age would have relied on short-term sickness benefit or Supplementary Benefit, the main means-tested safety net; older people would only have had access to a pension and means-tested supplementation. By the final year there was a wide-ranging set of benefits for disabled people, who had become the largest group of working-aged claimants, second in size overall only to elderly people. (This ignores children, who are indirect beneficiaries of the social security system since their parents receive Child Benefit on their behalf.)

In attempting to understand the generally upward trend in the receipt of disability and incapacity benefits, it is appropriate to begin first with the changed attitudes that led to the introduction and development of the various benefit schemes, topics addressed in Chapter 10 and 11 respectively. The impact of demographic factors is covered next in Chapter 12, and economic factors in Chapter 13.

TEN

Beliefs about disability

Summary

The introduction of new benefits in the 1970s reflected a shift in social attitudes to disabled people and recognition that society had a role in responding to their financial needs. Policy since then has, with rare exceptions, been a response to fears that the changed attitudes and benefit provisions may have created excessive, or indeed illicit, demand for benefits.

Survey evidence on the extent of disability has proved influential, increasing the climate for policy reform, although the definition and measurement of disability and incapacity has proved very difficult. It is possible that people may have fewer inhibitions about reporting impairments, particularly minor ones.

The public awareness of disability as a legitimate reason for benefit receipt appears to have increased, and it may be more acceptable for people to define themselves as 'disabled' and to seek out appropriate benefits.

It is possible that changing conventions about who should work have made it more acceptable for disabled people not to be in employment. However, there is evidence that many disabled people themselves want work, but may not believe they have much practical chance of getting a job.

The receipt of Incapacity Benefit is greatest in regions of high unemployment, and ill-health early retirement has increased. These trends are believed to reflect the diversion into 'hidden unemployment' or premature retirement. However, it has not been proven that these trends invariably represent a deliberate choice by individuals to positively choose a life on benefit.

The key to understanding the growth in benefit recipiency by disabled people is to recognise the change in the way that society has understood and responded to disability issues. In the early part of the 20th century, disability was virtually invisible in benefit policy, largely limited to a response to catastrophic events, such as war or industrial injury, where compensation was both practical and morally clear-cut. Only gradually did policy come to address both the opportunity and additional costs of disability. For the purposes of state Income Support, 'disability' encompasses both short and long-term absences from work, through sickness or physical or mental impairments. Most of the early schemes were based on physical impairments, with mental health and learning disability recognised later on (Brown, 1984).

Improvements to the system resulted from concern, generated from the mid-1960s onwards, that disabled people were poor, as those on benefit long-term tended to be reliant on means-tested benefits, without any assistance towards the additional costs generated by impairments. Reflecting the 'rediscovery of poverty' among the affluence of the day, organisations such as the Disablement Income Group (DIG) and the Disability Alliance campaigned for better incomes for disabled people. The Attendance Allowance and other benefits can be counted among DIG's achievements in the early 1970s. However, the campaign for better incomes for disabled people subsequently attracted the criticism, from adherents of the social model of disability, that it focused on the *symptoms* (poverty) and not the *cause* of disabled people's exclusion from society, such as reduced labour market opportunities (Oliver and Barnes, 1998). Alongside the pressure for improved benefits for disabled people grew a parallel (but largely separate) vocal and active civil rights movement, drawing on the ideals of the social model. This developed swiftly during the 1980s and 1990s, with the principal aim of achieving comprehensive anti-discrimination legislation. The campaign for equal status for disabled people undoubtedly influenced public awareness of disability, as well as a policy change from the then government in the mid-1990s, culminating in the enactment of the 1995 Disability Discrimination Act (DDA). Indeed the 'individual' model, stressing a needs-based approach, may well have been most influential in policy makers' development of disability benefits, while the 'social' model, personified in the well-publicised actions of some disability activists, may have helped to raise public consciousness about discrimination in the wider society.

Profoundly positive though some of these changes are, it is also important to reflect on negative attitudes and assumptions. Wider changes in the economy and benefit system, discussed in more detail in Chapters 11 and 13, may have established perverse incentives. Certainly, concern has been expressed that increased uptake of disability benefits is due partly to unemployed people exaggerating their impairments in order to receive the higher paying benefits.

This chapter divides into three major sections. The first documents the changing ideological perspective on disability and its consequences for benefit receipt. The middle section illustrates some of the problems of measuring the prevalence of disability that make it difficult to establish whether disability is increasing. The third section focuses on personal perceptions of disability and their impact on claimant behaviour.

Historical developments

Compensation schemes were developed in Britain before the Second World War, and benefits to cover short-term sickness were introduced with the creation of the postwar National Insurance Scheme. However, most of the benefits for disabled people and carers were introduced during the 1970s. These changes added contingencies to the National Insurance system (such as Incapacity Benefit), as well as extending non-contributory benefits payable on the basis of tests of disability rather than National Insurance Contributions or means. Non-contributory benefits now include income-replacement benefits (such as Severe Disablement Allowance) and benefits to compensate for the extra costs of disability, such as Disability Living Allowance. Although an oversimplification, it is helpful to contrast the differing policy approaches evident in each of the last three decades.

The 1970s

During the 1970s, strategic policy on social security had a number of goals: to lessen reliance on means testing by raising benefits above the means-tested Supplementary Benefit level; to pay benefits that would not be eroded by inflation; to extend earnings-related benefits such as State Earnings Related Pensions (Barr and Coulter, 1991). More specifically, for people with an impairment or illness, there was a new recognition of the impact of long-term sickness (before then benefit had been payable only for short-term sickness). This resulted from powerful pressure group activity, as well as research findings that disability featured prominently as one of the causes of poverty (Ogus et al, 1995). This led to the introduction of National Insurance (Invalidity Benefit) and non-contributory benefits (Non-Contributory Invalidity Pension, and the separate Housewives' Non-Contributory Pension for married women), and Invalid Care Allowance for carers. The development of non-contributory benefits was seen as an alternative to extending the contributory scheme for people who had been unable to pay recent contributions, by allowing them to claim as of 'right', without the stigma of means testing, in such a way as to gain the "psychological advantage of membership of the National Insurance community" (Brown, 1984, p 215).

The National Insurance-based Invalidity Benefit consisted of a flat-rate pension, dependant's allowances, and additional allowances based on age. The fact that one of the elements was called a 'pension' meant that, in subsequent years, governments came under pressure to confer more favourable treatment on that group of claimants than for short-term benefits (Ogus et al, 1995). Over the same period, Attendance Allowance and Mobility Allowance were also introduced, originally with a focus on physical impairments.

The 1980s

After the expansion in benefits for disabled people in the 1970s, the focus of policy development shifted, in the 1980s, towards enhancing work incentives and better targeting (Barr and Coulter, 1991), as it was believed that out of work benefits were sufficiently high to discourage people from returning to work. The main policy goals with respect to disability benefits during this time were to reduce administrative costs, eliminate sex discrimination, and scale back the industrial injuries scheme (the state 'no-fault' scheme for work-related injury and illness) (Ogus et al, 1995). Industrial injuries benefits were reduced, from the abolition of Injury Benefit in 1982, the abolition of Industrial Death Benefit and three of the special allowances in 1986, and the withdrawal of Reduced Earnings Allowance from 1990. Provision for short-term sickness was gradually transferred from the state to employers and, in 1984, the Non-Contributory Invalidity Pension and the Housewives' equivalent were replaced by Severe Disablement Allowance as a result of European directives on equal treatment.

The policy response to high levels of unemployment during this period led to changes in conditions of entitlement for Unemployment

Benefit, and included targets for the Employment Service for claims not pursued (Campbell, 1999b). This may have encouraged some movement from Unemployment Benefit to Invalidity Benefit (further discussed in Chapter 14).

Reviews of social security in 1985 excluded disability benefits, as the government had commissioned surveys of disabled people which had not then reported. When published, it revealed unexpectedly high levels of impairment among people of working age, and limited take-up of the extra costs benefits. A White Paper, *The way ahead* (DSS, 1990), was published in 1990, and proposed the amalgamation of Attendance Allowance and Mobility Allowance into Disability Living Allowance. This entailed the addition of lower rates of benefit to target those who could not previously have claimed, such as people requiring guidance and supervision because of sensory impairment or learning disability. The White Paper's proposals led to the introduction of Disability Living Allowance in 1992, which has been retained, with minor changes to administration and entitlement, for those in residential or hospital accommodation.

The 1990s

Despite the expansion of provision represented by the introduction of Disability Living Allowance, policy developments in this decade were largely driven by intensified concern about social security spending. Particularly important were worries about the increased numbers of claimants, including disabled people, and the greater length of time that people were spending on benefit. It was then, in part, a response to the outcome of the informal policies operating in the 1980s, which encouraged the movement from Unemployment Benefit onto Invalidity Benefit, and to the explicit aims of increasing take-up of the extra costs benefits following the disability surveys.

The government reaction in the early 1990s was to emphasise better targeting (by tightening eligibility or changing categories for benefit as well as means testing) and greater self-provision (see Oppenheim, 1994). Following administrative changes to Invalidity Benefit, new legislation was implemented in 1995, replacing Invalidity Benefit by Incapacity Benefit. The new regime tightened eligibility criteria through a new test of incapacity (the 'All Work Test'), and changed the structure of the benefit with two principal aims. The first was to reduce the number of recipients and, indeed, there has subsequently been a 30% fall in flows into Incapacity Benefit at 28 weeks from men aged between 50 and 64. The second, restricted to new claims, was to reduce the amount of benefit payable, through abolishing the earnings-related addition, ending the choice of claiming benefit for five years after pension age, and reducing some of the additions payable with the basic benefit. This change was complemented by the introduction of Jobseeker's Allowance which tightened the conditions of entitlement for unemployment-related benefits and strengthened the sanction regime.

The same concerns have exercised the new Labour government, particularly the doubling of workless households that has occurred over the last 20 years, much of it linked to sickness and disability (HM Treasury, 1999). Labour Force Survey statistics indicate that households with at least one member sick or disabled doubled between 1984 and 1996 (Bell et al, 1997). During this time there was also a 10% increase in the proportion of working-age women who were sick or disabled, and a 17% increase among similar women aged 50-59 years (Bell et al, 1997). The increase for all men ranged from 31% in 1984 to 41% in 1996, the largest percentage point increase occurring between 1991-96 (Bell et al, 1997). These figures may reflect changes over time in how people perceive and report conditions which affect them, as well as deteriorating health experiences of people on low incomes (see below).

In response to these concerns, the new government introduced a package of reforms in its 1999 Welfare Reform and Pensions Act which:

- changed the National Insurance Contribution conditions for Incapacity Benefit;
- introduced an offset of Incapacity Benefit of 50 pence in the £ where people receive occupational or private pensions of more than £85 a week, excepting people who also receive the highest rate of the Disability Living Allowance care component;
- extended the higher rate of the Disability Living Allowance mobility component to three and four year olds;
- introduced a Disability Income Guarantee, an increased premium for those on Income Support also receiving the highest rate of the Disability Living Allowance care component; and
- abolished Severe Disablement Allowance for new claims, and passporting younger disabled people (under age 20, or under 25 for those in higher education or training) to Incapacity Benefit.

The first change sought to stem the transition from unemployment to incapacity benefits by making it harder for formerly unemployed people to claim Incapacity Benefit on the basis of contributions made within three years of the claim. The second proposal, to offset income above £85 from an occupational or personal pension, aimed to reduce the amount of Incapacity Benefit to people who also received substantial payments through early ill-health retirement, as amounting to 'double provision'. Both proposals attracted opposition from disability organisations and parliamentarians. Underlying these reforms was the belief that the numbers of people claiming benefit on the grounds of sickness and disability had increased so rapidly that it could not be explained by a decline in health. This view was strengthened by the concentration of Incapacity Benefit claims in areas of former heavy industry, which was taken as evidence that this benefit was hiding unemployment rather than assisting workers who developed a health problem or disability and had to cease work.

The final change brings younger people who would formerly have qualified for Severe Disablement Allowance into the National Insurance scheme, in some senses a step further than the 1970s developments. However, it also removes the non-contributory access to benefits for people (often married women) who do not have enough recent contributions, although the numbers likely to be affected are relatively small (5,000, expected to be in the middle of the household income distribution – see *Hansard*, 16 November 1998, col 397w, House of Commons).

In summary, having first in the 1970s accepted the responsibility to respond to the financial needs of disabled people, successive governments sought to place curbs on expenditures by reducing the growing number of beneficiaries.

Defining disability

Clearly, estimates of the number of disabled people will be sensitive to the definitions and measures used. In 1980 the World Health Organisation (WHO) devised a system of classification based on the experience of an individual in a linked sequence; a *complaint* causes an *impairment*, which limits activity (*disability*) and so creates disadvantage (*handicap*) (described in Berthoud et al, 1993). The Office of Population Censuses and Surveys (OPCS) adapted this classification for use in disability surveys in the mid-1980s. Now revised, the latest classification replaces *disability* with 'activities', and *handicap* with 'participation', and includes environmental factors (WHO, 1999). This reinforces the view of 'disability' as a social or relative concept, or as a 'dual' model encompassing both the impairment and the disadvantages created by social and economic barriers (Berthoud et al, 1993; Howard, 1999).

Despite the complexities and difficulties in measurement, the evidence points to an increase in people experiencing or reporting impairment. However, none of the surveys are directly comparable over time. The momentum for introducing benefits for disabled people in the 1970s was partly generated by the 1971 survey of the prevalence of disability conducted by the OPCS. A further OPCS survey in 1985 constructed a ten-point measure of overall severity of disability, based on an assessment of functional limitations across 10 areas (such as locomotion, personal care, continence). This produced an estimate of 5.7 million disabled adults resident in private households in Great Britain (Martin et al, 1988). Another official study suggested that, by 1996/97, the number of disabled adults had increased to 8.5 million – 20% of the adult population (Craig and Greenslade, 1998). The latter survey was based on a follow-up sample to the Family Resources Survey (FRS), and designed to measure the incomes and resources of disabled people rather than to compare prevalence estimates. However, the FRS follow-up showed an increase in the rate of disability across all age groups, but a fall of 25,000 in those most severely disabled, while far more people appeared in the lowest two categories of severity.

The size of the overall increase led to concerns about the comparability of the two estimates, despite the fact that the latter survey used the same severity scales as the OPCS (and asked additional questions designed to model entitlement to disability benefits). Subsequent analysis of the FRS follow-up survey indicated that the differences could not be accounted for by methodology alone; it could be that the context in which questions are asked might also be important, and it is an area worthy of further investigation (Grundy et al, 1999). It may possibly be a reflection of changes in the socio-economic and employment climate (we discuss some possible influences in Chapters 12 and 13).

Other concepts and measures have informed the policy debate. The General Household Survey (GHS) has included self-reported measures of the limitations on everyday activities, while the Labour Force Survey (LFS) uses similar self-reporting techniques to assess impairments or ill-health that limit paid work. The measures used in the LFS have recently been changed to incorporate the definition of disability in the 1995 Disability Discrimination Act (Cousins et al, 1998). The new questions, adopted in Spring 1997, were estimated to have reduced reported levels of disability by 10%. Even so, they indicated that about five million people of working age have a disability, about one million more than revealed by the FRS estimates (Berthoud, 1998a). This reflects differences in the definitions used, with the LFS picking up more people with illness or minor impairment.

While empirical evidence about the prevalence of disability has importance in influencing policy, concepts such as disability and incapacity for work for benefit purposes can be slippery when applied to a particular individual, as many people do not fit a precise category over time. Indeed, people in receipt of disability benefits may describe themselves to researchers in different ways – as having a disability, illness or impairment (Rowlingson and Berthoud, 1996). In particular, people on incapacity benefit may describe themselves as long-term sick (83%), early retired (23%) or unemployed (8%) (Beatty and Fothergill, 1999b).

Avoiding work?

As in the 1970s, the development of new or extended disability benefits can signal society's approval or recognition of particular contingencies or circumstances (such as incapacity for work or the additional costs of impairment). However, policy concerns have shifted to potentially perverse consequences of policy and to possible unwelcome changes in individuals' attitudes and behaviour as a result of the very existence of those benefits.

There is, for example, a suggestion that it has become more socially acceptable to be out of work because of ill-health or impairment (Berthoud, 1998b), perhaps reflecting prevailing changes in the economy or employer behaviour. Certainly, research into public attitudes suggests that people who are willing to work but are unable to do so because of long-term illness are seen as a more deserving group (Williams et al, 1999). Also, the introduction of Incapacity Benefit as a contributory benefit may have reinforced the view of subsequent generations of claimants that they had a 'right' to claim because they had already paid in National Insurance contributions.

The results of a search for evidence of these kind of developments that may have added to caseloads are reported in the remainder of this section.

Beliefs about disability

One possible explanation for the growth of numbers on disability benefits is that more people are defining themselves as disabled. Berthoud has speculated that this may be so, as disability becomes seen as comparable with retirement (1998a). When work is scarce, being 'sick' may carry less stigma than being unemployed (Bartley and Owen, 1996). Berthoud has also suggested that conventions about who should work have changed, and that it is increasingly acceptable for people not to take employment if their impairments make it difficult for them to do so (Berthoud, 1998b).

Clearly, it is very difficult to disentangle higher prevalence of disability from a lowering in the threshold of disability that people report. However, comparison of the OPCS disability surveys, the FRS and the Health Survey for England supports the view that, across all age groups, there has been an increase in the rate at which people report that they experience ill-health or disability. Likewise, comparison of the two disability surveys in 1985 and 1996/97 reveals that more people reported they were permanently unable to work in the 1990s than in the 1980s (Grundy et al, 1999). People may have fewer inhibitions about reporting impairments, possibly linked to changing social attitudes towards disability and health.

The success of the disability and welfare rights movements may have raised public awareness about disability, publicly as well as politically, and shifted the perceived responsibility from the individual to society and government. Over two thirds of the public now believe that more should be spent on disabled people who are unable to work, although the focus may be on helping those who are on benefit long-term, rather than simply seeing disabled people as a more deserving group (Hills and Lelkes, 1999). For those involved in public service or politics, disability has become an increasingly important element of an equal opportunities agenda (although in most cases far less developed than race or gender). As a consequence, more people may have come to recognise their disability and to apply for benefits, and possibly to view benefits as a viable alternative to continued employment (particularly in a changing labour market).

Beliefs about work

More people might be claiming disability benefits for a range of other reasons that policy makers might consider inappropriate. As already mentioned, faced with a bleak labour market, people might avoid the futile hassle of looking for work and gain a higher income by choosing a disability benefit. They might hold beliefs (realistic or otherwise) about the state of the labour market, and about how their impairment affects their ability to work and their prospects of finding suitable work. They might also feel that employers would be unsympathetic to taking them on (Ritchie and Snape, 1993).

There does not appear to be much evidence, however, that large numbers of claimants are disinclined to work if they could, or that the proportion of disabled people not working has greatly increased. Based on LFS data, the proportion of disabled people of working age in employment in 1997 (40%) was virtually the same as in 1984 (38%), when the first reliable data was collected (Berthoud, 1998a). The actual numbers of disabled people in work has gone up from 1,266,000 to 2,289,000, but this seems to be a reflection of the overall increase in people reporting disability during this time (Cousins et al, 1998).

A survey of 2,000 working-age disabled people in mid-1996 also found little evidence of 'discouragement' among economically inactive disabled people (Meager et al, 1998). Only a few of them reported that they were not looking for work because they believed that there were no jobs available, or that none would be financially worthwhile, or that their impairment would prevent them working. Many Incapacity Benefit recipients have had long periods of stable employment before claiming, which does not suggest they are work-averse. In one study of Incapacity Benefit recipients, half said that they wanted a full-time job, although only 6% were actually looking for one (Beatty and Fothergill, 1999a). Similarly evidence from a study of claimants in rural areas suggests that about a third of people now on Incapacity Benefit looked for work when their last job ended (Beatty and Fothergill, 1999b). On the other hand, the same study suggested that, over time, older men in particular became 'detached' from the labour market. From a peak at the start of a spell of sickness or disability, the expectation of working, the desire to work, and job search were all reported to decline. How far this reflects a rational readjustment to the limitations imposed by their condition or disability, and a positive choice of a life on benefit in preference to work, is unclear.

Labour Force Survey estimates indicate that one million people on one of the incapacity benefits have some interest in work, although over 656,000 would not be able to do so within at least a fortnight (*Hansard*, 9 March 1998, WA22-26, House of Lords). Survey evidence that has considered work aspirations, alongside people's own assessments of their ability to work both immediately and in the longer-term, reveals that, of people who would like to work, a minority expected to do so immediately. Only 42% of those wanting to work were confident that they would ever be able to do so and only six out of ten of these felt that this was possible within six months (Loumidis, 1999). Earlier research into those on the qualifying benefits for Disability Working Allowance suggests that the people who seem to have the best chance of finding work tend to be younger and better qualified, and to have a partner in paid work (Rowlingson and Berthoud, 1996).

Hidden unemployment

Incapacity Benefit claimants tend to be concentrated in areas of industrial decline, with the incidence of claims being greatest in areas that have the highest unemployment rates, although this association is far stronger for men than women (Holmes et al, 1991). In some districts, Incapacity Benefit recipients account for about 10% of the potential labour force (DSS, 1999b).

The geographical concentration of claimants in areas of high unemployment has been seen as evidence of 'hidden unemployment' in those areas, with suggestions that some 1.2 million people might have been diverted from unemployment to sickness (Beatty et al, 1997). However, there is no evidence of regional differences in the rates at which people *leave* Incapacity Benefit (Swales, 1998a). One alternative explanation that has been offered is that the geographical spread may better reflect the pattern of health inequalities (Macmillan, 1999a).

It does appear, however, that there may be a 'ratchet' effect between incapacity and unemployment, whereby Incapacity Benefit caseloads rise at times of high unemployment but do not fall to the same extent when unemployment declines (Berthoud et al, 1993; Berthoud, 1998b; see Chapters 12 and 13). Analysis of the FRS covering the 1980s suggests that the local unemployment rate was more important in 1980 and 1984 than in 1988 (Disney and Webb, 1991). The 'ratcheting effect' seems to be confirmed by Campbell's analysis of the LFS and the British Household Panel Survey for the period 1979-97. This indicates that while there may be some correlation between unemployment and economic inactivity in particular areas at a given point in time, this does not continue over a long period (Campbell, 1999b).

Early retirement

Another concern among policy makers is that Incapacity Benefit has provided a mechanism for early retirement funded by the state; this was the reason for reducing the level of Incapacity Benefit paid to claimants with substantial occupational and private pensions (see also Chapter 11).

Men in manual jobs are more likely to take retirement on grounds of ill-health than those in non-manual work (42% compared with 33%; see Bone et al, 1992). This has been particularly so among local authority employees; over three quarters of retirements in 1995/96 were earlier than the normal retirement age, and 55% of male manual staff retired on grounds of ill-health. Moreover, the proportion of local authority staff retiring for health reasons gradually increased from 1990/91 to 1995/96 (Audit Commission, 1997). A later survey (1999) suggests that early ill-health retirements in local authorities are falling, but less rapidly than *other* early retirements, and there remain variations between authorities (Audit Commission, 2000). Differences over time and place may reflect the practice and procedures of pension fund trustees and employers as much as the rate of illness itself (Poole, 1997). Indeed, Campbell suggests that for disabled people, leaving the labour market may not always be a voluntary choice (Campbell, 1999b).

Although most Incapacity Benefit claimants are aged over 50, the prime age for early retirement, the age profile of claimants has remained fairly constant. If anything, the proportion of men aged 55-64 fell slightly, from 60% of recipients in 1978/79 to 56% in 1992/93, partly due to a growing number of younger claimants remaining on benefit for longer (Berthoud, 1998a).

Nevertheless, successive governments have sought to prevent Incapacity Benefit being used to finance early retirement. In the early 1990s, 35% of Invalidity Benefit recipients, typically men aged over 50, received an occupational pension on the grounds of incapacity. In 1995, the earnings-related supplement to Incapacity Benefit was withdrawn for new claims on the grounds that this amounted to double provision. It also used to be possible for people to receive Incapacity Benefit after retirement age, and many of the claimants with an occupational pension fell into this category – 67% of men with occupational pensions were aged over 65 and 52% of women were over 60 (Lonsdale et al, 1993). However, since 1995, people reaching pension age have no longer been entitled to claim long-term Incapacity Benefit, which naturally resulted in a sharp decline in the numbers of people receiving Incapacity Benefit over this age (DSS, 1999c). The present government's legislation to reduce the value of Incapacity Benefit to claimants with an occupational pension was partly justified by the fact that a quarter of recipients had incomes in the top two quintiles of the income distribution (Table 10.1).

Table 10.1: Position of Invalidity Benefit recipients in the household income distribution (%)

	Bottom quintile	2nd quintile	3rd quintile	4th quintile	Top quintile
All Invalidity Benefit recipients					
Before housing costs	20	34	23	17	8
After housing costs	21	32	22	17	9
Invalidity Benefit recipients with occupational pensions					
Before housing costs	7	23	26	28	16
After housing costs	6	21	25	29	20

Note: Income *includes* Invalidity Benefit. Figures relate to unequivalised income, and do not take account of variations in the size and composition of the households in which individuals live.

Source: The Department's Households Below Average Income (HBAI) series based on the FRS for 1996/97

So, while policy has repeatedly changed during the last 10 years in response to the perceived consequences of disability benefits – the erosion in the attachment of people to work, subsidised early retirement and hidden unemployment – the empirical evidence that these are major drivers of increased caseloads is not strong. Nevertheless, each may still have played a small part.

What has been learned

Changing social attitudes, together with the increasingly evident financial costs of disability, translated into political demands for government to introduce of a series of new cash benefits for disabled people during 1970s, and to more generous extra costs benefits in the early 1990s. However, from the 1980s onwards, concerns about increasing caseloads caused policy makers to tighten eligibility criteria, although at certain times over the last 30 years policy has tacitly encouraged the uptake of incapacity benefits as a means of holding down the claimant unemployment rate. Policy has increasingly been shaped and presented as a response to the inappropriate use of disability benefits by people who should either be considered as unemployed or have additional resources to cover incapacity.

There is, however, little evidence that large numbers of people receiving disability benefits have actively been choosing a life on benefit in preference to working. More likely is the possibility that individuals' perceptions of disability have been shaped by the context of a growing social awareness. Disability construed in this way may be a relative social concept more than an absolute one.

ELEVEN

Institutional factors and disability benefits

Summary

Aspects of the benefit regime and its implementation are implicated in the growth of disability benefit caseloads. This applies to both Disability Living Allowance and Incapacity Benefit.

Until recently **Disability Living Allowance** *was payable for 'life'*, the effect of which has been to set caseloads on a trajectory of sustained growth.

The introduction of self-assessment for **Disability Living Allowance** *may have helped to increase benefit up-take*, while the appeals system and welfare rights activity may help partially to explain geographic variations in take–up.

Caseloads have also been inflated by changes in other institutions, notably in health and social services, through the closure of long–stay hospitals, with the result that more disabled people of working age are living in the community. A more proactive implementation of unemployment benefits by the Employment Service may also have inflated **Incapacity Benefit** caseloads to a degree.

Likewise, the activity of GPs has been proposed as an important determinant of **Incapacity Benefit** claim levels, but *there is no evidence that changes in GPs' behaviour explain the growth in caseloads.*

Fraud was suspected as a factor in boosting disability benefit caseloads, notably **Disability Living Allowance**, although the evidence to

> date suggests that fraud and error are unlikely to be of sufficient
> scale to explain the extent of growth.
>
> It is not possible to establish how important increased take-up has
> been in explaining rising caseloads.

Chapters 9 and 10 revealed that a major factor explaining the rising
number of people claiming disability and incapacity benefits is the
increased availability of such benefits. Supply has fostered demand.

But there is a series of more or less subtle ways in which welfare
institutions have influenced caseloads, and these are the focus of the
current chapter. Aspects of the benefit regime are considered first, before
an examination of the influence of administrative procedures.

Benefit regime

The structure of benefits for disabled people has changed, not only in
the scope of provision, but also in terms of the ways in which disability
and incapacity are assessed, and in the use made of the appeals system to
establish precedent. Moreover, developments in other areas of social
security and social policy may also have affected demand for disability
benefits.

Benefit changes

Nine new benefits for disabled people were introduced in the period
1971-99, and many other changes made that will have served to increase
caseloads (see Chapters 2 and 9). To take an example of the latter, the
merger of Attendance Allowance and Mobility Allowance into Disability
Living Allowance in 1992 deliberately broadened the scope of provision
(principally through the introduction of two new lower rates of benefit),
and hence the numbers receiving benefit. It was anticipated that some
300,000 more people would be entitled to the new lower rates of benefit
(*Hansard*, 21 November 1990, col 314, House of Commons).

The publicity surrounding the introduction of benefit changes can
also generate new demands. In the run-up to the General Election in
1992, the launch of Disability Living Allowance was accompanied by
considerable publicity. As a result, inflows increased dramatically in the
early months of the new benefit, both from new claimants and from

those already receiving one component who claimed the other. This surge of claims created a backlog of cases waiting to be decided, which created pressure to clear claims quickly, often at the expense of the quality of decision making (see, for example, Social Security Select Committee, 1998). The initial surge generated 450,000 claims over a three-month period between February and April 1992, more than double the number of comparable claims during 1991 (Social Security Select Committee, 1993). Subsequently, new claims fell back to around 500,000 per year, until 1997/98 and 1998/99, when they declined to 461,000 and 398,000 respectively. (The proportion of applicants who received an award remained fairly constant over the period, at around half.)

Certain features of the design of the benefits introduced over the last 30 years may have encouraged people to claim continuously for long periods of time. It is evident, for example, that the public perceive disability and incapacity benefits as providing long-term, usually lifetime, support (Stafford, 1998). The fact that disability benefits require some degree of medical corroboration serves further to confirm and legitimate long-term receipt.

Long-term awards

Indeed, until recently, Disability Living Allowance was assessed on a lifetime basis. About three quarters of existing awards of Disability Living Allowance, and around half of the flow of new claims (some 200,000 a year), are for 'life' – defined as an 'indefinite period' during which the person's needs remain the same (Social Security Select Committee, 1998). This proportion would appear to be similar to the pre-1992 system, when 70% of Mobility Allowance awards were for life, and the coverage of the scheme was narrower (*Hansard*, 21 November, 1990, col 351, House of Commons). However, policy concern that some people may have been receiving allowances for 20 years without scrutiny, resulted in the 1999 Welfare Reform and Pensions Act, which contains provision to clarify the meaning of 'life'.

Most benefits are now subject to regular review, which may have the effect of shortening the average period of time that people spend on benefit and, hence, the size of the caseload. Concerned not to 'write off' the stock of claims, the government is developing methods of 'active case management', such as the Periodic Enquiry process for Disability Living Allowance, and the piloting of a 'Keeping in Touch' exercise for Incapacity Benefit (*Hansard*, 5 April 2000, col 250 WH). At the same time, Personal Advisers (via the New Deal for Disabled People and 'ONE' pilots) are being used to coax disabled people back to work. However, early experiences of the Periodic Enquiry process for Disability Living Allowance recipients suggest that in only a minority of cases does the person's need for assistance change to the extent that the benefit award is affected.

Keeping working age benefits after pension age

Disability Living Allowance can be paid over the age of 65 where entitlement began before that date, and some 440,000 recipients are now over that age – 146,000 more than in 1994 (DSS, 1999c).

Similarly, almost a third of the growth in Invalidity Benefit awards has been attributed to the numbers drawing benefit for five years after pension age, as the tax-free status of Invalidity Benefit made it more advantageous to do so than to switch immediately to a pension (Berthoud, 1998b). Whereas in 1983/84, 59,000 men over the age of 65 were receiving Invalidity Benefit, by 1994/95, the last year before the reforms, this had risen to 233,000 (DSS, 1999c). The pattern for women aged over 60 was similar, with the number rising from 9,000 in 1983/84 to 66,000 in 1994/95.

Since then, pensioners can only continue to receive Incapacity Benefit if they were entitled to Invalidity Benefit before April 1995 and also reached pension age before that date. By 1998/99 the number of people receiving Incapacity Benefit after pension age had fallen to 40,000 men and 12,000 women, and there had been a corresponding doubling of the numbers who had transferred from Incapacity Benefit to Retirement Pension, to 365,000.

Changes in contribution conditions

As Incapacity Benefit is a contributory benefit, caseload growth is affected by changes to the contribution conditions. The abolition of the married women's reduced stamp from 1975 is likely to have had some impact on the rise in claims from married women. A growing number of married women in the labour market and paying contributions has been estimated to have increased the Invalidity Benefit caseload by some 16% (Berthoud, 1998a).

A further example is the rule for linking periods out of work for the purpose of establishing which are the relevant years during which National Insurance Contributions have to be paid, an obscure but potentially additional factor affecting both flows onto benefit and their duration. For example, flows of unemployed people onto Invalidity Benefit may have been increased by the ability to rely on contributions paid in an earlier period of employment *prior* to unemployment, rather than immediately before the period of incapacity. Before 1995, it was easier to link periods on different benefits together; these rules were changed to make it more difficult for people to claim Incapacity Benefit without a recent work record.

The abolition of non-contributory access to the benefit by people who had suffered an industrial injury from 1995 may also have reduced some of the flows onto benefit from this (very small) group of people.

As movement to the higher rates of benefit is largely dependent on the time already spent on benefit, returning to benefit after leaving can mean that people have to start again on the lower rates. This may have deterred some recipients from leaving benefit to try employment (Ritchie and Snape, 1993). Until 1980, people could leave Invalidity Benefit for up to 13 weeks before losing their right to higher rate benefit. Since then the linking period has been only eight weeks (now 52 weeks if moving into work and satisfying the rules as a 'Welfare to Work' recipient).

Medical corroboration and self-assessment

As already noted, the medical profession has traditionally played an important part in the administration of benefits for disabled people and, in doing so, perhaps legitimated long-term receipt. However, the role of GPs differs between benefits and has varied over time. A certificate from a GP is required to begin a claim for Incapacity Benefit, possibly followed at a later stage by a medical examination by a Benefits Agency Medical Service doctor (now operated under contract to the private company SEMA rather than directly by the Benefit Agency) to ascertain if someone qualifies. Before 1995, the GP's certificate carried more weight throughout the process.

In contrast, Disability Living Allowance was introduced in 1992, with a deliberate move away from medical examinations towards self-assessment, to be backed up by further evidence from GPs, and only in a minority of cases by examination. This strategy was a response to the disability lobby arguments that an automatic medical examination was humiliating, inappropriate and provided little more than a 'snapshot' of someone's needs. However, confronted by a rapidly rising caseload, the then government revised administrative procedures. The changes included requiring further corroborative evidence for the higher rate of the mobility component in 1996, thus moving away from self-assessment as the main source of information for a claim. This change has been credited with the substantial fall in new claims already noted above (DSS, 2000a). Further changes involved curtailing entitlement when people were in residential care or long-term hospital stay, and a fraud review instituted to justify re-examining awards made for life. The vast majority of claims are now supported by medical evidence (Table 11.1).

Table 11.1: Percentage of new awards of Disability Living Allowance by component and type of evidence

Benefit component	Claim pack only	Factual report from GP or consultant	Medical exam
1992-93			
Care component	49.5	24.7	21.9
Mobility component	45.0	27.6	22.5
1997-98			
Care component	16.0	47.9	31.0
Mobility component	9.0	51.7	35.0

Source: derived from *Hansard*, 17 March 1998, col 537-8w, House of Commons

Appeals

People who have been refused an award for either Incapacity Benefit or Disability Living Allowance may appeal against this decision. It has been suggested that in the case of Disability Living Allowance, the appeal system and the impact of legal judgements, creatively used by welfare rights groups, has expanded the scope of the scheme and may have added to overall numbers. However, the evidence suggests that decisions made on points of law by Social Security Commissioners (largely concerning people with communication needs) seem not to have resulted in significantly more claims from this group. In only 2% of all awards would a decision have been made differently as a result of these cases (Swales, 1998b).

In the case of Incapacity Benefit, a DSS-commissioned study of people disallowed showed that half of these subsequently appealed (Dorsett et al, 1998). Many of the claims were reinstated, meaning that the process resulted in a short-term churning of the caseload; most decisions were reached within four months, although successful appeals took longer.

There is evidence that the existence of a welfare rights service can have a significant impact on whether people appeal and how successful they are. The recent success rate of Incapacity Benefit appeals in Glasgow, which exceeds that in other cities, has been credited to local welfare rights activity (Adams, 1999). However, it is impossible to discern whether changes in the funding and effectiveness of the welfare rights movement has contributed substantially to the increase in claims. Likewise, it is difficult to judge whether a series of changes in decision-making procedures and in the appeals system between 1996 and 1999 will affect the number and success rate of appeals and impact on claimant numbers. However, statistics suggest that the success rate for claimants may be in decline. In 1994 some 59% of claimants successfully appealed against a decision about Invalidity Benefit; by 1998 the success rate for Incapacity Benefit was only 37% (DSS, 1999c).

Policy interactions

It is important not to see disability and incapacity benefits in isolation. A longstanding policy concern is that disability benefit caseloads are in part determined by the characteristics of other benefits. For instance, the level of Invalidity Benefit, being paid at a higher rate than Unemployment Benefit or Invalid Care Allowance, has been thought to be one factor influencing whether people claim one or the other (Ritchie and Snape, 1993). The time limit for contributory Unemployment Benefit (12 months until the introduction of Jobseeker's Allowance) was also thought to have been a factor contributing towards the growth in numbers claiming Invalidity Benefit (Public Accounts Committee, 1991). In particular, the benefit rules for incapacity and unemployment can give incentives for people to claim the former rather than the latter, although it can also result in people being shunted between the relevant agencies and simply swapping benefit entitlement over a period of time. In the mid-1990s, one in four unemployed claimants reported an impairment or health problem limiting their work, and 18% of these changed from unemployed to a sick or disabled status within the space of two years, together with 3% of those who did not mention ill-health or impairment at the outset (Shropshire et al, 1999). However, as noted in Chapter 10, there is little evidence confirming that the majority of people make this transition as the result of genuine choice.

Nonetheless, it is possible that changes in other benefit regimes have affected claims for incapacity benefits. For example, during the 1970s and early 1980s, the Unemployment Benefit regime had comparatively lax implementation of conditionality. This began to change by the mid-1980s, with the introduction of the 'Actively Seeking Work' test in 1989, and more checking of claimants, notably beginning with the Restart programme of interviews from 1986 (Philpott, 1990). These changes may have led claimants to believe that Unemployment Benefit was more 'pressurised' than Invalidity Benefit (Ritchie and Snape, 1993). At that time, people on Invalidity Benefit were offered few incentives to help them find work. Another part of the Employment Service was concerned with helping disabled people to obtain and retain jobs, but this Disablement Resettlement Service (now Disability Employment Advisers) tended to concentrate on unemployed disabled people, and had relatively little interest in Invalidity Benefit claimants (Ritchie and Snape, 1993). A recent qualitative study suggests that some claimants perceived signing on for work as a 'hassle' (especially where the chances of getting work were slim), which might have precipitated a migration to incapacity benefits (Macmillan, 1999b). The same research, however, showed that medical testing for incapacity benefits could act as a deterrent.

The way in which health service and social care institutions operate can also have an influence on the inflow or duration of benefit claims. For instance, there is qualitative evidence that the growth of Invalidity Benefit claims has been related partly to the management of waiting lists for hospital treatment. People have been advised by their doctors not to work while waiting for an operation or treatment (Ritchie and Snape, 1993). General practitioners (discussed below in relation to gate-keeping) may also have played a role in shaping people's expectations of health and the prognosis of their condition, which may have affected perceptions of whether they should claim a particular benefit or not.

More directly, the fundamental policy shift in health, towards the closure of long stay hospitals and their replacement by care within the community, is likely to have had an impact on the numbers of people claiming disability benefits. In particular, people will have been more likely to need Disability Living Allowance and associated benefits if living independently in the community (Social Security Select Committee, 1998). While the total number of people who were resident in institutions grew between 1981 and 1991, Census data indicates that the number of people of *working age* fell by around 15%, to 98,000 (OPCS Census data for 1981 and 1991). Similarly, changes in the pattern of health and social care for people with mental health problems have shifted towards more community-based services, and at the same time numbers of people being referred for specialist services has increased. In England and Wales there were over 300,000 new attendances at psychiatric outpatient clinics, an increase of 40% over the decade ending 1997/98 (Matheson and Summerfield, 2000). First contacts with community psychiatric nurses have also increased, from 418,000 in 1992-93 to 618,000 in 1997/98 (Matheson and Summerfield, 2000).

This reinforces the view that more people of working age may have been living in the community and claiming benefit, although the small scale of these numbers suggests that the overall impact on disability benefit caseloads is likely to have been relatively limited. Also, in the absence of adequate community care services, some people providing informal care may have chosen to claim Invalidity Benefit in their own right, rather than the smaller Invalid Care Allowance, when they had a National Insurance record.

Overall, therefore, most of the exogenous changes of policy that have occurred over the last three decades are likely to have added to the number of disabled people claiming benefits. Much social security policy after the 1970s aimed to put a brake on caseload growth, but did not stem the upward trend until the latter half of the 1990s when, of course, the economy also began to recover (Chapter 12).

Implementation

The focus now shifts from policy to a consideration of policy implementation on caseload numbers.

Massaging the unemployment count

There is some evidence that during the 1980s, with the decline of manufacturing industries, the shake-out in manual jobs and the growth in long-term unemployment, people were encouraged by Employment Service staff to sign off the unemployment register and to claim Invalidity Benefit instead (Campbell, 1999b). This had the effect of enhancing claimants' incomes – Incapacity Benefit is paid at a more generous level than Jobseeker's Allowance/Unemployment Benefit – and of keeping the claimant count down, which was advantageous for political reasons. Also, claimants were under no obligation to look for work.

Part of the context for this action was the introduction of the aforementioned Restart programme, designed to impose greater conditionality on recipients of unemployment-related benefits. This consisted of an interview with an Employment Service counsellor, intended to link people into a range of job search activities and training programmes. Restart operated nationally from July 1986, for people unemployed for 12 months or more, and from April 1987 for those who had been out of work for six months, and was credited with a substantial reduction in the unemployment caseload (Philpott, 1990). However, whereas government ministers claimed that Restart had worked by getting people into jobs, the Opposition used the same data to complain that the scheme was only cosmetic (Philpott, 1990).

A later survey of 5,000 participants for the Employment Service indicated that Restart did explain some of the movement out of unemployment and into 'non-unemployed claimant status' (including, but not exclusively, Invalidity Benefit; see White and Lakey, 1992). However the *additional* effect exerted by Restart was found to be smaller than expected, and probably only short-term (occurring during the first six to 12 months or so of a claim). The authors speculate that this was because the movements into this status were already strongly controlled by other influences. Moreover, some 36% of participants had a health problem or disability, which may in any case have led many to be referred to specialist Disablement Resettlement Officers. It is probable, therefore, that it was not the deterrent effect of Restart that precipitated a movement onto sickness or invalidity benefits, but rather the formal interview which drew the attention of Employment Service staff to the poor health condition of many participants, especially men aged 40-60.

Fraud and error

Fraud became a major concern of the DSS in the mid-1990s, and a series of benefits have been targeted for a 'review' of fraud activity. The Benefits Agency is now stepping up efforts to curb error and fraud across a range of benefits, including Incapacity Benefit (Benefits Agency, 1999)[1].

The most publicised fraud initiative concerning disabled people was the Benefit Integrity Project, which focused exclusively on the caseload receiving the higher rates of Disability Living Allowance. In 1996, fraud investigators estimated that 12% of Disability Living Allowance claims could be fraudulent (Benefits Agency, 1997). Subsequently, the Benefit Integrity Project started in the run-up to the 1997 General Election on 28 April 1997, but closed in March 1999, with much fewer than expected cases of fraud having been established. Evidence suggests that only a minority of people were claiming inappropriately or at the wrong rate, so the scope for fraud and incorrectness as a factor in the growth in claims appears limited. After a year-and-a-half, only 79 cases had been investigated for fraud and none referred for prosecution (Social Security Select Committee, 1999).

Since the Labour government came into power in 1997, there has been a subtle change in language used to describe attempts to verify Disability Living Allowance and awards of other disability benefits. The emphasis has shifted from fraud to overall correctness, stemming from the complexity of a benefit that people do not fully understand, and which may be 'systems error' as much as individual error (Social Security Select Committee, 1998). In fact, the government's own advisory body (Disability Living Allowance Advisory Board, 1998) emphasised administrative factors in explaining increased Disability Living Allowance caseloads. As well as take-up and appeals, including increased welfare rights activity (discussed below), the Board noted:

- a significant rate of incorrect payments and a noticeable degree of overstatement of need; in 63% of cases the award was deemed to be in conflict with the facts;
- Adjudication Officer practices that include insufficient understanding of the disabling condition; inadequate corroboration by the claimant's GP; failure to request medical evidence; failure to select the most appropriate source of medical evidence; misinterpretation of medical evidence; managerial pressures for throughput targets; and a widespread tendency to give life awards, overlooking the potential for improvement;
- a significant degree of avoidable physical and psychological disablement resulting from lack of investment in local clinical and rehabilitation services.

An official review of 1,200 case papers also concluded that 13% of payments were in error (Swales, 1998b). However, Berthoud (1998a) has concluded that this error rate could not explain the six-fold increase in the number of attendance and mobility payments over the past 15 years (excluding the lower rates).

Local variation and GPs as gatekeepers

It is frequently proposed that GPs, who before the Incapacity Benefit changes in 1995 were expected to issue certificates to verify a claim and its continuation, have in some cases and some areas been 'soft' on claimants, or been intimidated into giving sick notes.

Research evidence suggests that GPs were ambivalent towards their role in the certification process for Invalidity Benefit, but that many were unaware of departmental guidance concerning incapacity for work (see, for example, Ritchie and Snape, 1993). The British Medical Association (representing the interest of GPs) has expressed concern that the involvement of doctors in the administration of benefits increases workloads and can jeopardise the doctor–patient relationship (Social Security Select Committee, 1997). The latter concern may be taken as an admission that GPs can be placed in an invidious position. Moreover, a study in Glasgow also found a widespread belief – particularly common among Benefits Agency staff – that people who had been made redundant would go to their GPs to be signed off sick (Adams, 1999). Nevertheless, it is very difficult to substantiate such claims, since data that could have allowed the correlation between major plant closures and Incapacity Benefit receipt to be assessed was not collected below national level prior to 1996.

However, there is little evidence that GPs were more strict in the 1970s than in the 1980s or 1990s, and therefore little to suggest that changes in the attitudes of GPs have contributed much to the increase in benefit claims (Berthoud, 1998a). As far as Disability Living Allowance is concerned, GPs have little involvement beyond verifying diagnosis and condition, often as part of the claim form or on request from the Benefits Agency (for which they are paid).

If the activity of GPs helps to explain the geographic variation in the prevalence of claims for disability benefits, if not the trend over time, they are unlikely to be the only administrative factor involved. There is evidence that the administration of Disability Living Allowance also varies markedly between Disability Benefit Centres. Both the process by which decisions are made, including the type of evidence on which a decision is based, and the outcomes and success rates, vary between centres (Hirst, 1997). Similarly, some regional centres (such as Leeds) seem to be less likely to make Disability Living Allowance awards for children than other centres (Roberts and Lawton, 1998).

In summary, there is conflicting evidence about whether the way that policy was implemented significantly affected claimant numbers. There is a widespread belief that in an era of structural economic change, unemployed people were directed towards incapacity benefits that offer higher benefits and no commitment to seek work. Both GPs and the Employment Service are said to have been instrumental in this process. However, the necessary data to test this belief is lacking and such evidence as there is suggests that while this may have been a factor, claims that this alone can account for the tripling of the Invalidity Benefit caseload are much exaggerated (see Chapter 13).

Take-up

Although the increased take-up of benefits may be a factor increasing claimant numbers, statistical series only exist for income-related benefits, which in the main do not identify disabled claimants of these benefits separately. Estimates of Income Support take-up do, however, suggest that people receiving Attendance Allowance and Disability Living Allowance are more likely to be entitled to Income Support but have not claimed it (DSS, 1999d).

Although there are no official estimates of Incapacity Benefit take-up, Berthoud (1998a) has estimated that some 42% of the growth in the Invalidity Benefit caseload could be accounted for by increased take-up among the eligible population.

Take-up of Attendance Allowance in the mid-1980s was 85% for those of working age and 73% for pensioners. At that time the take-up of Mobility Allowance by working age people was 67% (Martin and White, 1988). The data available for the take-up of Disability Living Allowance and Attendance Allowance, suggests that it remains comparatively low (Table 11.2). Figures for the late 1980s suggested that take-up was especially low among people with medium–severe disabilities, despite the fact that they would have extra costs to meet. This group was targeted by the 1992 change that expanded coverage of Disability Living Allowance. Even so, take-up estimates based on the 1996/97 disability survey still reveal quite limited take-up, not reaching above 80% even among the most severely disabled people (Craig and Greenslade, 1998). Among severely disabled people, the numbers receiving the care component have hardly changed, although the numbers of mobility component claims have increased; the main area of growth seems to have been in the middle–severity range (Table 11.2).

Table 11.2: Take up rate of selected benefits (1996/97)

Benefit	Take-up rate
Disability Living Allowance – care	30-50%
Disability Living Allowance – mobility	50-70%
Attendance Allowance	40-60%

Source: Craig and Greenslade (1998)

The complicated structure of disability benefits, and the complexity of rules, can *inhibit* take-up (Hedges and Thomas, 1994). Research also suggests that take-up is lower for those benefits that are conditional on type and severity of disablement and the extent and type of care needed, because of the difficulty people have in recognising their eligibility without additional help and advice (Costigan et al, 1992, quoted in Corden, 1995). Indeed, claims may also have been encouraged by welfare rights and local authority activity, the latter encouraging people to claim disability benefits as a contribution towards charges for community care services (Berthoud, 1998a). Take-up is also comparatively low when there is a test of disability, including methods such as a medical examination (Hedges and Thomas, 1994; Corden, 1995). The introduction of self-assessment in 1992 was intended to eliminate some of the problems caused by insensitive medical examinations, and so to increase take-up. Early research, however, indicated that people still had worries about giving the wrong answers and emphasising the negative aspects of their condition (Hedges and Thomas, 1994).

Were it possible to increase take-up it is clear that caseloads could rise still further, almost doubling the take-up of the benefits listed in Table 11.2 (Craig and Greenslade, 1998).

What has been learned

Until recently, institutional arrangements have emphasised medical corroboration of new claims rather than regular reviews of benefit, perhaps contributing towards the duration of disability benefit awards. The behaviour of 'gatekeepers' to benefit such as GPs can also have an impact on claimant numbers. Other factors include benefit rules allowing people to retain entitlement after pension age as well as publicity surrounding the introduction of new claims, notably Disability Living Allowance.

Disability Living Allowance has, for the most part, been paid for life, and recent attempts to introduce periodic review of eligibility have not led to significant numbers leaving benefit. An important consequence of this is that caseloads may continue to increase until such time as the number of benefit terminations exceed the number of new applicants. Given that the prevalence of impairments begins to increase rapidly when people approach late working life, and their age-specific life expectancies are in the upper seventies, one would not expect caseloads to stabilise until 30 or so years after introduction.

In addition, a number of other changes, including self-assessment, welfare rights activity and local initiatives and, perhaps most important, the closure of long-stay hospitals and the introduction of community care, have probably all increased the number of new cases. The effect of these is to delay further the point at which caseload stabilisation occurs.

Note

[1] A review of fraud and error in Income Support and Jobseeker's Allowance suggests that disabled people are only half as likely to commit fraud than lone parents, but twice as likely as pensioners (DSS, 2000h). About 5.6% of cases were thought to be fraudulent and 4% were in error.

TWELVE

Demography and benefits for disabled people

Summary

Increased longevity and the acquisition of impairment in late old age are perhaps the major factors behind the increased caseloads of disability benefits claimed by people over retirement age.

Demographic trends have limited the growth in the number of people of working age claiming disability benefit, but appear to have been more than offset by increased ill-health and disability.

The increased prevalence of impairment may also reflect the advances in medical science that enable people to survive, albeit with some degree of impairment, *and the higher incidence of poor health in certain areas and among people in the lower socio-economic groups.*

The increased prevalence of certain health conditions, notably mental health problems, may also have added to caseloads.

Institutional changes, both within social security policy and implementation, and in policy interaction with other areas like health and employment, will have contributed to the growth in caseloads. However, the question remains whether the increasing numbers of recipients of disability benefits reflect a rise in numbers of people who have developed an impairment, or simply an artefact of the way that benefit rules have been framed and applied. For instance, how significant is the ageing population and worsening health? Certainly, since the chances of developing impairment increase with age, one might expect – other things being equal – an ageing population to be associated with a higher incidence of impairment. The difficulty is that other things are seldom equal and, as has already been discussed, social attitudes towards disability have changed markedly over the last 30 years, measurement has changed and improved, and people have possibly become more prepared to exercise their right to provision.

An ageing population

A key characteristic in the ageing of Britain's population since 1971 has been the 44% increase in the number of people/pensionable age, over a period when total population increased by less than 7% (Chapter 2). Not surprisingly, therefore, the most obvious impact of an ageing population can be seen in the increased numbers of people of pensionable age who are in receipt of benefits to cover the extra costs associated with disability (largely Attendance Allowance – the increase in numbers of older people continuing to receive Disability Living Allowance was considered in Chapter 11). But even within this group, the incidence of impairment is concentrated among older people. Some 80% of the over-85s can expect to have developed some impairment and therefore to be more likely to need care. One estimate puts the care needs of an 80-year-old as between five and ten times those of a 60-year-old (see Le Grand, 1991).

Attendance Allowance is restricted to people aged over 65 at the time of their first claim, who are so severely disabled that they need a lot of help with personal care or supervision. Almost half of claims from men, and about two thirds from women, are from people aged over 80. Given that the number of people aged over 80 rose by 225% between 1971 and 1997, a significant part of the growth in caseload for Attendance Allowance can be explained by this factor alone. Indeed, over the period between 1984/85 and 1998/99, the number of people aged 80 and over claiming Attendance Allowance increased four-fold and accounted for 61% of the total increase in caseload, while the number of claimants aged under 70 hardly changed (Table 12.1).

Table 12.1: Growth in the Attendance Allowance caseload (1984-99)

	1984	1989	1994	1999	% change (1984-99)	% contribution of caseload growth (1984-99)
Men						
65-69	16	25	27	16	0	0
70-74	21	26	65	66	214	5
75-79	20	33	60	98	390	8
80 and over	30	58	124	169	463	15
Women						
65-69	18	30	39	21	17	0
70-74	27	38	99	112	315	9
75-79	35	59	123	200	471	17
80 and over	108	219	425	552	411	46
All	275	539	962	1234	372	100

Source: DSS (1999c)

However, there is evidence that this increase was not solely the result of changed demographics or morbidity. The number of disabled pensioners is estimated to have risen by a quarter between the mid-1970s and the mid-1990s (Berthoud, 1998a). Likewise, the proportion of pensioners receiving disability benefits has increased, from 4% in 1979 to 20% in 1997/98 (DSS, 2000b).

Proportional increases of similar magnitude have been recorded in the up-take of Attendance Allowance within the last five years alone. This suggests that take-up has been increasing, perhaps due to increasing awareness and greater willingness to claim benefit entitlement, perhaps also encouraged by local authority and welfare rights activity (see also Chapter 11). However, Attendance Allowance take-up estimates remain at only 40-60% (Craig and Greenslade, 1998).

The prevalence of impairment increases with age even within the working age population. A third of people aged between 55 and 59 responding to the LFS report some disability (Sly et al, 1999). Sixty-eight per cent of men of working age who received Incapacity Benefit in 1998/99 were aged 50 or over, and 52% were 55 or over. Likewise, 46% of people in receipt of Disability Living Allowance were aged 50 or over, even though this benefit is non-contributory and is available to all age groups, including children.

Age is also related to the duration of claims. Claims for Incapacity Benefit, for example, have been shown to lengthen as people grow older, particularly for those over 55 (Holmes et al, 1991; Erens and Ghate, 1993). The fact that, in 1998/99, men aged 50 or over, accounted for only 48% of people receiving the short-term rate of benefit but 71% of those in receipt of the long-term rate, is illustrative of this.

However, while the higher incidence of impairment among older age groups is consistent with the pattern of benefit receipt, it does not help to explain the growing caseloads among people of *working age*. Over the period 1971 to 1991, which saw a rise in the number of people receiving Invalidity Benefit (now Incapacity Benefit), the number of people in the population aged 50-60 actually fell by more than 680,000 (although by 1997 was beginning to increase). More women, of course, were in work at the end of this period than at the beginning, and thereby eligible for benefit on account of their contribution records, but even in 1994 women only accounted for 29% of the caseload (compared with 21% in 1984 and 18% in 1974). Another significant element in the growth of Invalidity Benefit was the increase in the number of people over pensionable age staying on that benefit rather than choosing to claim Retirement Pension instead (as discussed in Chapter 11).

In sum, the ageing of the population is a very important factor in explaining increased disability benefit caseloads among the retired population, but does not adequately account for growth of benefit receipt among the working age population.

Increasing ill-health and impairments

Berthoud (1998a) calculated that 13% of the expansion of Invalidity Benefit claimants that occurred between the mid-1970s and the mid-1990s was due to a growth in the numbers of the working age population with impairments.

Certain conditions (particularly mental health problems) have become more prevalent among people claiming Incapacity Benefit over time, which may reflect inflows to benefit and duration of claims. Back problems, osteoarthritis, and depression, as the reasons given for claiming Invalidity Benefit, increased the fastest between 1980 and 1994 (Campbell, 1999b). More recently, a study using Benefits Agency records of Incapacity Benefit claims in Glasgow – the city with the highest number of people claiming incapacity benefits in the UK – notes that the most prevalent diagnosis for claims is now mental ill-health (Adams, 1999).

This is confirmed by national statistics which show that by 1998/99 'mental and behavioural disorders' had become the largest single 'cause of incapacity' for both men and women (DSS, 1999c). (A year earlier musculoskeletal problems had been a marginally more important factor for men.)

The increase in mental ill-health conditions may be a reflection of poverty and deprivation as well as the stresses imposed by modern society. In 1995, the first comprehensive survey of mental illness showed that one in six adults of working age had suffered from some type of mental health problem in the week before interview. The most common problems were 'neurotic' conditions, such as anxiety and depression (Meltzer et al, 1995, reported in DoH, 1999). Social factors seem to increase the risk of mental illness, with the incidence being higher among those who are widowed, divorced or separated, homeless or in prison, and among children cared for away from home (DoH, 1999). It also appears that unemployed people are twice as likely, and urban dwellers one-and-a-half times more likely, to suffer depression than those in work or living in rural areas. Higher amounts of reported stress also seems to be associated with isolation, economic inactivity in men, and lone motherhood (Rainford et al, 2000). The policy change away from hospitalisation (see also Chapter 11) towards a greater emphasis on community treatment will also have added to the growth in people claiming disability benefits.

It is difficult to establish whether the change in the profile of impairments among Incapacity Benefit claimants is a cause or consequence of the changing duration of benefit claims. Research in the early 1980s indicated that Invalidity Benefit claimants with mental, nervous and circulatory conditions were more likely to stay on benefit for longer than others with injuries or digestive problems (Holmes et al, 1991). Those with multiple health problems (and older people) also remained on Invalidity Benefit for the longest periods (Erens and Ghate, 1993; Lonsdale et al, 1993). Ritchie and Snape's (1993) qualitative examination of Invalidity Benefit claims highlighted the increase of certain conditions and illnesses, particularly mental health problems, where employment opportunities were declining. They also noted evidence of claims by people with conditions that were once fatal, but which, with increased rates of survival, mean that people remained on Invalidity Benefit for longer.

The impact of trends in ill-health and impairment on the pattern of receipt of other benefits such as Disability Living Allowance has been less explored than in the case of Incapacity Benefit. Advances in medical science can mean that some people are born, or survive accidents, when without the latest medical technology, they might have died. Research on how these advances might affect the growth in benefit claims does not appear to have been undertaken. However, such people might survive with severe impairments that would make them eligible for benefit which they might receive for long periods. There is also some evidence to suggest an increase in children and young people developing some impairment. Infant mortality overall fell by 67% between 1971 and 1997, though death rates for the poorest and for children born outside marriage were higher (Matheson and Summerfield, 2000). At the same time, the numbers of families registered as eligible for help from the Family Fund, a charity assisting severely disabled children under the age of 16, have increased ten-fold from 1974, to 105,000 in 1999 (Family Fund, 1999).

To be eligible for Disability Living Allowance, a child under the age of 16 has to require more supervision, guidance or attention than a child of the same age and gender without the impairment. Children over the age of five are eligible for the mobility component, and of any age (provided the conditions can be met in babies) for the care component (before 1990 the age limit was two years). The number of children and young people under the age of 16 receiving Disability Living Allowance has increased by 54,000 between 1995 and 1999 (DSS, 1999c).

People with malignant diseases made up 12% of new awards of Disability Living Allowance in 1998/99, but only 2% of the caseload, which probably reflects the fact that survival rates are still comparatively low. On the other hand, analogous comparisons indicate that people with arthritis and people with learning difficulties are likely to claim Disability Living Allowance for comparatively long periods.

Growing health inequalities

Ill-health is not the same as disability. Although poor health can become disabling, disabled people are not necessarily ill (see Berthoud et al, 1993 for further discussion). There is some overlap between these categories, however, and some evidence that variations in health may also be reflected in the prevalence of disability.

A prominent viewpoint is that the numbers of claimants exceed what might be expected from the level of ill-health and disability in society overall; in particular, the rise in Incapacity Benefit recipients is contrasted with the lack of evidence of a substantial deterioration in the general health of the population. Set against this view, however, is a body of evidence about the disparities in ill-health and inequality between different localities and socio-economic groups. A consideration of these inequalities, rather than looking at the average for the nation as a whole, may help to explain (in part) some of the disparity.

Regional patterns

The Health Survey for England reveals variations in the prevalence of disability, with fewest in the NHS Executive regions of Anglia and Oxford, and highest in the North West. This pattern is evident even among people with the most severe impairments, which suggests that the regional differences are not simply due to people with less severe impairments opting out of work when the labour market is difficult. It has also been suggested that studies linking unemployment and Incapacity Benefit claims may reflect the distribution of ill-health rather than simply the impact of labour market variation (Macmillan, 1999a).

According to at least one measure, death rates, regional health inequalities increased between 1981 and 1991. Moreover, for some groups (especially younger men) death rates rose in absolute terms (Benzeval et al, 1995). Likewise, morbidity rates (ill-health) for people under the age of 65 also rose over the same period, from 2% to 4% as measured by Census responses. Furthermore, morbidity rates in the areas with the poorest health increased by much more with up to an eight-fold increase in Glasgow and the North East (Shaw et al, 1999).

The prevalence of benefit receipt by disabled people is also high in the North West, although in 1997/98 a slightly higher proportion of households in Wales and the North East were reliant on either Incapacity Benefit or the care component of Disability Living Allowance (Table 12.2). The similarity in the geographic distribution of the different benefits is marked, and could be taken to reflect variations in the buoyancy of the regional economies, the distribution of poverty (see below), or to variations in Employment Service practice (Chapter 10). On the other hand, Disability Living Allowance, which follows the regional pattern, is payable by the DSS irrespective of other income or work status, although only 5% of recipients are in employment (Berthoud, 1998a). Similarly, the distribution of Attendance Allowance recipients is also skewed towards the regions with highest numbers of working age people receiving disability benefits. In Wales, 32.7 people per thousand receive

Attendance Allowance, as do 25.9 per thousand in the North West, compared with a Great Britain average of 22 per thousand population (DSS, 2000d).

Table 12.2: Households by benefit receipt and region (1997-98)

%of households

	IB	SDA	DLAC	DLAM	AA	IIDB	WP
			Benefit received				
North East	11	1	7	8	2	2	2
Wales	11	1	7	8	6	1	1
North West and Merseyside	10	2	6	8	3	1	1
Scotland	9	1	5	6	4	1	1
Yorkshire	8	1	5	6	3	1	1
East Midlands	7	1	5	5	3	2	1
West Midlands	6	1	5	5	4	1	1
England	6	1	4	5	3	1	1
Eastern	4	–	3	3	3	1	1
London	4	1	4	4	3	–	–
South East	4	1	3	3	2	1	1
South West	4	–	3	4	4	1	1
Great Britain	7	1	4	5	3	1	1

Key
IB   Incapacity benefit
SDA   Severe Disablement Allowance
DLAC   Disability Living Allowance care component
DLAM   Disability Living Allowance mobility component
AA   Attendance Allowance
IIDB   Industrial Injuries Disablement Benefit
WP   War Pensions
Source: FRS (1997-98)

The above figures refer to Great Britain. It is instructive, however, to consider the situation of Northern Ireland. There, disability surveys similar to the 1980s OPCS surveys discussed in Chapter 10 were carried out between 1989 and 1990. They revealed a higher incidence of disability in the region than the Great Britain average (174 adults per thousand population compared with 142). In 1996 the Northern Ireland population receiving Attendance Allowance or Disability Living Allowance was twice as high as Great Britain's, partly reflecting this higher incidence of impairment. There are also similar trends in the growth of benefit caseloads over time, with increases in Invalidity Benefit recipients, from 41,000 in 1986 to 78,000 in 1996 (Geddis et al, 1997).

Socio-economic patterns

The differences between regions could also reflect a broader pattern of material deprivation. There is evidence of a socio-economic gradient for poor health and disability. The 1995 Health Survey for England showed that men in social class V were almost three times as likely to have an observed serious disability than men in class I, and women four times as likely. Similarly, with measures of poor health, the poorest men are almost four times more likely to report a long-term limiting condition as professional men. In the 45-64 age group, 48% of unskilled manual men reported some illness or disability which limited their activity, whereas only 17% of professional men did so (Howarth et al, 1998). Although there is no precise correlation between responses to such surveys and claims for benefit, this data does suggest that there has been a growth in the pool of *potential* claimants in the poorest socio-economic groups over the past 20 years.

Within regions, there may also be some connection between poor health and disability in more localised areas of deprivation. For instance, medical respondents in Adams' (1999) study of Glasgow highlighted the links between deprivation and ill-health which were felt to contribute to the above-average incidence of Incapacity Benefit claims in the city. He also uses the Jarman Index, developed to allocate deprivation payments to GPs in England, to compare overall scores with the other English cities studied. This revealed that, with the exception of Manchester (which has a bigger ethnic minority population), Glasgow had a higher level of deprivation than the other cities.

Local deprivation or local unemployment may also be a factor affecting the numbers claiming Incapacity Benefit. There is evidence that inflows to Incapacity Benefit during the 1980s were highest in areas like Wales, which had suffered industrial decline, and lowest in London (Holmes et al, 1991). Likewise, the scale of Glasgow's manufacturing decline in the early 1980s, deeper and more intense than any other city in Europe, may have had an impact on the high level of Incapacity Benefit claims (over 40,000) in the city (Adams, 1999). Unemployment and the impact of the economy is considered in more detail in the next chapter.

More poverty, more ill-health?

Given these socio-economic differences, many commentators have associated ill-health with poverty and worklessness, although the precise relationship between the three remains unclear. There is some suggestion that the sequence of causation may start before someone is made redundant or loses their job. As already noted (Chapter 10), significant numbers of people in employment report some ill-health or limiting condition (even if not sufficient to justify a claim for disability benefits). This may be exacerbated by job insecurity and the anticipation of unemployment (Wilkinson, 1996). Indeed, about a quarter of unemployed people claiming Jobseeker's Allowance also have a health problem or disability that affects the kind of work they can do (Trickey et al, 1998).

Other groups of claimants appear to suffer disproportionately from health problems, and in the case of lone parents it is known that poor health is increasing. In 1991, 15% of lone parents reported a longstanding illness, but by 1995 this figure had risen to 29%; 7% of lone parents were unhealthy throughout the entire four-year period (Ford et al, 1998). The same study also found that one in four lone parents had at least one child who suffered from a long-term illness over this period. Whether in this case the ill-health or impairment pre-dated or post-dated the benefit claim is unclear.

One study of an industrial town in the North West found one-and-a-half times the expected number of people in receipt of Disability Living Allowance mobility awards at the higher rate (Noble et al, 1997). The authors speculate that this could be the result of a greater concentration of people with impairments among low-income households, together with perhaps more incentive to take up benefit entitlement if other incomes are low.

It is likely, then, that the eligible population for incapacity and extra cost benefits may be drawn disproportionately from groups that are already at risk of poor health, although the direct evidence is difficult to establish. The impact of the economy, implicit as an underlying factor in the health trends described in this section, particularly in creating the preconditions for poverty and worklessness over recent years, is considered in the next chapter.

What has been learned

Demography has played an important role in increasing the use of disability benefits by retirement pensioners, with growth in the number of people aged 80 and above – who are most prone to impairment – being exceptionally high.

Among people of working age, demographic trends with falling numbers of people aged over 50 should have reduced the prevalence of morbidity. However, there is evidence that the poorest individuals, those without work and those living in areas of high deprivation, may have become more likely to experience poor health and disability, which will have increased the numbers of people eligible for benefits. It is also very probable that there is a spiral of causation in which poor health increases the risk of worklessness and worklessness increases the risk of poor health.

Among children, improvements in medicine and prenatal and perinatal care may have given life to those who would in earlier generations have died. Some of the children who have survived may nevertheless have impairments that qualify them for benefit, thereby adding to benefit caseloads.

THIRTEEN

The economy and disability

Summary

The link between the economy and caseloads is likely to be most direct in the case of Incapacity Benefit.

Incapacity Benefit caseloads rose at a constant rate throughout most of the period to 1999.

The growth was primarily the result of fewer people leaving benefit, resulting in an increase in the length of spells that people spent on benefit.

Benefit claims increased as a direct result of more women working, who, when they became disabled, were entitled to benefit on account of their contribution record.

Increased job entry requirements may have left disabled people without substantial qualifications or work experience doubly disadvantaged in their search for employment. Disabled people are seen as a risk and financial liability by some employers.

It is commonplace to attribute much of the growth in the numbers of people claiming disability benefits to changes in the economy. A process usually singled out is the decline in manufacturing industries, leading in particular to inflows onto Incapacity Benefit from men formerly working in manual trades. However, the realisation that more disabled people were working in the recession of the 1990s than in the more buoyant part of the 1980s suggests that the world is more complex than received wisdom, or the understanding that sometimes drives policy (Berthoud, 1998b). While repeated recessions have undoubtedly impacted on disability benefit caseloads, account needs to be taken of the needs and behaviour of employers, as well as the process by which workers move into economic inactivity.

This chapter concentrates largely on Incapacity Benefit, as it has a more direct relationship to the labour market than additional costs benefits. However, it should be borne in mind that the consequence of economic change in creating poverty may have a knock-on effect on claims for extra costs benefits (see Chapter 12).

There are two main ways in which changes in the labour market may have had a direct influence on the people claiming Incapacity Benefit. The first, the increasing participation of women in the labour market, has had a straightforward effect. As a consequence of working, more women have become eligible for Incapacity Benefit on account of being able to satisfy the National Insurance contribution conditions – the proportion of female recipients rose from 19% in 1972/73 to 32% in 1998/99. Berthoud (1998a) has attributed 16% of the growth of Invalidity Benefit claims between the mid-1970s and mid-1990s to the increasing numbers of married women in work and paying National Insurance contributions (as discussed in Chapter 11).

The second labour market influence on caseloads relates to the impact of the changing nature of labour demand. Here the effects are multifaceted and contested. The next section is devoted to the dynamics of Incapacity Benefit in an attempt to disentangle what the literature reveals about the impact of recession and the secular trend towards higher unemployment. The second section is focused on the changing nature of labour demand and the action of employers, although, in reality, the various labour market developments are interlinked.

The dynamics of Incapacity Benefit

The complex nature of any relationship between unemployment and the caseload of Incapacity Benefit is demonstrated in Figure 13.1. This plots the claimant unemployment count for each year between 1971 and 1999 against the Incapacity Benefit caseload (short-term higher and long-term rate), and the total of people receiving incapacity benefits, including those in the first 28 weeks of sickness. While unemployment fluctuated substantially over this period, there was a secular upward trend in Invalidity Benefit caseloads that only ended with the replacement of Invalidity Benefit by Incapacity Benefit in 1995. The subsequent fall in the Incapacity Benefit caseload after 1995 was more marked than the decline in total incapacity, suggesting that the benefit

Figure 13.1: Rate of change in incapacity benefits and claimant count (1971-99)

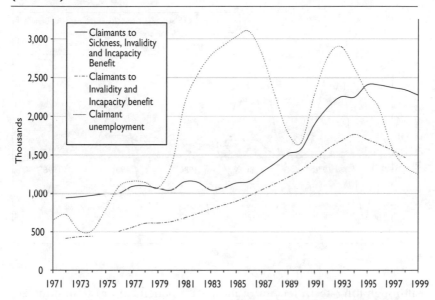

change, in combination with other factors, led to a reduction in the inflows and duration of benefit receipt. (The influence of some of the other 1995 changes, such as the removal of the option to remain on benefit rather than claim a pension, was discussed in Chapter 11).

The fall in the Incapacity Benefit caseload came later, and not as fast as the fall in unemployment, with the result that by 1998 more people were in receipt of Incapacity Benefit than were receiving Jobseeker's Allowance.

It is worth noting that 'credits-only' cases, people who are incapable of work but who do not meet the contributory conditions for receipt of benefit, have not fallen along with the caseload as a whole, and by November 1999 totalled 764,500. In the quarter ending November 1999, 'credits-only' cases accounted for 45% of all new claims, compared with 39% of a slightly smaller total of new claims in the quarter ending May 1995. Little is known about this sub-group except that they will have had to satisfy the test of incapacity and thus be excluded from benefit for other reasons.

There was clearly no direct one-to-one relationship between rising unemployment and the increasing claims for incapacity benefits. During the period 1971 and 1986, when unemployment increased almost five-fold to an all time high, total incapacity increased by less than a quarter,

Figure 13.2: Unemployment and incapacity (1971-99)

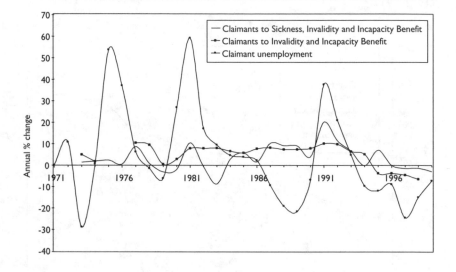

although long-term receipt of incapacity benefits more than doubled. The association between unemployment and receipt of Incapacity Benefit is clearer when the rate of change rather than the total caseload is considered (Figure 13.2). Throughout the period from 1973 to 1994, except around 1980 when benefit up-take scarcely changed, the caseload for Incapacity Benefit (previously Invalidity Benefit) increased at a constant rate of around 7% or 8% per year. However, total incapacity fluctuated rather more, rising at times of recession to 10% in 1980/81 and 20% in 1990/91. Even so, these increases were much less than the corresponding rises in unemployment (59% and 38% respectively). Moreover, rapid increases in incapacity were also evident in the late 1980s, when unemployment was falling fast.

It is difficult to compare any of these trends with the number of people becoming ill or incapacitated – measured as the number of people submitting a claim at the beginning of a spell of sickness – because of the distortions introduced by repeated policy changes. However, it appears that over the last 30 years the growth in new claims that occurred in between bouts of policy change was much less than the rise in Incapacity Benefit caseloads. Year-to-year variation in the number of new claims was also comparatively low.

The year-on-year increase of 133,000 in the Invalidity Benefit caseload that occurred between 1990 and 1991 was of exceptional magnitude, and was followed by the second highest proportional increase the following year. The increase coincided with an abrupt downturn in the economy that saw claimant unemployment rise by 38%. But the processes involved do not seem to have been exceptional. The increase in claims far exceeded the comparatively small increase in the number of people beginning spells of sickness, indicating that the increase occurred because of a fall in the numbers leaving benefit. A change of this magnitude is unlikely to have occurred through a change in attitudes to work, which suggests that the main reason was the drop in labour demand. As noted below, many disabled people looking for work share the same impediments as long-term unemployed people, over and above the impairment.

The in-flow began falling in 1993/94, but the numbers claiming Invalidity Benefit continued to rise until 1994/95 on account of the lengthening periods of receipt.

Time spent on Incapacity Benefit

The increase in the length of time that people claim Invalidity Benefit has been a sustained long-term trend. It is known to have increased in the nine-year period to 1983/84, particularly for older claimants (over 55), those living in poor housing, and people with particular conditions (mental health problems, nervous and circulatory disorders) (Holmes et al, 1991). It would appear that people who would have experienced intermittent spells on incapacity benefits in the 1970s remained permanently on benefit in the 1980s. Between 1985 and 1995 the average duration of Incapacity Benefit claims increased substantially, from three to five years (DSS, 1998e), and is now more than six years. Moreover, once people had been on Incapacity Benefit for more than a year, the proportion leaving was low, generally less than 10% a year, a pattern that has been sustained (Bell et al, 1997).

All this suggests that, to the extent that fluctuations in the economy affect caseloads for incapacity benefits, the effect works primarily through reducing movements off benefit, which in turn causes people to spend an increasing amount of time off, or out of, work. It would appear that the rate of increase in the number of people sick for up to 24 weeks increases in the early part of a recession. A proportion of this comparatively large cohort remains on benefit and moves onto higher-rate short-term benefit, and then onto the long-term rate after a year. However, the cohort is overshadowed by the large size of the existing caseload, meaning that it has comparatively little effect on the rate of growth of the caseload. It is for this reason that the Invalidity Benefit caseload increased at a remarkably constant rate until 1994. It should not be forgotten, however, that this constant relative rate translated into a very substantial rise in the annual increase in caseload. This increased from 19,000 between 1972 and 1973 to 86,000 between 1994 and 1995.

The characteristics of the current 'stock' of claimants can be seen as a reflection of the social and economic conditions of the 1980s, since a shift in entry or exit patterns may take 10–20 years to work through (Berthoud, 1998a). For example, over half of current Incapacity Benefit claimants are aged over 50, and people tend to have received benefit for long periods (six years on average). However, although the proportion of all over-50s who are economically inactive has grown, from 7% in 1975 to 28% in 1997, the bulk of the rise took place between 1975 and 1986 (EPI, 1998). Since then the main growth has been in inactivity rates for younger people.

To summarise, while formal modelling is still required, the secular rise in the number claiming Incapacity Benefit appears to be driven by a sustained long-term fall in the proportion of people leaving benefit. There is no evidence of increased numbers of people newly claiming benefit, although the proportion moving onto the long-term rates appears to rise during recessions.

Routes onto Incapacity Benefit

There has been a substantial increase in the proportion of Incapacity Benefit recipients who were previously unemployed, from 4% in 1982 to 47% in 1998 (Figure 13.3 and Table 13.1). (It should be noted that data in Table 13.1 do *not* include people who were receiving a National Insurance credit for incapacity ['credits-only' cases] and who may [or may not] also have been receiving Income Support.) It is very unlikely that this increase is due entirely to a rise in the proportion of claimants *moving on* to Incapacity Benefit who were previously unemployed. Certainly, fewer than 47% of unemployed claimants move directly onto Incapacity Benefit; other research suggests that a third or less of Incapacity Benefit recipients start their claim from unemployment.

The research includes a DSS-commissioned study of 1,545 Invalidity Benefit recipients who began receiving benefit between January 1991 and March 1992 which found that only 18% had been unemployed at any time in the three years (between 1989-91) before their Invalidity Benefit claim started (Erens and Ghate, 1993). Eleven per cent had

Figure 13.3: Number of Incapacity Benefit recipients unemployed prior to claim

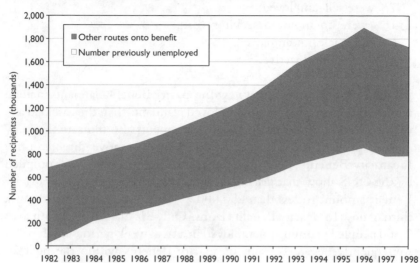

Source: DSS Statistics given to *The Guardian*, March 1997

Table 13.1: Employment status of Incapacity Benefit recipients prior to claim

	As at 31.3.96		As at 31.3.97		As at 31.3.98	
	Numbers	**%**	**Numbers**	**%**	**Numbers**	**%**
Employed	860,000	45	787,000	44	789,000	46
Self-employed	133,700	7	121,700	7	111,500	7
Unemployed	882,000	47	875,900	49	806,000	47
Total	1,894,600	100	1,797,900	100	1,728,500	100

Source: DSS, personal communication, February 2000

claimed unemployment–related benefits for less than a year. More recently, a survey of 500 workless men in rural areas indicated that about a quarter were unemployed immediately before their Incapacity Benefit claim, although this study was based on respondent recall (Beatty and Fothergill, 1999b).

Similarly, a study of people *leaving* Incapacity Benefit revealed that fewer than one in five of this group were actually signing on prior to their claim, and that there were many different routes onto benefit (Dorsett et al, 1998):

50% were off sick with sick pay from employer;
19% were employed, not sick;
7% were self-employed;
16% were unemployed/seeking work;
6% were sick not employed;
4% were other inactive.

All these studies confirm that new Incapacity Benefit claimants include a smaller proportion of ex-unemployed claimants than the caseload as a whole. Studies of movements between benefits also indicate that only a small proportion of unemployed claimants move directly onto Incapacity Benefit. Claimant count and administrative data compiled by the ONS show that *flows* from Jobseeker's Allowance to Incapacity Benefit amount to less than 250,000 a year – accounting for about a third of new Incapacity Benefit claims. Only 8% of a national sample of 2,500 people becoming unemployed in a two-week period in July 1995 subsequently began to claim Incapacity Benefits within the next 22 months (Trickey et al, 1998).

Part of the reason for the accumulation of former unemployed claimants in the Incapacity Benefit caseload must be because they remain on benefit longer than other groups. The available evidence for this is, as yet, only circumstantial. A study of people receiving Invalidity Benefit indicated that those with limited skills were the least likely to leave benefit (Erens and Ghate, 1993). Given that people who are unemployed are less skilled than the labour force as a whole, it is at least possible that people who move onto Incapacity Benefit via unemployment are less skilled than those who move directly from employment to Incapacity Benefit.

Some of the explanation for the preponderance of formerly unemployed claimants in the Incapacity Benefit caseload is also likely to lie in the rapid movement between benefits that some claimants experience. Many claims for Incapacity Benefit are comparatively short-lived. This is illustrated by the fact that only 35% of people who claim the short-term lower rate of Incapacity Benefit move onto the higher rate of benefit (normally after six months). Similarly, only 15% of claimants 'progress' from this higher rate to the long-term rate of benefit (normally after one year) (*Hansard*, 15 December 1997, col 74w, House of Commons). People moving onto Incapacity Benefit from unemployment are more likely than other groups to receive benefit at the lower rate and, as would be expected, people receiving lower rate (ie short-term) benefit are more likely than longer-term recipients to leave benefit (Swales, 1998a).

There is also evidence of differential 'churning', movement backwards and forwards between unemployment-related benefits and Incapacity Benefit, especially at the lower rates. Although between March 1995 and August 1997 about 21,000 people a month moved onto Incapacity Benefit from Jobseeker's Allowance, 15,000 changed benefit in the opposite direction (Edgeley and Sweeney, 1998).

The trajectories taken by people leaving Incapacity Benefit differ according to employment history and the trigger for leaving benefit. Two thirds of claimants who voluntarily leave Incapacity Benefit go into work, but only one in ten of those disallowed benefit – a group that includes disproportionate numbers of formerly unemployed people – do so (Dorsett et al, 1998). Furthermore, two fifths of those who are disallowed benefit were back in receipt of Incapacity Benefit 12 months after leaving it (Swales, 1998a). Part of this 'churning' is the direct result of administrative procedures. For example, people can receive Jobseeker's Allowance pending an appeal against an Incapacity Benefit refusal; one in nine people who subsequently won their appeal spent some time after their disallowance on Jobseeker's Allowance (Dorsett et al, 1998).

To conclude, it seems likely that no more than a third of new Incapacity Benefit claims result from people moving from unemployment, rather than almost half as might incorrectly be deduced from the caseload statistic reported in Figure 13.3. The difference is due partly to churning, with people moving temporarily onto unemployment-related benefits while awaiting the results of appeals, and for other reasons. It is also probable that the category 'unemployed' used in the official statistics is slightly inflated by the inclusion of people who might more accurately be called 'workless'. These could include claimants receiving Maternity Allowance, Widowed Mothers Allowance, approved training credits, and jury service, as well as those signing on as unemployed. But the main reason is likely to be the accumulation of formerly unemployed claimants as a more disadvantaged group with very limited prospects of ever moving off benefit.

Disability premium

Although this chapter is focused on Incapacity Benefit, it is important to note that the numbers of credit-only cases, as well as those receiving means-tested Income Support with disability premium, have continued to grow since 1995, at a time when the Incapacity Benefit caseload has been falling. In November 1995, 724,000 people on Income Support received a disability premium, and by November 1999 this had grown to 940,000 (DSS, 2000b). Inflows and outflows appear to have remained constant (with most moving from other benefits rather than being entirely new claims), suggesting that caseload growth is due to the accumulation of long-term recipients. Forty-six per cent of people receiving the premium in November 1999 had done so for more than five years.

Cross-benefit data reveal that 1.22 million out of 2.8 million people of working age in receipt of sickness or disability benefits also received Income Support (DSS, 2000e). Of these, 623,000 (50%) were credited with incapacity credits only (and so received no benefit). A total of 270,000 (22%) received Incapacity Benefit, 231,000 (18%) received Severe Disablement Allowance and 532,000 (43%) received Disability Living Allowance. Some claimants may have been in receipt of income maintenance *and* extra costs benefits and so qualified for the premium on either ground.

The incapacity test is common across Income Support Disability Premium, Incapacity Benefit and National Insurance Credits (the up-take of which, it will be recalled, has also continued to increase since 1995). This suggests that changes to the medical controls for Incapacity Benefit are less important in explaining recent trends in caseloads than alterations to other features of benefit eligibility (discussed in Chapter 11) and external factors. There is little direct evidence that falls in Incapacity Benefit had led to the increased up-take of National Insurance credits or the Income Support Disability Premium.

The nature of work and fitness for employment

Higher Incapacity Benefit caseloads are also consistent with a structural change in the nature of labour demand that may have served to marginalise disabled and lower-skilled workers. Labour demand has shifted away from valuing traditional manual skills towards preferring softer people-friendly skills, advanced technical expertise and flexibility. Demands for higher productivity mean that the employment threshold has risen, squeezing out the less demanding jobs that may once have been held by disabled people. It is known, for example, that to be in work, men aged 20-59 had to be in better health in 1993 than 1973 (Bartley and Owen, 1996). Likewise, whereas in 1979, 72% of men in the lowest socio-economic group were in work despite long-term health problems, by 1993 only 43% of the corresponding group were employed. In this context it is important to note that the growth in employment among disabled people has exclusively been among women, and that the proportion of disabled men in work fell by 10% for those aged under 50, and by 20% for those who were older (Grundy et al, 1999).

Some labour market changes will have advantaged certain disabled people. The decline in manual work may have had little impact on those disabled people with an impairment affecting their ability to undertake jobs involving heavy physical work or lifting. (In one study this group accounted for over a third of disabled people who reported constraints on the kind of work they could do – see Meager et al, 1998). The same study indicated that the impairments most likely to have a work-related impact were mental health problems, learning disabilities, mobility problems and visual impairments (the latter affecting the type rather than the amount of work – Meager et al, 1998).

However, disabled people who are in work are more likely to be qualified than those who are economically inactive (Meager et al, 1998). Similarly, the evidence both from the early 1990s and more recently has shown that disproportionate numbers of Incapacity Benefit recipients have low educational attainment and limited work experience. In the earlier period 57% of Invalidity Benefit recipients had no educational qualifications at all (Lonsdale et al, 1993), a proportion that had fallen only marginally by 1999 (Arthur et al, 1999). Some 29% of Incapacity Benefit recipients who, in 1999, responded to an offer of help to assist them into paid work under the New Deal for Disabled People had no qualifications, and 61% had not worked for more than two years.

Not only do significant numbers of disabled people share the same labour market vulnerability as other unskilled people, they also have to confront the limitations that arise from their impairment and the attitudes of others. Seventy-nine per cent of people volunteering for the New Deal for Disabled People believed that their health condition would mean them taking more than 20 days sick leave each year, 73% thought that they would need several breaks a day, and 42% felt that they would need someone to help them at work.

In the context of excess labour supply that has been an enduring feature for much of the last 30 years, employers may well have become more selective about whom they employ. This selection may have resulted in more people with impairments being excluded from the labour market, at the same time as greater social acceptance of people not taking work if their impairments make it difficult for them to do so. Employers' responses to illness and disability (either in making people redundant or a reluctance to recruit once people are receiving benefit) has been identified in qualitative research as one of several factors influencing the growth of Invalidity Benefit claims (Ritchie and Snape, 1993).

Arthur et al (1999) identified two broad groups of employer on the basis of qualitative research conducted in 1999. The first were mostly larger organisations with specialist support departments and access to external sources of support. The second did not have the same active commitment to employing disabled people, but said that they did not discriminate. They generally had little experience of employing disabled people or specialist support, either internally or externally. Whereas the first group recognised some challenges associated with employing disabled people, the latter saw the same concerns as major obstacles. However, the researchers noted that the good principles espoused by employers in the first group were not always evident among staff involved in recruitment or management.

The concerns that employers had were that impairments might conspire to limit the productivity of disabled people, and that there could be difficulties relating to the working environment, raising issues about both safety and access. Some found it difficult to envisage the type of support or adjustments that could make a post acceptable; such employers often had an image of disabled people that emphasised more severe impairments. Others were concerned about the financial costs entailed, and employing disabled people was generally seen to involve uncertainty and risk (although the limited evidence so far suggests that the costs of adjustments are minimal, for example, Watson et al, 1998). Significant numbers of disabled people seeking work felt that employers discriminated against them: 46% said that employers thought them to be too sick or disabled, and 34% felt that other people's prejudices made it difficult for them to work. Specialist staff in the Employment Service supported this view.

While the evidence is not available to determine whether employers' attitudes have changed over time, it is possible that increased competitiveness will have made employers more risk-averse in making appointments, even at a time of more liberal attitudes towards disability. (While employers may believe disabled people to be less productive than others, disabled people themselves tend not to share that perception – of those reporting that their impairment would have an impact on work, only 17% said that this meant they were less productive – Meager et al, 1998.) Whether this amounts to direct discrimination is unclear. So far, research has shown that employers are more likely to turn down a suitably qualified disabled person for a job than someone without that disability. However, other studies suggest that remarkably few people report that they experience discrimination directly; according to a survey for the DfEE, only around one in six disabled people of working age said they had experienced discrimination or unfair treatment by an employer (Meager et al, 1998). Similarly, there is little evidence of age discrimination; only 5% of people aged 45-69 (and 7% of 50-54 year olds) believed they had been discriminated against in one or more job applications because they were too old (McKay and Middleton, 1998). However, the impact of the 1995 Disability Discrimination Act, discussed in Chapter 9, may highlight both good and bad practice. Early experience suggests that experience of a Disability Discrimination Act case is likely to have an impact on employer policy and practice, highlighting the need for better awareness among staff (Meager et al, 1999).

The economy has clearly had a significant impact in influencing the inflows and durations of claims, which in turn may have influenced the views and behaviour of gatekeepers to benefit, as well as the context within which benefit rules are drawn up and operate (discussed earlier in Chapter 11).

What has been learned

Any link between slack labour demand and increasing claims for Incapacity Benefit is complex, and is not reducible exclusively – if at all – to the simple notion of unemployed people choosing a more generous and 'passive' benefit in preference to less generous and more stringent Jobseeker's Allowance. Caseloads rose steadily between 1971 and 1994 against a background of massively fluctuating unemployment, and did so primarily as a result of people moving off benefit less quickly, rather than because more people were newly claiming benefit. The proportion of Incapacity Benefit claimants who move onto benefit from unemployment has increased over time, partly reflecting high levels of unemployment, although even by the mid-1990s only one out of every 12 people who became unemployed began to claim incapacity benefits within 22 months (Trickey et al, 1998). To the extent that firms are confronted by increasingly vigorous competition, it is possible that disabled people, especially those with limited qualifications, have become more disadvantaged in the scramble for work. Almost certainly, the threshold of employability has risen as the demand for both soft and technical skills has increased, and some, possibly many, employers could perceive employing disabled people to be both a financial liability and a risk. Increasing numbers of employers may have considered that market conditions meant this risk was no longer one worth taking.

FOURTEEN

Understanding the growth in disability benefits

Summary

Increasing recognition of the financial and opportunity costs of disability, and public perceptions that views of disabled people were 'legitimate' long-term welfare recipients, were important factors in the growth in benefit caseloads They led to the introduction of new benefits, and possibly higher up-take.

The changing economy and labour market may have contributed to increasing benefit caseloads, especially to longer periods on benefit. Market-led requirements for firms to be more productive and competitive may have also reduced job opportunities and lengthened spells on benefit, thus excluding some disabled people from the labour market.

There has also been some increase in the reported prevalence of disability, perhaps also linked to greater public awareness of disability.

Trends in increasing worklessness, poor health experiences for some groups of people, as well as an ageing population, may also have contributed to the growth in disability benefit caseloads.

The precise pattern of factors determining caseload size varies between different benefits, not least because of the diverse circumstances of disabled people claiming benefit.

Figure 14.1: Understanding disability benefit caseloads

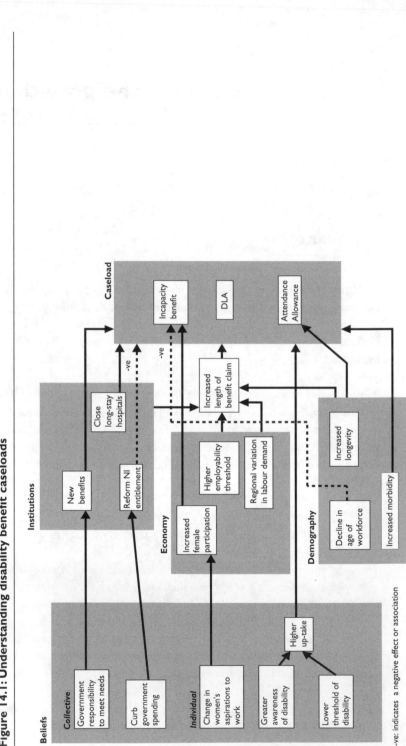

-ve: indicates a negative effect or association

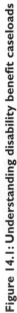

The growth in the caseloads of most benefits for disabled people in the last 30 years has been dramatic. Disabled people now constitute the largest group of benefit recipients after retirement pensioners, and one fifth of pensioners now receive a disability benefit. Perhaps the most important reason for the growth has been the change in public attitudes towards disability, and recognition that the state has a duty to support disabled people financially (Figure 14.1).

Ironically, as disabled people's organisations have been campaigning for better civil and employment rights, the numbers dependent on benefit have grown dramatically.

Changes in attitudes towards disabled people over time may also reflect the subjective nature of some conditions, depending on the interaction between the person's impairment and their environment. Having a more positive 'label' than 'unemployed', people may have been more inclined to take up benefits that are based on an assessment of impairment. In a sense, like poverty, disability may be a relative concept.

However, despite this common feature, the experience and circumstances of disabled people are very diverse, and the relative importance of the multiplicity of factors leading to the growth in the numbers claiming individual benefits varies. Therefore, each of the main types of benefit (Incapacity benefit, Disability Living Allowance, Attendance Allowance and Income Support for disabled people) are discussed in turn, identifying the factors that seem to have most bearing on the inflows and, more importantly, the outflows that lead inexorably to longer spells of receipt.

Main factors influencing benefit caseloads

Incapacity Benefit

By definition, all Incapacity Benefit recipients must have had some connection with the labour market in order to have satisfied the National Insurance conditions for benefit receipt. The increase in the proportion of women employed has directly increased the number of claims, but there is little evidence that new claims increase greatly in line with the cyclical fluctuations in the labour market. Before 1995, GPs had a greater role in sickness certification, and in some circumstances may have been sympathetic to claimants who may have had some capacity for work but little prospect of getting it. However, it is not evident that GPs' approach to their patients has changed significantly over the last

30 years in ways that could account for much of the increase in caseload, and since changes in 1995, the role of GPs has been reduced. The extent to which people are claiming when their health does not warrant it, or when they 'should' be unemployed, is unclear.

It is apparent that people have remained on benefit for longer, for a combination of reasons including limited job opportunities, deteriorating health conditions, perhaps some reduced motivation after a period of looking for work, and the fear of losing benefit if attempting work. Incapacity Benefit claimants disproportionately live in regions of high unemployment, where the chances of getting a job are slight, and the flexible labour market may have made it harder for some people with an impairment to work, especially for former manual workers. Many recipients are also over the age of 50, and will have been out of work for a number of years, and the chances of returning to work are slight on both counts.

Berthoud (1998a) has estimated the relative importance of the various demographic, economic, and institutional factors to the tripling of the Invalidity Benefit caseload between the mid-1970s and mid-1990s. Of this increase:

- 29% was due to people over pension age continuing to draw Invalidity Benefit in preference to the retirement pension, as the former was tax free;
- 16% consisted of an increasing number of married women in the labour market who had been paying National Insurance Contributions before they became disabled;
- 13% is explained by a gradual increase in the proportion of working age population with impairments;
- 42% derived from the genuine growth in the take-up rate of claiming Invalidity Benefit among a stable population of disabled people (Berthoud, 1998a).

The 18% fall in caseloads since 1995 is perhaps most easily attributable to those reforms affecting eligibility to the National Insurance benefit (such as removing the chance to opt to remain on Invalidity Benefit for five years after pension age), as numbers of those receiving incapacity credits have continued to increase. Both the number of new spells of sickness and the number of new claims for Incapacity Benefit has fallen, albeit slightly, each year since 1995, something unprecedented since the benefit reforms of the mid-1980s. Unemployment has also fallen over this period, but given the lack of any association between change in unemployment and claims for Incapacity Benefit in earlier periods it is difficult to gauge how influential the buoyant economy has been in facilitating the fall in caseloads.

Disability Living Allowance

Receipt of Disability Living Allowance is not dependent on employment status, so any link between caseload and labour market conditions is likely to be indirect.

Claims were increasing prior to the 1992 introduction of, and extension to, extra costs benefits, perhaps because people had become more willing to identify themselves as disabled and so potentially eligible for benefit. However, claims surged as a result of government publicity at the time of the 1992 reforms.

Somewhat surprisingly, there is some evidence that the proportion of people claiming Disability Living Allowance is highest in regions and areas of high unemployment. This may reflect the distribution of poor health as well as administrative practices, and to the extent that suspicion that people may be exaggerating their impairments to claim benefit is true, this could be a further reflection of the pressures of living on a low income. The closure of long-stay hospitals will also have increased claims for Disability Living Allowance, for the most severely disabled people who moved from institutional care to live independently in the community.

Perhaps more important than all of these considerations is the simple fact that the majority of Disability Living Allowance awards have been for life. This means that the numbers on benefit will inevitably have grown as people become disabled and claim benefit at a time when comparatively few recipients either recover or die. Although the new emphasis on reviewing the stock of claims may reduce some of the caseload, evidence to date suggests that the impact of this initiative is likely to be small. Furthermore, people receiving Disability Living Allowance before the age of 65 can continue to receive it after pension age, which maintains the caseload levels.

Attendance Allowance

A major driver in the increasing numbers receiving Attendance Allowance is the demographic trend of increasing longevity, especially of those who are aged over 80. There is some evidence of regional variations in benefit receipt, similar to the patterns for other benefits. However, it is also likely that take-up has increased, perhaps as a result of local authority and welfare rights campaigns.

Income Support for disabled people

As eligibility for the disability premium is largely based on receipt of other disability benefits, the growth in numbers of disabled people receiving Income Support is thus likely to reflect increases in receipt of benefits for extra costs and incapacity, and the range of factors affecting each. However, there has also been an increase in numbers of 'credits-only' cases, where the test of incapacity is satisfied but no payment of Incapacity Benefit is made as the other conditions are not met. As a result, the institutional factors affecting Incapacity Benefit trends may well have been less important to the growth of credits-only cases, but other factors (such as the impact of the economy and demographic pressures) may have exerted more of an impact on this group. Some of the 'credits-only' cases will also be eligible for Income Support, which may have fuelled the growth of the premium.

Labour market exclusion

Although there is little evidence that the number of people claiming disability benefits has been much influenced by economic downturns, there are many reasons for believing that the labour market is less amenable to disabled people than in the past. Greater competitiveness, and demands for higher productivity from more skilled employees, may all serve to deter employers from hiring people with impairments; employers may have become more risk averse and more concerned to avoid perceived additional costs. If so, this adds an economic dimension to the social relativity of disability discussed above, and cautions against expectations that caseloads will necessarily fall substantially, even if the labour market continues to tighten.

A further factor that may prevent a fall in caseloads is the length of time for which many claimants have been outside the labour market. Although there is evidence that significant numbers of people on incapacity benefits still retain an attachment to work, others may have become 'discouraged' and given up looking for work. Another important factor is the great store employers place in their recruitment decisions by recent work experience, which places many disabled claimants at a significant disadvantage. This reinforces the 'ratchet' effect identified by Berthoud (see Chapter 10), that prevents caseloads falling in an era of high labour demand as quickly as they rise when and where demand is slack. The process of exclusion from the labour market or entrapment on benefits may be exacerbated by geographical factors. The greater likelihood of people on low incomes, who are more likely to be living in areas of high unemployment, developing an impairment or illness, suggests that one should not be entirely surprised by the geographical concentrations of Incapacity Benefit (or Disability Living Allowance) claims.

Individual choice and a welfare class?

Developments since 1971 have resulted in a situation where today well over four million people are claiming disability benefits, most of them for very long periods. Given that this multi-fold increase in claims occurred within a generation, it is not surprising that some commentators portray this as another example of increased dependency and a growing welfare class.

It is important, however, to recognise the diversity among people claiming disability benefits. Around a third are pensioners and many are very old and severely disabled. About 4% of claimants are children, and the vast majority of the remainder are of late working age, most having spent the majority of their adult lives in almost continuous employment.

There is precious little direct evidence that significant numbers of people – even those in their pre-retirement years – have chosen deliberately to live on disability benefits. Campbell's (1999b) work suggests that the sheer scale of the numbers of older men leaving the labour market cannot be explained solely by individual choice. While some people do move backwards and forwards between the categories of 'sick and disabled' and 'unemployed', nearly one fifth of the working age population report a longstanding illness or disability, as does more than a tenth of the total workforce, which makes such churning inevitable. Even the recent fall in Incapacity Benefit claims, which seems to be linked to administrative changes, does not provide incontrovertible evidence of deliberate choice. Income Support and National Insurance credit caseloads have risen unusually fast over the same period, leaving the number of people claiming some form of disability benefit only marginally down.

Possibly more fundamental forces are at play. Perhaps when a 'disability' category is created within the social security system, it is likely to be a response to an unmet need, and so will generate considerable demand that, at some point, is likely to be questioned by policy makers. This will then present difficult moral and political judgements about who is deserving of state aid and who is not. In a social security system which strives for objective and repeatable decisions, determining who is 'disabled enough' for benefit purposes is an inherently subjective one, and can create perverse incentives (Mashaw, 1998). For example, tougher eligibility criteria can reduce incentives to leave benefit to take up work.

Growing civil rights and welfare rights campaigns may have contributed to personal as well as public awareness of disability, and as a result more people may have overcome inhibitions about claiming benefit. For Disability Living Allowance and Attendance Allowance, the available evidence points to predominantly institutional and demographic factors, whereas for Incapacity Benefit, labour market exclusion and associated institutional changes have probably been more significant.

Part 4
Benefits for children and families

FIFTEEN

Trends in receipt of benefits by children and families

Summary

Some benefits are only available to families with children – Child Benefit and Family Credit *– while the level of other benefits is higher if dependent children are living with the applicant,* for example, Housing Benefit and Income Support.

Child Benefit is paid on behalf of all children under 17 and to young people aged 17 and 18 who are in full-time non-advanced education. Family Credit is available on a means-tested basis to people working 16 or more hours each week if they have dependent children.

Child Benefit was claimed on behalf of a million children in 1999, down since its introduction in 1997. However, the number of families receiving Family Credit or its earlier equivalent rose by more than eleven-fold, to 788,000, between 1971 and 1999.

The number of families with children claiming Income Support or the earlier benefit equivalent tripled between 1971 and 1999, to 1.4 million.

Housing Benefit was received by 1.4 million families with children in 1998, an eight-fold increase over 1990.

Identifiable benefit expenditure on families with children increased, from 16% of total social security spending in 1978/79, to 18 % in 1998/99.

British governments have used the concept of benefits for children and families as a way of categorising social security expenditure since at least the mid–1970s. This reflects the importance attached to children –

defined for the purposes of social security as all children up to the age of 16 and 17 and 18 year olds in full-time non-advanced education – and particularly to the avoidance of child poverty. The presence of children increases the risk of adult poverty, not least because there are more mouths to feed and less hours available to engage in paid work. Also, under a regime that features a sizeable volume of means testing, the existence of children assumes additional significance in relation to work disincentives. If the level of out–of–work benefits varies according to household size, benefits are likely to be higher for families with children, and work disincentives correspondingly greater.

Families with children can apply for the full range of social security benefits depending on their circumstances. However, some benefits are available solely on account of the fact that they have children. Universal, non-contributory Child Benefit, is paid for all children in full-time, non–advanced education. Maternity Allowance is paid for 18 weeks to women who have paid full National Insurance contributions at the earliest starting 11 weeks before the baby is due, and a Maternity Grant is paid to mothers receiving certain means-tested benefits. In other cases, families with dependant children receive a higher benefit. This applies to income-based Jobseeker's Allowance, Income Support and Housing Benefit. Finally, two in–work benefits, Working Families' Tax Credit and Disabled Person's Tax Credit, are only available to people who have children.

The number of children on whose behalf Child Benefit is paid has fallen noticeably since its introduction in 1979, reflecting falling birth rates (Figure 15.1). In contrast, the numbers of families with children in the caseloads of all other relevant benefits increased markedly between 1971 and 1998, although in a number of cases a downward trend became evident from the mid-1990s onwards (Figures 15.2 and 15.3). As a consequence, whereas in 1974 only 6.4% of all under 16 year olds relied on means-tested state benefits, by 1994 this figure had risen to just over 25%. Moreover, the increase in reliance on means-tested benefit was even more marked for children aged under five; the proportion living in families receiving means-tested benefits grew from 6.6% to 29.1% between 1974 and 1994 (Evans, 1998).

Figure 15.1: Numbers receiving Child Benefit

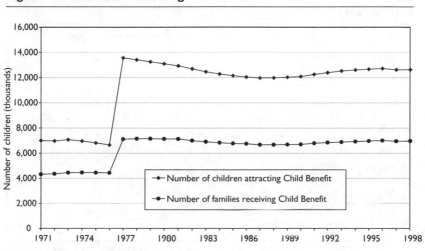

Source: DSS (1999c)

Figure 15.2: Number of families with children receiving Income Support and Housing Benefit

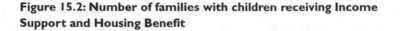
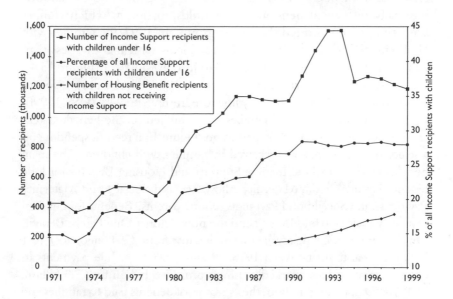

Source: DSS (1999c)

Figure 15.3: Families receiving Family Credit (formerly Family Income Supplement)

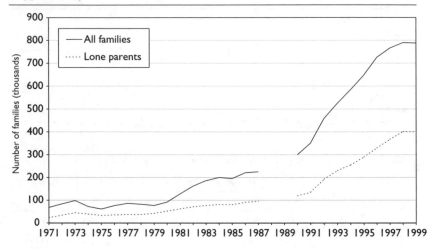

Source: DSS (1999c)

The increased reliance of families with children on benefits occurred over a period during which the incidence of child poverty increased markedly. At the same time, the composition of the poverty population changed, from one dominated by people living in childless families, especially retirement pensioner households, to one in which families with children constituted the largest group. In 1997/98, families with children accounted for 54% of all individuals with incomes less than half of the national average, compared to just 36% in 1971 (Figure 15.4). Likewise, over the shorter period 1979 to 1997/98, the proportion of children living below this poverty line rose from 9% to 24% (DSS, 1999f).

The increased reliance of families with children on the benefit system has led inevitably to a rise in expenditure. Figure 15.5 records spending on a selected range of benefits received by families with children. The main benefits counted include Income Support and Housing Benefits for lone parents, Family Credit, Maternity Allowance and Social Fund Maternity Payments, and Social Fund Payments to lone parents. Benefits for children primarily include Child Benefit and the now defunct One Parent Benefit. On these measures, expenditure on families rose from £2.4 billion to £10.1 billion in real terms between 1978/79 and 1998/99, while payments to children increased less markedly, rising from £5.8 billion to £7.3 billion. In 1978/79, spending on both these groups of benefits paid to families and children accounted for 16% of total social security expenditure, but by 1998/99 this proportion had moved upwards to 18%.

Figure 15.4: Families and children as a proportion of all individuals with incomes less than half the average (before housing costs)*

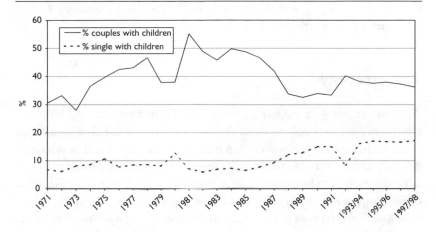

* Figures for 1994/95 onwards are based on analysis of the Family Resources Survey. The Family Expenditure Survey was used in earlier years.

Source: Goodman and Webb (1994); and DSS (1999b)

Figure 15.5: Spending on benefits for families with dependent children*

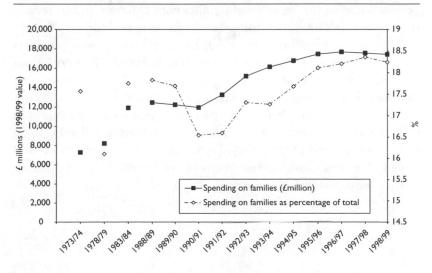

*1973 estimated.

Source: DSS (2000a); Evans (1998)

The above figures understate the true rise in benefit spending on families with children because they exclude payments to the children of unemployed people, and of disabled people claiming Disability Living Allowance and Incapacity Benefit.

The strategy

All four drivers – demography, the economy, institutions and beliefs – are implicated in the growth in the numbers of families with children claiming benefits that has occurred since 1971, but the interrelationships between the drivers are unusually complex. Particularly important has been the growth in lone parents, resulting from a decline in the institution of marriage and the permanency of conjugal unions. This in turn has followed from changes in the social and economic aspirations of women, and in beliefs about the sanctity of marriage. At the same time, labour market developments have encouraged employment of women but reduced the proportion of jobs that pay sufficient to support a family with children above the poverty threshold. Increased unemployment has also led to a growth in the proportion of workless families, with the result that the risk of children living in households reliant on benefits has risen. Finally, the government has responded at different times with policies to boost the incomes of families with children, and to reduce the numbers of families claiming benefit for long periods.

There is no ideal order in which these different sets of processes should be covered. The chosen strategy is to begin, in Chapters 16 and 17, with descriptions of the demographic and economic changes that have exerted an upward pressure on caseloads. Chapter 18 then addresses the shifts in values and beliefs that have underpinned developments in demography and labour market participation, leaving Chapter 19 to provide an account of the policy developments that in part reflect and embody the same changes in demography and beliefs. Chapter 20 offers a reflective overview.

SIXTEEN

Aspects of the demography of family life

Summary

The number of marriages fell from 370,000 in 1971 to 182,000 in 1997, and the number of people cohabiting increased to comprise 7% of all heterosexual couples.

The divorce rate in England and Wales increased by 42% over the slightly shorter period 1973 to 1997, and the evidence is that cohabiting unions are more short-lived than marital ones.

The birth rate fell, but the proportion of births that occurred out of wedlock increased from 8% to 38% between 1971 and 1998; many such births were to cohabiting couples.

The number of lone parent families tripled to 1.7 million between 1971 and 1998. The proportion caused by widowhood and separation declined, while those due to divorce, the breakdown of cohabitation or a non-resident relationship increased.

The number of lone parents receiving Income Support increased from 213,000 in 1971 to 972,000 in 1998, and demographic changes conspired to exacerbate the prevalence of child poverty.

The period since 1971 has witnessed radical changes in family demographics, some of which, such as later childbirth and falling fertility, are continuations of long established trends. Others, for example increased divorce and the rapid growth in the number of lone parent households, are more recent phenomena. The net result of these changes is that Britain in 1998 was characterised by fewer first marriages, higher rates of divorce, more cohabitation, more lone parents and smaller families than was the case in 1971. The decline in family size will have exerted a downward pressure on claimant caseloads, but it is the increased instability of relationships and the consequent upward trend in lone parenthood that has most influenced the level of benefit receipt. Not only have the numbers of lone parents receiving benefit increased but, so too, has the proportion reliant on means–tested support. In 1971 there were only about 570,000 lone parents, of whom 37% were receiving means–tested Supplementary Benefit. By 1998 the number had grown to 1.7 million and of these, 972,000, 58%, claimed the corresponding benefit, Income Support.

This chapter is divided into four parts. The first part describes the decline of marriage and the growth in cohabitation, the second charts the consequent rise of lone parenthood and the third documents the fall in family size. Finally, the impact of demographic change on benefit caseloads is briefly reviewed.

Marriage, cohabitation and divorce

Marriage remained the preferred form of heterosexual partnership in the late 1990s. Some 63% of people aged 16 to 69 had been married at some point in their lives, and over 90% of couples living together were married (Shaw and Haskey, 1999). However, marriage certainly became less frequent in the period 1971 to 1998, with each successive generation being less likely to marry than the preceding one.

The high point for first marriages was 1969, when almost 400,000 took place, after which numbers fell precipitously to about 370,000 in 1971, and to 280,000 in 1976. The number of marriages remained fairly constant through to the late 1980s, when the year-on-year fall in marriages accelerated, with the result that only 182,000 marriages were recorded in 1997, the latest year for which information is available (The Stationery Office, 2000a). The marriage rate received a boost in the early 1970s, with a marked increase in second marriages following the enactment of the liberalising 1969 Divorce Law Reform Act in 1971 (see Chapter 18). In 1973 there were 16.3 marriages per 1,000 resident population (in England and Wales), a figure which had fallen to 13.1 by 1990 and to 10.4 in 1997. Age at first marriage fell for successive birth cohorts up to those born in the 1950s, but subsequently rose.

Figure 16.1: Divorce and marriage rates in England, Wales and Scotland

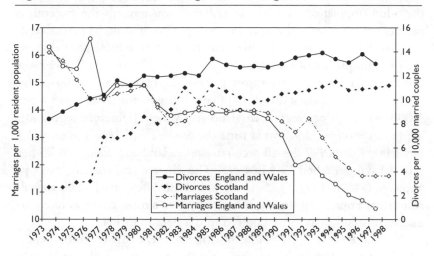

Source: TSO (2000a)

As marriage declined, cohabitation increased. Estimates of cohabitation before 1979 are unreliable, but between then and 1996 the number of cohabiting couples rose from 367,000 to 1.56 million, about 7% of all heterosexual couples (Shaw and Haskey, 1999). Over this period the number of people cohabiting without having previously been married increased markedly; for example, about 27% of women aged between 18 and 49 were cohabiting in 1996, compared with just 8% in 1979. On the other hand, although divorced men and women were both more likely to cohabit than other groups, the propensity for men to do so declined markedly during the 1990s.

Cohabitation is generally the prelude to marriage; however, the proportion of relationships that develop in this way has been falling. For example, the proportion of men who began cohabiting in their late twenties and who went on to marry their partner declined from 95% of those who began cohabiting in the early 1970s to 63% 20 years later. Not surprisingly, the same pattern is evident for women. The principal reason for marrying after cohabitation was the desire to strengthen the relationship; a third of partners give this as a factor. One fifth note the arrival of, or desire to have, children.

The younger a person begins cohabiting, the less likely they are to get married and, since the average age at which cohabitation begins has fallen over the last two or so decades, one would expect the number of cohabitations that end in marriage to continue falling. However, taking the adult population as a whole, cohabitation remains the exception rather than the rule; by the mid-1990s only 12% of adults had cohabited, and less than 1% reported that they had lived in five or more partnerships.

If the frequency of marriage fell between 1971 and the late 1990s, the rate of marriage dissolution increased. The divorce rate in the immediate aftermath of the 1969 Divorce Law Reform Act was 8.4 per 1,000 marriages per year in England and Wales. (Different legislation applies in Scotland, and at that time the divorce rate there was only 2.7 per 1,000.) By 1997 the divorce rate in England and Wales was 13 per 1,000, having reached 13.9 in 1993. The divorce rate was still lower in Scotland (11% in 1997; 11.2% in 1998) but the differential had narrowed. Marriages contracted during the 1980s were almost twice as likely to end in dissolution as those entered into a decade earlier.

Marriage, however, remains considerably more stable than cohabitation. Irrespective of birth cohort or age at the start of a relationship, cohabitation is more likely to end than marriage. Moreover, more marriages preceded by periods of cohabitation are dissolved than those where cohabitation has not taken place.

These developments – especially the increase in divorce, the growth of cohabitation and the comparative instability of such unions – all increased demand on the social security system during the 1970s to 1990s. Most importantly, they contributed significantly to the growth in lone parenthood described in the next section. However, it should also be recalled that relationship breakdown frequently impacts on employment, and usually leaves at least one partner with a lower income.

Empirical studies of the dissolution of married and cohabiting relationships in Britain during the early 1990s revealed that two thirds of women and two fifths of men experienced a decline in income as a consequence (Jarvis and Jenkins, 1998). Whereas men on average were better off after a relationship split, women averaged a 75% fall in income, and children a 77% decline in household income, before payment of benefit. The proportion of women in employment fell from 47% to 35% after splitting up, and the proportion of men declined from 75% to 65%. Following separation, the effect of social security was to help reduce the loss in income to 17% and 14% for women and children respectively.

Lone parenthood

In Britain, lone parents are formally defined to comprise a mother or father living, without a spouse (and not cohabiting), with his or her never-married dependent child or children aged either under 16 or from 16 to (under) 19 and undertaking full-time education (DHSS, 1974). Single parents are taken to have conceived out of wedlock, which it used to be assumed also meant outside a stable relationship, an assumption that has become anachronistic with the growth in cohabitation.

The total number of lone parent families has grown continuously since 1971, and the reasons for lone parenthood have also changed (Figure 16.2). The proportion of lone parent families headed by a woman rose from 88% in 1971 to 93% in 1998, and the number of dependent children living in lone parent families almost tripled, from about 1 million in 1971 to 2.9 million in 1998 (The Stationery Office, 2000b). Seventeen per cent of women born in 1958 had become lone parents by the age of 33, in 1991 (Payne and Range, 1998).

Figure 16.2: Number of lone parents and their dependent children

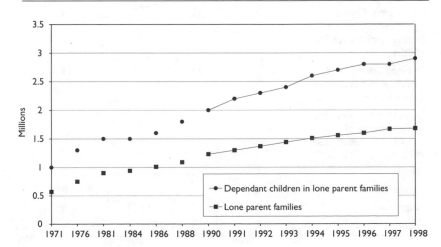

Source: Haskey (1998)

The prime reasons for the increase in lone parent families between 1971 and 1991 were higher separation and divorce rates. As a consequence, the proportion of lone parents who had been widowed fell, from 29% of the total in 1971 to 4% in 1998 (Table 16.1). However, during the early 1990s, which witnessed an acceleration in the growth of lone parenthood that subsequently subsided, there was a marked increase in the number of never-married mothers who had either separated from, or never lived with, a partner (The Stationery Office, 2000b). By 1998, 39% of lone mothers had never been married, and a survey, conducted four years earlier, found that just under half of this group had never cohabited (Marsh et al, 1997). Of the cohort of lone parents born in 1958, a quarter did not have a partner immediately before becoming a lone parent, and 17 had never had one. Nearly half of the latter group became lone parents as teenagers and three quarters had become mothers by the age of 23 (Payne and Range, 1998).

Table 16.1: Trend in families

	1971	1981	1991	1998/99
Lone parent families (000s)	570	900	1,300	1,680
Lone parent families as percentage of families with dependent children	8	12	20	24
Children born outside marriage as percentage of live births	9	14	31	38
Types of lone mothers, as percentage of families with dependent children:				
Single	1	2	6	9
Divorced	2	4	6	8
Separated	2	2	4	5
Widowed	2	2	1	1

Sources: Bryson et al (1997) and TSO (2000b)

Linked to the change in composition, the average age of lone parents has been falling. Over a third of single mothers are aged less than 25, whereas the peak ages for divorced and separated mothers are the early and late 30s respectively and, for widows, the early 40s. Male lone parents are, on average, older than lone mothers. Teenage births fell from 10% of the total in 1971 to 7% in 1998, but whereas, in 1971, 74% of teenage mothers were married at the birth, this was true of just 11% in 1998.

There is some evidence that the time people spend as lone parents has fallen slightly, again due to the change in composition; single mothers tend to remain as lone parents for less time than other groups (McKay and Rowlingson, 1998). Based on data gathered in the mid-1980s, 50% of single mothers re-partnered or otherwise ceased being a lone parent within three years, whereas the median length of lone parenthood was around five years for divorcees and eight years if separated or widowed. It follows, therefore, that the long-term growth of lone motherhood has been the result of an increase in the number of people becoming lone parents rather than lone parents remaining so for longer.

Partly as a result of the increase in single lone mothers, the economic circumstances of lone mothers has worsened over the last 20 years. The proportion of lone parents with an income below 50% of the median grew from 57% to 70% between 1984/87 and 1992/95 (Shouls et al, 1999). Similarly, while the number with access to a car rose from 30% in 1979/83 and 35% in 1984/87 to 44% in 1992/95, the disparity between lone mothers and other mothers increased.

The proportion of lone parents receiving means-tested Income Support and its predecessors rose markedly, from around 37% in 1971 to 70% in 1993, but then fell to 58% in 1998 (Figure 16.3). The reason for the rise in reliance on Income Support is generally attributed to the increase in the number of younger single, that is, never married, lone parents, who also tend to have younger children who inhibit employment (McKay and Rowlingson, 1999). The reasons for the subsequent fall in claims for Income Support are still unclear. However, it is likely to reflect the changes in government policy, modifications to Family Credit and possibly the creation of a Child Support Agency to increase maintenance payments from absent parents, and the general improvement in labour demand, in particular for women (Bradshaw, 1998).

Up-take of universal One Parent Benefit (abolished in 1999) increased from its introduction in 1977, reaching a plateau of around 60% to 65% in the late 1980s (Figure 16.4). Claimants of means-tested benefits received no financial benefit from One Parent Benefit since it counted as income, which probably set a ceiling on the level of claims.

Figure 16.3: Proportion of lone parents receiving Income Support

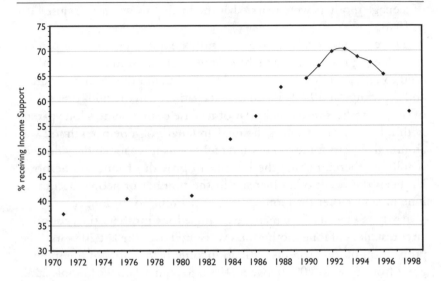

Source: Authors' calculations

Figure 16.4: Proportion of lone parents receiving One Parent Benefit

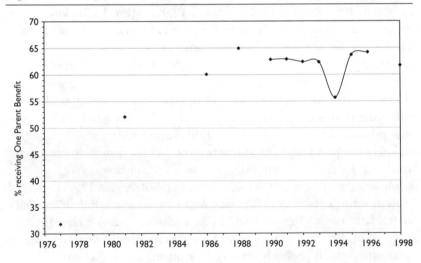

Source: Authors' calculations

Family sizes of one and two parent families

Fertility began falling in 1964, and had already declined to 15.8 per 1,000 population by 1971 (The Stationery Office, 2000a). By 1998 it had fallen to 12.1, the lowest level ever recorded. Total period fertility, the number of children a women is likely to have in total, declined from 2.36 in 1971 to 1.7 in 1998. The increase in cohabitation, in particular, resulted in a very large rise in the proportion of births which occurred outside of wedlock, from 8% in 1971 to 38% in 1998.

As a result of the declining birth rate, the number of children aged under 16 in Britain decreased from 13.7 million in 1971 to 11 million in 1998. Average family size also fell slightly between 1971 and 1998, on account of the declining birth rate (Table 16.2). This may have exerted downward pressure on child poverty, to the extent that poverty is concentrated in large families; the proportion of families with three or more children fell from 9% to 4% between 1971 and 1998.

There was, however, an increase in the average number of children living with *single* lone mothers. This was probably largely due to the increase in the number of cohabiting couples having children, and subsequent separations. However, a minority of women do give birth while they are lone parents: 9% of the 1958 birth cohort of lone parents did so, although two fifths were already pregnant when they became lone parents (Payne and Range, 1998). Similarly, 15% of lone parents who remained without partners between 1991 and 1995 had another child or became pregnant during this period, as did another 9% of those who re-partnered for some of this period (Ford et al, 1997). However, 70% of all the births to women who were lone parents in 1991 were to women who were married or cohabiting in 1995.

Table 16.2: Average number of dependent children per family

	1971	1981	1996	1998
Lone parent families	1.79	1.60	1.73	1.7
Couple families	2.03	2.07	1.85	1.9
Single lone mothers	1.25	1.19	1.56	
Separated lone mothers	2.03	1.81	2.08	
Divorced lone mothers	1.93	1.75	1.75	

Source: Hasley (1998)

The net result of the fall in birth rate and rising cohabitation is that, between 1971 and 1998, the proportion of lone parent families grew from 7% to 24% of all families with dependent children. Whereas, in 1971, about one child in 12 lived in a lone parent family, by 1998 almost one in four did so. In 1998 lone parent families were 11 times more likely to be reliant on Income Support than other families with children.

What has been learned

The number of people marrying declined between 1971 and 1998, and fertility fell to the lowest level on record. On the other hand, the proportion of people cohabiting increased, especially among younger age groups, and the number of divorces rose. Since relationship breakdown typically leaves one person worse off financially, can lead to job loss and, where, there are children, to lone parenthood, the net result of demographic change over the period was to increase the number of people in need of means-tested supplementation.

Even allowing for the social security safety net, the demographic changes cited above contributed to a substantial rise in poverty among children. Between 1979 and 1997/98 the proportion of children living in households with less than 50% average incomes increased from 9% to 26%[1]. In 1997/98, 48% of children in lone parent households were living in poverty compared with 24% in 1979 (DSS, 1999f)[2].

Notes

[1] A change in the statistical series with the FRS replacing the FES may cause this growth to be understated. In 1995/96 the FRS indicated 22% of children had incomes below 50% of average income, whereas the FES recorded 26% before housing costs.

[2] The increase may again be understated. In 1995/96, the FRS indicated that 35% of children in lone parent households had incomes below 50% of average and the FES, 50%.

SEVENTEEN

The economy and the family

Summary

Employment among women with employed partners increased markedly between the 1970s and 1998, but remained static among women with partners who were sick, disabled or unemployed.

This resulted in a polarisation of employment between 'work-rich' and 'work-poor' households.

Employment among lone parents fell noticeably between 1971 and 1994, but had recovered slightly by 1998. The fall, adding about 120,000 to Income Support caseloads, was linked to the changing characteristics of lone parents and to an increasingly competitive labour market, rather than to a lack of willingness to work. More lone parents were young, with pre-school-aged children, and had limited qualifications and work experience.

The proportion of men who were low paid approximately doubled between the early 1970s and 1996. Over a similar period there was a four-fold increase in the risk of poverty among families with at least one person in work.

However, the rise in the number of individuals in poor families of working age, from 3.1 million in 1971 to 8.5 million in 1997/98, was due mostly to the increased proportion of workless families.

Over a million working families were added to claimant caseloads between 1971 and 1998.

Virtually all the changes in the labour market, documented in Chapters 4 and 13 that have conspired to increase benefit receipt – the decline in manufacturing, higher unemployment, higher employability thresholds – of course affect families with children. Suffice, therefore, to focus here on three issues that have special poignancy for families, and which have contributed both to an increase in child poverty and higher caseloads: the polarisation in wages, the fall in working by lone parents, and increased worklessness more generally. First, however, it is important to acknowledge that more mothers working is of financial benefit to themselves and their families.

Mothers' employment

One of the most profound changes in the labour market that has occurred during the last three decades is the increase in women's participation in the labour market, both in absolute terms and relative to men. In 1998, 69% of women and 81% of working age men were in paid work – a gender gap of 12%. In 1971 only 57% of women worked and, since 94% of men then had jobs, the gap was 37%.

There are a number of reasons why this transformation occurred. The pattern of labour demand shifted in women's favour. Maternity rights legislation now allows nearly two thirds of women to return to the same employer after childbirth. The educational achievement of women has increased faster than men and the gender gap in wage rates has fallen (Desai et al, 1999). But perhaps most important of all, women's attachment to work and career aspirations have risen as part of the social re-evaluation of women's roles, which will be discussed further in Chapter 18.

The re-evaluation of roles has meant that more mothers are prepared to take paid work, and to do so when their children are still quite young. This is evident from Figure 17.1, which shows that between 1981 and 1998, the proportion of mothers with pre-school-aged children who were working increased from 32% to 52%. Even more dramatic was the increase in the proportion of mothers with a baby less than a year old who were working, which rose from 19% to 44% over the same period. In contrast, employment rates among women without children remained virtually unaltered through the 1970s, 1980s and 1990s. Although women with young children mostly worked part-time, these developments speak volumes for the changed economics of family life.

Figure 17.1: Female employment rates according to the age of the youngest child

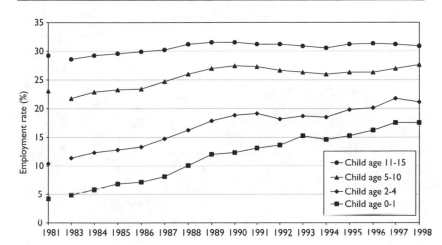

Source: Desai et al (1999)

The increase in female employment rates that occurred over the last 20 years is attributable almost entirely to women with employed partners (Figure 17.2). For example, whereas, in 1981, 52% of mothers with a partner in work themselves had a paid job, by 1998 the proportion had risen to 73%. By way of contrast, the proportion of mothers with a partner who was unemployed, sick or disabled that went out to work was virtually unchanged. Part of the reason was that the partners of employed men were, on average, better educated than those who had partners who were out of work. Another factor, however, was that the female partners of many unemployed men would have found much of their gain in wages offset by loss of their male partner's means-tested Jobseeker's Allowance[1]. Also, the one-earner family lacks the additional financial flexibility that allows dual earners to buy child and domestic care that makes two people working easier.

The precise motivations for women working – notably, the balance between financial necessity and self-fulfilment – are complex and under-studied. The receipt of two incomes can enhance lifestyles and, in circumstances where it is the norm for both partners in a family to be working, help to establish the consumption standards that are collectively desired by the community. Equally, it is known that in 1991, women earning reduced the incidence of poverty experienced by couples by a third (Harkness et al, 1997). Indeed, during the 1990s, the only way a

Figure: 17.2: Female employment rates according to partner's employment status

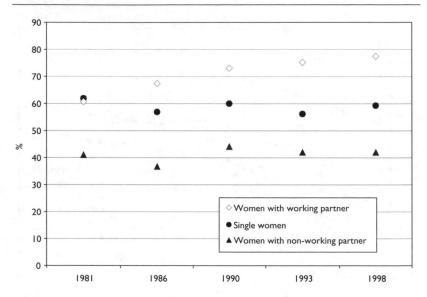

Source: Desai et al (1999)

family on benefits could guarantee escaping poverty was for both parents to secure full-time jobs; one job left 37% of families in poverty; one full-time and one part-time job left 7% poor (Iacovou and Berthoud, 2000).

These developments, creating 'work-rich' households, contrast with the processes that generated increasing numbers of 'work-poor' families: unemployment, the increase in lone parenthood, and worklessness generally. Both have nevertheless conspired to increase the numbers claiming benefit.

Lone parents and employment

In 1998, lone parents were nearly 20 times more likely to be without work than other families of working age and, therefore, also to suffer the financial deprivation and risk of social exclusion that that entails (The Stationery Office, 2000b). Moreover, whereas other mothers have been going out to work in ever greater numbers, the proportion of lone mothers working fell from 48% in 1979, the earliest year for which figures are available, to 39% in 1993 – lower than in all OECD countries

Figure 17.3: Employment rates of women with children

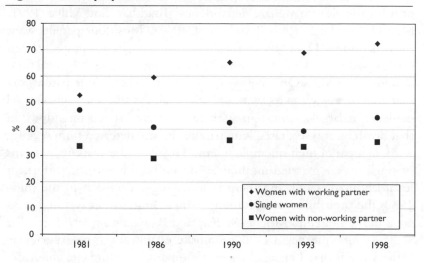

Source: Gregg et al (1999)

except Ireland, New Zealand and the Netherlands (Bradshaw, 1998). By 1998 the employment rate of lone mothers had recovered to over 44% (Figure 17.3).

The decline in employment by lone mothers has received more investigation than the recent rise. It would appear to be due to the change in the composition of lone parents. Widows, separated and divorced women, who used to predominate among lone parents in the 1970s, tended to be older and have better qualifications and work experience than later cohorts of never-married lone parents. Not only were they more able to compete in a labour market that was less tight than in later years, and to command higher wages as a result, they were also less constrained domestically because their children tended to be older (Browning, 1992). The proportion of lone parents with under school-aged children increased from 34% to 46% between 1982/83 and 1992/93 (Bryson, 1997). It has also been suggested that labour market changes may have led to increasing competition for low-skill, low-paid jobs, to which many lone mothers are restricted by their domestic circumstances and lack of skills (Payne and Range, 1998). The growing material deprivation suffered by lone parents, described in Chapter 15, which tends to make people risk averse in their behaviour, may also have reduced flexibility vis-à-vis the labour market (Dobson et al, 1995).

The factors that stop lone mothers from working appear to have more to do with barriers to employment than an unwillingness to work or a predilection to welfare dependency (Bradshaw and Millar, 1991; McKay and Marsh, 1994; Bryson et al, 1997). Most lone parents want to work – some 43% of those not already working have repeatedly been categorised as 'work-ready', with 42% deferring work, usually until their children are older. Only between 7% and 11% of all lone parents say that they never want to work (Hales et al, 2000). The behavioural evidence is largely consistent with lone parents' stated intentions, in that divorced and separated lone parents are not deterred from seeking work in areas of high unemployment. However, the working patterns of single, never-married mothers are more sensitive to the pattern of local labour demand, and there is some suggestion that in the mid-1980s the probability of becoming a single lone parent was higher in areas of high unemployment (McKay and Rowlingson, 1998).

Many lone mothers lack the requisite qualifications or experience. Others are deterred by an absence of informal or affordable childcare; over half of lone parents have nobody or just one person who could provide short-term childcare (Bradshaw and Millar, 1991; Bryson et al, 1997; Hales et al, 2000). Ill-health, of either their own or their children or other members of the household is another factor (Finlayson and Marsh, 1998). Lone parents are themselves between 50% and 70% more likely than other mothers to report a limiting longstanding illness (Shouls et al, 1999).

The recent increase in the numbers of lone parents working may well reflect the sustained upturn in the economy. It could reflect the ageing of lone parents and their children in the claimant population as the rate of growth in lone parents has slowed. Research has also shown that the receipt of regular child maintenance from absent parents provides lone parents with the financial security to make the transition into work, and it may be that the Child Support Agency, established after 1991, is beginning to ensure more regular payments.

Whatever the reasons, the fall in labour market participation by lone parents between 1979 and 1994 probably accounted for in the region of 120,000 additional claims for Income Support, that is, about 16% of the increased claims from lone parents and 5% of the rise in the total claimant caseload. Moreover, the decline in employment of lone parents will have added significantly to total social security spending. Single payments to cover exceptional needs, and now Social Fund loans, go mostly to lone parents, and lone parents have increased as a proportion of claimants receiving Housing Benefit.

Wage polarisation and low pay

One result of the growth in wage inequality that occurred in the late 1970s and 1980s, described in Chapter 4, was to increase the proportion of jobs that were low paid. This not only resulted in rising levels of poverty among working families over the last 30 years, it also increased benefit receipt in two ways. First, it led to the introduction and increasing take-up of in-work, means-tested benefits and second, it reduced the financial benefit of working that may, at the margin, have deterred some people from doing so.

The prevalence of low pay, defined as two thirds of the median for all earners, fell sharply from 1973 to a low of 17% in 1977, because of a rise in female wages. Thereafter, the extent of low pay among women remained fairly constant, while the proportion of low paid men approximately doubled. By 1994 women were two-and-a-half times more likely than men to be low paid, whereas at the beginning of the 1970s (actually, 1968) their chances of being low paid were six times those of men. Taking a threshold of £4.50 per hour, 36% of women were low paid compared with 17% of men (Stewart, 1999).

Table 17.1 reveals the overlap between poverty and low pay. Only 11% of low-paid workers live in poor households which, of course, reflects the fact that most low-paid workers are women and that most are part of a dual income household. However, the table also demonstrates that the presence of children massively increases the chances of a low-waged worker being poor. Twenty-six per cent of men with a partner and children on low wages were poor, as were 33% of lone parents, compared with 4% of single men. Furthermore, while the vast majority of poor households contain nobody in employment, when they do they are 76% likely to be low paid. Moreover, largely because of the increased prevalence of low pay, the chances of a household with at least one person working full-time being in poverty increased from 3% to 15% between 1979 and 1997/98 (DSS, 1999f).

The association of in-work poverty with the presence of children was one reason for the introduction of in-work benefits, although the principal intention, especially in the case of Family Credit introduced in 1988, was to redress the supposed disincentive effects created by the increased prevalence of low pay. The pay available from entry level jobs fell relative to benefit levels, reducing the value of work. Evaluation of the scheme revealed that, while Family Credit did facilitate some people, especially lone parents, returning to work, its principal function was to help people on low incomes remain in work, acting also as a

Table 17.1: Poverty and low pay

	% of low paid* who are in poor† households	% of employees in poor† households who are low paid*
Male		
Couple, with children	25.7	64.4
Couple, no children	3.6	79.8
Single, with children	32.7	91.0
Single, no children	4.2	58.5
Female		
Couple, with children	9.7	81.4
Couple, no children	3.7	63.0
Single, no children	9.0	83.8
Total	10.5	76.4

* Low pay defined as £4.50, which in 1997 approximated to two thirds male median earnings.
† Poverty is defined as half net equivalised household income.

Source: Stewart (1999)

safety net when earnings faltered (Walker with Ashworth, 1994; Bryson and Marsh, 1996). For lone parents, 80% of whom worked less than 30 hours per week, Family Credit facilitated the juggling of childcare and employment and provided an element of financial security, that, like maintenance payments, enabled them to risk working. But rather than acting as the transitional benefit that Family Credit was expected to be, it, like Family Income Supplement before it, rapidly became a mechanism for the long-term supplementation of low wages.

When combined with the introduction of in-work benefits, a by-product of the growth of low pay was, therefore, to create a group of families who had failed to escape reliance on benefit even by securing paid work. At least 790,000 families found themselves in this position in 1998 (Figure 15.3).

Worklessness

Unemployment, the growth, the number of lone parents, and the polarisation of wages all contributed to the rise in worklessness that characterised the period 1971 to 1998. This, in turn, increased poverty

Figure 17.4: The growth in workless households

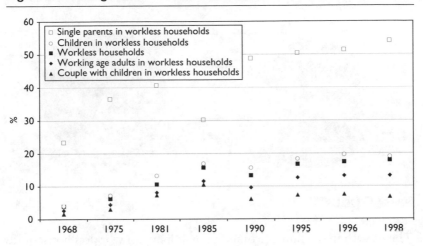

Source: Gregg (1999)

and benefit caseloads. What is still disputed is how far the structure of social security itself added to the rise in worklessness.

Excluding pensioners, the proportion of households where no one worked more than quadrupled between 1971 and 1998, from 4% to 18% (Figure 17.4). Over the same period, the proportion of all working aged adults living in workless households increased from less than 3% to 13%, and the proportion of children from 4% to 19%. The risk of individuals in a workless household being poor changed only slightly, but the proportion of poor people living in households where no one worked rose markedly, from 29% in 1971 to 51% in 1996. Therefore, despite the increased incidence of low pay, the major cause of poverty shifted from inadequate wages towards the absence of work. To illustrate, 30 years ago 65% of poor children had at least one parent working, but by 1995/96 the number with a working parent had almost halved to 37% (Figure 17.5). Indeed, while a fifth of the overall increase in child poverty can be attributed to the rise in lone parenthood, the larger portion is due to the fact that so many more children had one or both parents without paid work (Gregg et al, 1999b). Moreover, much of the poverty experienced by childless families was long-term. In August 1999, nearly 800,000 children had been living on means-tested benefits for at least five years (HM Treasury, 2000).

Figure 17.5: Distribution of child poverty according to household type

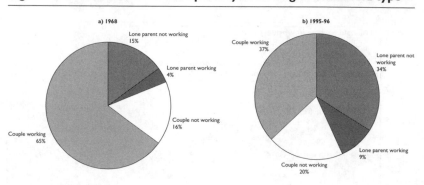

Source: Gregg (1999)

The growth in the number of individuals living in workless households over the somewhat shorter period 1979 to 1996/97 is known to be attributable to increases in lone parenthood, economic inactivity – principally as a result of long-term illness and disability – and unemployment in the ratio 3:3:2 (DSS, 2000a). It is also the case that the available employment in Britain is concentrated in employment-rich households, as explained above, more so than in any other OECD country (OECD, 1998). This tends to direct attention to the characteristics of the British social security system and its heavy reliance on means testing. Economic modelling has determined that a third of the rise in worklessness is due to changes in family structure and the availability of employment (Gregg et al, 1999a). Much of the residue has been interpreted to result from the interaction of low-paid jobs with the tax and benefit system causing work not to pay, which has, in turn, fostered the polarisation into 'work-rich' and 'work-poor' households.

However, the econometric models employed to date fail to take adequate account of four sets of drivers identified in this book, especially the changing institutions and underlying shift in public attitudes, beliefs and ideology. Account needs to be taken of the complex pattern of influences identified in earlier chapters that determine employment rates, levels of disability and the nature of family relations.

Whatever the precise web of causation, the net result is that in 1998 1.4 million families received Income Support or income-related Jobseeker's Allowance, whereas in 1971 Supplementary Benefit aided just 430,000. National means-tested, in-work benefits, such as Family Credit, that in 1998 supported 870,000 families, and Housing Benefit that provided for 357,000, did not exist in 1971. Neither did specific incapacity benefits that also now cater for unknown numbers of families with children.

What has been learned

Changes in the labour market appear to have had a more detrimental effect on the self-sufficiency of families with children than other groups. Falling wage rates at the bottom of the labour market made it increasingly more difficult for families to acquire an acceptable standard of living without both parents working or recourse to in-work social security benefits. By 1998 over a million families in work had need of in-work benefits, and it is the intention of the Labour government that this number should rise still further.

But most of the increase in both poverty and benefit expenditure, although less clearly in claimant numbers, was due to rising worklessness. This was as a result of growing unemployment, lower employment among lone parents and, as discussed in Chapter 13, increased incapacity among prime age males. But it was exacerbated by the concentration of employment in dual earner households. Indeed, households where someone was already in employment accounted for most of the employment growth that occurred between 1971 and 1998. To those who had, more was again given, leaving the social security system to support the increasing number of families without work.

It is clear that the gulf between families with no earner and the increasingly typical two-earner household widened between 1971 and 1998. The structure of the benefit system, dependent as it is on means testing most of those available for work, and with different systems of provision on each side of the employment divide, may hinder people returning to work. But the evidence presented in this and earlier chapters shows that most of those who do not work have other more self-evident impediments to employment – limited skills, inadequate childcare, an impairment.

Note

[1] This problem – which research suggests was less important than originally thought (McKay et al, 1997) – was recently countered by the introduction of a Back to Work Bonus, which allows families to reclaim part of the income lost (Ashworth and Youngs, 2000).

EIGHTEEN

Beliefs about the family and poverty

Summary

Increased divorce, cohabitation and lone parenthood reflect profound changes in sexual attitudes and relations. Sex and procreation have come to be separated from marriage.

Stigma associated with cohabitation has almost disappeared, but is still attached to lone parenthood, the growth of which during the 1980s and 1990s provoked moral panic among some policy makers.

Lone parenthood is often viewed as the lesser of two evils by lone mothers, generating financial, legal and housing problems but offering an escape from unsatisfactory relationships, and occasionally from unemployment and low status work.

Employment and employment opportunities for women are still influenced by traditional gender divisions of unpaid and paid work. Nevertheless, gender-based differentials in the labour market narrowed noticeably between the 1970s and 1990s, although improvements were limited to full-time work.

Low female wages extend the time that lone parents and couples with children spend on benefit (since a woman's wage is typically insufficient to take a family off benefit and out of poverty). *However, a second earner even receiving low wages can protect families' earners against poverty caused by low pay or unemployment.*

Poverty has been reinstated to the political lexicon after a period in the 1980s and 1990s when its existence was denied and attention focused almost exclusively on reducing claimant numbers.

The decline in marriage and the increase in divorce, cohabitation and lone parenthood described in Chapter 16, and the polarisation of work resulting from the rise in dual earner couples and worklessness, considered in Chapter 17, are important consequences of even more profound changes in sexual morality and gender roles.

Sexual activity has become increasingly separated from the institution of marriage, and the sexual and economic dependency of women on men has been challenged in principle and practice. These changes have reforged some of the structures of inequality, reshaped patterns of deprivation and called into question prevailing views on the causes of poverty and the legitimacy of claims on social security.

While policy and policy institutions have sometimes influenced events, typically they have lagged behind changes in private behaviour and public attitudes. For this reason, changing attitudes towards sexual morality, the economic autonomy of women and the nature of poverty are considered in this chapter before describing some of the formative changes in social security policy in Chapter 19. Clearly, however, personal values, political ideology and policy are not hermetically sealed from each other, and some reference is made in this chapter to policy developments.

Sexual morality, marriage and lone parenthood

The increase in extra-marital births and fall in the marital birth rate in the 1980s and 1990s, described in Chapter 16, is best interpreted with reference to changes occurring earlier. Exactly the same coincidence of trends was evident during the Second World War, but resulted from many marriages being thwarted by wartime disruption and death rather than from a fundamental change in morality (Land and Lewis, 1998). This was followed, in the 1950s and 1960s, by a widespread separation of sex and marriage that led to sharp rises in both marital and extra-marital births but resulted in little moral panic. Most premarital conceptions were legalised, lone parenthood was rare and stigmatised and, since divorce rates were still low, the institution of marriage appeared to remain intact.

Almost everything changed in the mid-1980s and 1990s. Sex continued to be separated from marriage, but divorce and cohabitation increased and, perhaps most important of all, marriage was separated from parenting.

Divorce and cohabitation

The 1969 Divorce Law Reform Act was an important facilitator of change, but was also a reflection of past changes. Marriage, at the beginning of the 20th century, was a duty that was supported by, and contributed to, a strict moral code. The code, though criticised in the inter-war period for the hypocrisy to which it (almost literally) gave birth, survived into the 1960s. It was then challenged by the notion that relationships should be built on love rather than be prescribed by law, and that neither extra-marital relations nor divorce were necessarily morally wrong. In this context, the 1969 Divorce Law Reform Act, enacted in 1971, replaced adultery, desertion, cruelty and insanity with 'the 'irretrievable breakdown of marriage' as the sole grounds for divorce. By taking a period of separation as evidence of irretrievable breakdown the Act moved some way towards introducing 'no fault' divorce, and precipitated a dramatic rise in divorce that levelled off in the late 1980s.

The increase in divorce was, as noted in Chapter 16, accompanied by an immediate decline in new marriages that accelerated in the 1990s, and by a rise in cohabitation. Cohabitation, possibly at its nadir in the 1960s, had been limited to the very poor and to those prevented from remarrying by restricted divorce laws, and was subject to pervasive social stigma. While post-marital cohabitation continued to grow after the 1960s, new pre-marital and non-marital forms also emerged; the former is undertaken as a prelude to marriage, the latter as an alternative to marriage, although in intent and reality this distinction often proves to be false. The new forms of cohabitation which began to come to the fore in the early 1970s had become majority practice by the 1990s (Haskey, 1995). Whereas, in the late 1960s, only 6% of women marrying for the first time had cohabited with their husband, by the mid-1990s 70% had done so. By that time, too, the social stigma associated with 'living together' had all but disappeared, and the term 'partner' had replaced 'husband or wife' in many official forms.

A further profound development, beginning in the 1980s, was the increase in procreation within cohabitation. This is mapped officially in the rising proportion of births outside marriage that are jointly registered: 45% in 1971, 79% in 1998. During the 1990s, three quarters of unmarried people jointly registering a birth lived at the same address.

Although cohabitation has become a norm, certainly for people under the age of 35, it remains a more fragile institution than marriage (Chapter 16). This has special significance in light of the increased births to cohabiting couples and, during the 1990s in particular, was a major factor in the rise of lone parenthood. Indeed, to the extent that cohabitation remains at all socially contested, being contrasted rhetorically with 'traditional family', it is because it is seen as a cause of lone parenthood.

Lone parenthood

Like cohabitation, lone parenthood has become 'normal' but, unlike cohabitation, it was viewed in policy circles as a moral and material problem for much of the 1990s. By the beginning of the 1970s, the perception of 'unmarried mothers' as abnormal and either unusually promiscuous or victims had been replaced by a less moralistic approach that sought responses to their undoubted material and emotional needs. In the 1980s, as divorce and relationship breakdown swelled the numbers of lone parents, concern grew about the public expenditure costs of lone parenthood which, by the 1990s, had developed into a moral panic in some policy circles. Fuelled by US writers, such as Charles Murray and Larry Mead, who in the context of US welfare provision saw lone parenthood as providing the foundation to a growing underclass (Chapter 1), policy sought not only to reduce government spending but also to reduce lone parenthood.

Under the third Thatcher and Major governments lone parents were presented as "coldly rational and calculating, determined to live a life of 'idleness' on state benefits" (Kiernan et al, 1998, p 278). The pursuit of reducing expenditure was supported by moral rhetoric that emphasised 'individual choice' and 'personal responsibility', and reform that sought to change the 'perverse incentives' that resulted from generous state provision. The long-term concern about 'liable relatives' – fraud in which fathers continued to live with lone mothers who claimed benefit – was extended to a concern that absent fathers were avoiding their responsibilities to support their children. Some of the same language was used by members of the incoming 1997 Labour government – Tony Blair is cited in Chapter 1– but, despite implementing the abolition of One Parent Benefit initiated by the Major government, their polices have focused on improved child provision and employment.

While attitudes at a policy level hardened against lone parents during the 1990s, social stigma within communities lessened, although it did not disappear. Whereas in the 1950s and 1960s the stigma against lone motherhood would have discouraged single women from having or keeping babies, this was not so in the 1990s (McKay and Rowlingson,

1998). Rather, lone mothers themselves did not identify with women who had deliberately got pregnant in order to receive social security and housing, and so dissociated themselves from much of the generalised stigma that existed.

Some mothers from poor economic backgrounds saw lone motherhood as an acceptable, even a desirable, alternative to unemployment or low-paid, low-status work. Most single lone mothers in the 1990s, however, became pregnant more or less by accident: contraception failed or was not used because they had trusted their partner, took risks or wanted to avoid being thought of as promiscuous. Moreover, the increased number of women who became lone mothers through relationship breakdown often felt that they had little choice; 20% mentioned violence, 31% adultery or infidelity and 15% substance abuse (Bradshaw and Millar, 1991). A third said that they did not get on anymore and a quarter that they no longer talked. Qualitative research indicates that, while few mothers regretted separation – indeed many felt that they had gained in self-esteem – they often initially felt ambivalence and even shame at their new status as lone parents (Leeming et al, 1994). Moreover, very few could contemplate a future alone.

In summary, cohabitation, divorce and lone parenthood have become new milestones in the life-course. Typically, none is entered into lightly, and each is seen as presenting risks. Lone parenthood, in particular, is understood to create problems – financial, legal and emotional – but women typically 'choose' it as a preferred solution to prior personal problems. It is considered to be better than being in a loveless or unhappy relationship or marrying an unsuitable father, and offers a secure, albeit low income for mothers, some of whom have few prospects. It is this last point that connects most fully with the concerns that drove policy towards lone parents throughout much of the 1990s.

Women and employment

It has already been established that the evolving pattern of women's employment was one of the most profound social changes occurring between the 1970s and 1990s, implicated in the polarisation of work and increasing claims for Income Support from lone mothers (Chapter 17). Equally, it can be seen as a major defence against further child poverty and an expression of greater gender equality. It can only be understood in terms of the changing aspirations of women, mapped onto a labour market still shaped by a sexual division of labour.

Immediately after the Second World War, policy makers were convinced that married women with young children should be looking after them at home rather than being in paid work (Land and Lewis, 1998). The labour market was structured to meet men's needs and no attempt was made to facilitate married women working. A partial exception was made for lone parents, who were expected to engage in full-time work, with childcare being provided by family and friends or via the limited local authority daycare services, to which they were given priority access.

Labour shortages through to the 1960s led to attempts to recruit more mothers with school-aged children into the labour market and helped generate a momentum, reinforced by rising educational attainment and the re-emergence of the women's movement in the 1970s, towards more women working. However, the jobs typically available to women were very similar to the unpaid domestic activities that gender relations determined that they continued to do in the home (Lonsdale, 1987). Skills were undervalued and pay was low. Career advance was also inhibited by the priority that women were expected to give to childcare.

While women in 1998 still on average earned 25% less than men, the employment circumstances of women had improved markedly since the 1970s (Desai et al, 1999). As noted in Chapter 17, labour demand shifted in their favour as de-industrialisation took hold. Increasing numbers of women worked, including those with school and pre-school-aged children, although the employment of lone parents fell, for reasons discussed in Chapter 17. Employment legislation (the 1970 Equal Pay Act, the 1975 Sex Discrimination Act, and especially the 1975 Employment Protection Act and later enhancements) all improved conditions and enabled women to retain jobs after childbirth, adding continuity to employment. (Comprehensive childcare provision was also discussed in the 1970s but not implemented.) The wage gap between men and women reduced by over 13 percentage points between 1971 and 1998. Education and experience are now rewarded almost equally and there has been a narrowing in gender differences in the labour market with respect to age, education and job tenure in full-time work, which have all helped reduce earnings differentials.

However, the marked improvement in wages was restricted to women working full-time. In fact, forty-five per cent of employed women work part-time and the gender differentials among part-time workers widened between the 1970s and 1990s. As a consequence the pay penalty for women working part-time rather than full-time opened up

(Harkness, 1999). This penalty is important because it is evident that mothers continue to put their children before employment in a way that fathers do not. Sophisticated analysis has shown that the factors that determine a man's move off benefit relate almost exclusively to his human capital resources, whereas a mother's behaviour is associated with the age of her youngest child and her readiness for work (Iacovou and Berthoud, 2000).

The increased employment of women gives them access in their own right to contributory social security benefits (Chapters 14 and 22). In so far as families with children are concerned, it provides the only mechanism by which low status families can escape poverty and continued reliance on means-tested in-work benefits (Iacovou and Berthoud, 2000). It is also clear that a second earner protects a family from needing to claim means-tested benefits in the event of one party becoming unemployed.

On the other hand, the 25% differential between male and female wage rates makes it unlikely that a family can move into work entirely by means of the mother getting a job. This serves to increase the time spent on benefit, minimises families' financial robustness given the demands of a flexible labour market and reinforces the traditional division of labour. Combined with the additional financial penalty associated with part-time work, it also helps to explain the low employment rate of lone mothers.

Perspectives on family poverty

Since Labour came to power in 1997 this failure of people to work has been emphasised as a principal cause of poverty (Bennett and Walker, 1998). It is a somewhat different perspective than prevailed in 1971, when policy makers were still much influenced by the rediscovery of poverty in the 1960s based on a relative definition. For people of working age, poverty had been shown to be highest among families with children, and there was much concern about the extent of poverty among working families. The Labour government at that time had already increased family allowances, and reform of benefits for children was planned. However, a Conservative government was elected in 1972 and, adopting a selectivist approach, introduced means-tested Family Income Supplement for working families, which treated lone parents on a par with two-parent families. Rent Allowances and Rent Rebates were also introduced, and families in work were one group to benefit, although take-up was never great.

When a Labour government was returned in 1974 it received the Report of the Finer Committee, which confirmed the severe financial deprivation experienced by lone parents and suggested providing an income guarantee for lone parents. This was rejected (on grounds of cost), but instead a universal Child Benefit was introduced to replace Family Allowances, which was paid to the mother and extended coverage to the first child. (Family Allowances only applied to second and subsequent children.)

Policy attention was captured by rising unemployment during the 1980s, that had the effect of shifting the balance of causation of family poverty away from low pay to the lack of work. However, except for a brief period when Sir Keith Joseph, Secretary of State for Social Services, became interested in the possibility of deprivation being transmitted from one generation to the next, poverty was dropped from the political lexicon during successive Thatcher governments (Chapter 1). Poverty, defined in absolute terms, was taken not to exist in modern Britain, and such poor families as there were (defined relatively) were castigated for their own laziness and lack of will power – a response shared quite widely by the public of the day (Walker et al, 1984). Moreover, even the poor, it was assumed, would benefit from the 'trickle down' of wealth created in an entrepreneurial economy.

With such views prevailing in the 1980s and early 1990s, anti-poverty programmes were an anathema, and the main policy objective was to prevent social security expenditure from rising further. However, with the arrival of panel data, interest began to grow in the permanence of poverty and such dynamic phenomena as the low-pay-no-pay cycle in which some families found themselves trapped (Walker with Ashworth, 1994; Hills, 1998). The growth, too, in workless families – due to increased unemployment, incapacity and lone parenthood – began to be documented, and to inform Labour's thinking in opposition such that they entered government with a portfolio of Welfare to Work proposals.

New Labour ministers were also much taken by evidence which suggested that – echoes of Keith Joseph – a 'cycle of deprivation' existed whereby "deprivation in childhood can lead to low educational achievement and on to worse outcomes in adulthood and poverty and exclusion in old age" (DSS, 1999h, p 5). In March 1999, therefore, Tony Blair announced the policy goal of eradicating child poverty within 20 years (Blair, 1999) and subsequent policy statements have begun to devise strategies by which this goal is to be achieved (HM Treasury, 2000).

Poverty and social exclusion are now understood to be 'complex', 'deep-rooted', 'multidimensional' problems that have their roots in a lack of opportunities to work and to acquire education and skills, in childhood deprivation, poor housing, poor neighbourhoods and inequality in health. The declared strategy is to 'tackle the causes, not just the symptoms of poverty'. This is to be achieved by means of 'joined-up' government intent on creating a fairer society in which "everyone has the opportunity to achieve their full potential" and "investing in individuals and communities to equip them to take control of their lives" (DSS, 1999h, p 5).

For the most part this new strategy, which is recognised to be long-term, has yet to impact on the size of caseload numbers.

What has been learned

Increased claimant numbers arising from the growth in lone parents can only be understood in terms of profound changes in individual morality and gender relations that resulted in sex and child-rearing being separated from marriage.

Likewise, the growth in female employment reflects profound changes in the balance that women are prepared to accept between unpaid work in the home and paid work in the formal economy. However, the ability of women to earn enough to guarantee financial sufficiency for their family is still curtailed by gender-based inequalities in wage rates that continue to reinforce the traditional sexual division of labour. The effect is to prolong the time that both lone-parent and two-parent families spend on benefit and, hence, to increase caseloads.

Somewhat ironically, given that the British welfare system was designed primarily to provide relief from poverty (Chapters 1 and 2), preventing poverty was not an explicit policy goal throughout much of the period between 1971 and 1998. In the early 1970s low wages were seen as a key contributory factor to family poverty, whereas, by the mid-1990s, worklessness had come to be viewed as the primary cause (and, indeed, the underlying aetiology did change over this period, although both factors were always important). The more sophisticated analysis and policy agenda now being promoted by the new Labour government has yet to have had time to impact on claimant caseloads, although some early evidence is reported in the next chapter.

NINETEEN

Social security provisions for families and children

Summary

The number of families receiving financial assistance for their children was doubled in 1977 by replacing family tax allowances for the second and subsequent child by Child Benefit payable for all children.

A class of working families receiving means-tested benefit was created by the 1971 introduction of Family Income Supplement and by Rent Allowances and Rebates in 1972.

In 1998, lone parents constituted 49% of the 790,000 recipients of Family Credit, the successor to Family Income Supplement, that is, the year before it was replaced by Working Families' Tax Credit.

New Deal for Lone Parents, a voluntary scheme offering advice and support to lone parents seeking work, may have reduced Income Support caseloads by more than 3% over an 18-month period.

The 1991 Child Support Act sought to ensure that non-resident parents – mostly men – financially supported their children, but many refused or were unable to do so.

Deregulation of rents and ending 'bricks-and-mortar' subsidies for housing increased the Housing Benefit caseload.

Britain has never had a Minister for the Family and the Minister for Women is a creation of the new Labour government. Nor does it have a coherent family policy, governments generally preferring not to intervene directly in family matters (Kammerman and Kahn, 1980).

However, at various times, governments have accepted the fact that children increase the risk of families suffering poverty and have introduced policies to raise family incomes. They have also responded, if sometimes reluctantly, to social problems associated with new family forms, typically targeting specific population groups and relying on fiscal and benefit measures rather than promoting an explicit family policy.

It is apparent from earlier chapters that the growth in benefit claims from families with children was influenced by the activities of many social institutions other than social security: moral authorities including the church and other opinion leaders, the legal profession and employers were all agents of change. Space limits consideration in this chapter to key changes in social security policy that have impacted most directly on the numbers of parents and children receiving benefit.

Child Benefit and One Parent Benefit

The one single policy change that most increased the number of families receiving benefit was the introduction of Child Benefit in 1977. Reflecting pro-natalist, strategic considerations that were important in 1945, Family Allowances introduced into the tax system were allowed only for second and subsequent children. Replacing these allowances with universal cash benefits paid for all children, including the first, doubled the number of families receiving benefit (Figure 15.1). Making mothers the recipients of benefit, when formerly men had been the direct beneficiaries under a tax regime based on household income, the government signalled its intention to tackle child poverty and to offset some of the costs of child-rearing.

Child Benefit survived numerous attempts to abolish it during the period 1977 to 1998, most notably in the Fowler reforms of 1985-88. As a universal scheme, Child Benefit is expensive. Moreover, people concerned that benefit was being paid to affluent mothers, and those without children who believed that they were financing the lifestyle choices of parents, often did not appreciate the logic of horizontal redistribution. However, the option of clawing Child Benefit back from affluent families became untenable with the individualisation of the tax system.

In the event families, especially mothers, valued Child Benefit highly and were prepared to mobilise politically to protect it. Perhaps even more importantly, from a policy perspective, Child Benefit helped to offset the disincentive effects created by mean–tested benefits for unemployed people.

When Child Benefit was introduced, Child Benefit Interim for lone parents was implemented a year early, partly on account of evidence that they were particularly exposed to the risk of poverty. The interim payment was retained as a supplement to Child Benefit, and renamed One Parent Benefit in 1981, making explicit the principle that lone parents should receive additional benefits. This principle was also applied to out of work benefits, with the 1980 introduction of Supplementary Benefit and its transformation into Income Support in 1987.

However, in the context of frantic concern about the growth of lone parenthood, in 1996 the Major government proposed abolishing One Parent Benefit and the corresponding premium under Income Support. This, it was considered, would remove one of the perverse incentives encouraging lone parenthood, and save money. It fell to the incoming Labour government to promote the enabling legislation which, amidst considerable furore, it did. Indeed, the vocal opposition led to the Prime Minister briefly taking charge of social security, and contributed to the sacking of Harriet Harman, Labour's first secretary of State for Social Security.

Part of the reform involved introducing a higher rate of Child Benefits for the first child in lone–parent families – £17.10 instead of £11.45 in 1997 – which added a further financial incentive to take employment and acknowledged the higher work-related costs incurred by lone parents. However, when the value of Child Benefit for the eldest child was substantially increased from £11.45 to £14.40 in 1999, as part of the drive to reduce child poverty, the addition for lone parents remained unchanged. This was despite the fact that research cited to justify the increase also revealed that poverty was much greater among lone parent households (Middleton and Ashworth, 1997).

While the introduction of Child Benefit and One Parent Benefit increased the number of children receiving benefits, the recent changes affected expenditure rather than caseload size. (The resulting increase in financial incentives may have led some lone parents to move into employment, moving from out of work to in-work means-tested benefits.)

Family Credit and Working Families' Tax Credit

The introduction of Family Income Supplement in 1971, that was to develop into Family Credit and was exported into the tax system, as

Working Families' Tax Credit, in 1999, did most to introduce a new class of benefit recipient – the working family in receipt of means-tested benefit.

Family Income Supplement was introduced as a temporary measure, a negative income tax style change having proved impossible to implement, to improve the financial circumstances of low-paid workers with children. Since entitlement was means-tested and affected by the age and number of children, it worked on a principle similar to the notorious Speenhamland system of 1795, and was similarly criticised as a means of supporting employers paying low wages (McKay and Rowlingson, 1999).

Uptake, caseload numbers, and take-up, the proportion eligible claiming benefit, of Family Income Supplement remained low. By the time Family Credit was introduced, political opinion was moving to the view that subsidising wages was a price worth paying to get benefit recipients into work. Even so, the main aim was to facilitate a move off Income Support and into the labour market. The scheme was more generous with a lower taper – rate of benefit withdrawal with increased income – and the minimum qualifying hours limit was reduced from 30 hours work per week under Family Income Supplement to 24 hours and, in 1992 to 16 hours. These changes were of particular benefit to lone parents, who mostly work part-time, as was the introduction of a disregard to offset childcare costs in 1994. As a result of these changes the caseload increased from 221,000 in 1986 to 340,000 in 1991, and to 790,000 in 1998 (Figure 15.3). By 1998, lone parents accounted for 49% of recipients, and the ratio of lone parents receiving Family Credit to those on Income Support had risen to over 4 in 10, from 1 in 10 in 1979 (McKay and Rowlingson, 1999).

Early modelling of the Family Credit caseload (Walker with Ashworth, 1994) indicated that the largest number of claimants received benefit for a single six-month period – bridging the transition into work or the period when one member of a dual family was without work. However, long-term recipients came to dominate the caseload, with 36% of the caseload predicted to remain on benefit for more than six years, thereby emphasising Family Credit's role as a wage subsidy. There is also some evidence that Family Credit enticed lone parents off benefits into jobs without prospects, causing them to remain low paid and on benefit for longer than they might otherwise have done (Byson, 1999).

Despite these difficulties, the still more generous Working Families' Tax Credit is intended to reach 1.1 million people and, by first introducing a national minimum wage, Labour set a limit on the effective wage subsidy that employers stood to gain through the new credit. Locating the new scheme within the tax system – where Family Income Supplement was originally intended to be – allowed extra expenditure to be disguised as a tax cut, and in the long-term might enable better tax-benefit integration. It was initially intended to be paid by default directly to the wage earner rather than the mother, as had been the case since Family Credit was introduced, signalling its role as a work incentive rather than an anti-poverty measure. Opposition to this change led to a compromise whereby claimants can choose to whom the credit is paid. New plans to integrate support for children in Working Families' Tax Credit and Income Support into a children's tax credit, and to create a separate employment tax credit available to all low waged workers, aim to disentangle the incentive and child support functions of benefits.

New Deal for Lone Parents

New Deal for Lone Parents is the one Welfare to Work initiative introduced by the 1997 Labour government with explicit family-orientated objectives. Linked to the introduction of a £470 million National Childcare Strategy designed to ensure "good quality, affordable childcare for children aged 0-14 in every neighbourhood in England" (DSS, 1999h, p 8), the New Deal invites lone parents to make use of a voluntary service of support and advice. It is explicitly focused on helping lone parents into work, by assigning lone parents a personal adviser who provides assistance with job search, training and finding childcare, and gives advice on benefits. Prototypes were commenced in July and October 1997 and the scheme was implemented nationally in October 1998. Under the proposed ONE scheme, which is to provide a single gateway for all benefit recipients of working age, an initial work-focused interview is to become compulsory for all lone parents.

It will be recalled, from Chapter 15, that claims from lone parents for Income Support ceased rising in 1996, falling back from 1.05 million in 1996 to 972,000 in 1998, and to 940,000 in 1999. Despite the fact that the downward trend began before New Deal was implemented, it is important to ascertain how much of this fall can be attributable to the new scheme. Evidence from the prototypes indicates that 23% of targeted lone parents – that is, those with a child aged over five years and three months – participated in an initial interview. Personal advisers, with caseloads of 20 to 30 clients, placed an average of one lone parent into work every one-and-a-half-weeks (Hales et al, 2000).

Econometric analyses from the prototypes indicated mixed results. The impact of the scheme appeared to diminish over time, increasing the odds of lone parents leaving Income Support by 12% during the first six months of the scheme, but only by 5% 12 months later (Hasluck et al, 2000). Also, while the scheme appeared to benefit new claimants in areas of high unemployment, it did not do so in areas with medium to low rates. Nevertheless, it is estimated that the schemes led to a reduction of 1.54% in the caseload after six months, rising to 3.28% after 18 months. If these figures applied nationally, they could explain the bulk of the fall in claims observed between 1998 and 1999 (although not, of course, the fall in earlier years). However, other bases of comparison suggested that the impact of the scheme may have been less than the figures reported (Hasluck et al, 2000).

The Child Support Agency

In recognising the additional costs attributable to lone parenthood, the social security system creates an incentive for unscrupulous parents to pretend to live alone, even when the other parent or another adult is living with them. This dilemma has much exercised policy makers in Britain. As long ago as 1973, fictitious desertion and cohabitation cases accounted for 14% of fraud prosecutions, and took up nearly 40% of special investigators' time (Fisher Committee, 1973). However, during the 1970s and 1980s, fraud and liable relative work (the latter to try to ensure that maintenance was paid by non-resident parents) tended to be curtailed whenever work pressures in local social security offices increased. Liable relative work, in particular, was not vigorously pursued throughout much of the 1980s.

However, the situation changed in the context of rising numbers of lone parent claimants, escalating benefit expenditure and Margaret Thatcher's growing moral indignation that irresponsible men were fathering more children than they could afford (Maclean, 1998). Liable relative procedures were strengthened in 1990, and a White Paper published that proposed establishing a Child Support Agency to fix and collect maintenance payments on behalf of Income Support recipients (and, in time, other lone parents). Whereas policy had previously been to encourage lone parents to support themselves and their children single-handedly, it was now proposed to seek resources from non-resident parents – predominantly, of course, fathers.

The change removed the responsibility for setting maintenance from the courts. There had been concern that registrars had been setting maintenance low so as not to reduce the benefit entitlement of parents with care of the children, especially where the absent father was low paid or thought likely not to comply regularly with the maintenance, order. A complicated, although rather insensitive, formula was used to calculate maintenance, and longstanding arrangements fixed by the courts could be overturned. Lone parents with care of the children claiming Income Support – typically mothers – were, under all but the most extreme circumstances, obliged to reveal the name of the non-resident parent, but did not benefit from extra maintenance received, which continued to be treated as income. (Lone mothers in Family Credit were able to retain £15 of maintenance payments.)

The Child Support Act proved to be far more controversial than anticipated, something that was not helped by great administrative difficulty in establishing the system that led to numerous delays in processing claims. Also, many absent fathers, especially those with second families, refused or were unable to pay the increased maintenance, and supported a vocal lobby against the new system. The Act was subsequently reformed on a number of occasions, and the system is currently in the midst of being changed, with a much-simplified formula and provisions to enable lone parents on benefit to gain financially from maintenance payments. It has even been suggested (Land and Lewis, 1998) that the failure of the Child Support Agency triggered the reforms to Family Credit during the 1990s, as a result of policy makers turning to earnings rather than maintenance as the means of cutting lone parent caseloads.

It is very difficult to assess what impact the child support reforms had on benefit caseloads. By 1999, 864,000 full assessments had been made, but the evidence is that, despite the extensive powers of the Child Support Agency to enforce payment, substantial amounts of maintenance remained unpaid (Clarke et al, 1996). Indeed, by 1994, the percentage of lone mothers receiving regular maintenance payments was still the same as before the Agency was established (around 30%), although the overall amount paid in maintenance had increased because absent fathers were assessed to pay more (Marsh et al, 1997). Where maintenance is in payment, a small number of people will have been 'floated off' Income Support and rather more may have been helped into work, reducing numbers on Income Support, but inflating Family Credit caseloads.

There is also the possibility that some absent fathers may themselves have moved onto benefit, in order to reduce the level of maintenance payments due. In 1999, 25% of non-resident parents who had been assessed by the Agency were on Income Support, 13% on Jobseeker's Allowance and 3% on disability benefits (DSS, 1999c). What, if any, proportion of these families were receiving benefits as a result of the Child Support Agency is unknown, but the number certainly suggests that a significant minority of the parents with care of the children would not stand to receive much in maintenance payments.

Housing Benefit

While the introduction of Family Income Supplement and later policy developments created the intellectual argument for providing cost benefits to working families' children, Housing Benefit increased the number of recipients almost by accident. In 1998, around 315,000 families with children, 180,000 of them lone parents, seemed to be receiving Housing Benefit while working (DSS, 1999c).

Housing Benefit is also available on a means-tested basis to people who are not working, including disabled and unemployed people, and to people without dependent children. It therefore straddles the four groups of welfare recipients used to structure this book. In briefly reviewing its development here, many of the most pertinent points apply to groups of claimants discussed elsewhere.

The enormous geographic variation in housing costs defeated Beveridge when constructing the foundations of Britain's welfare provision, and still frustrates welfare reform. A statement on the latest reform of Housing Benefit has been awaited for some months. The national antecedents to Housing Benefit, means-tested Rent Allowances and Rebates, were introduced in 1972, as an explicit aspect of housing policy, and to standardise the haphazard system of rent subsidisation that had been developed by local authorities. A key aim was to try to reinvigorate the private rented sector. Supplementary Benefit – the means-tested safety net for people not working – continued to meet the full cost of claimants' rent and mortgage interest payments.

Then, in the early 1980s, as part of an attempt to contain costs, the first moves were made towards redirecting the housing subsidy away from generalised 'bricks-and-mortar' support to benefits targeted on low-income individuals. To support this change, a unified Housing Benefit system was introduced in 1982 that tried to amalgamate housing payments to Supplementary Benefit recipients with Rent Rebates and Rent Allowances. (The scheme was reformed again in 1988 when it proved to be administratively inoperable – see Walker with Hedges,

1985; Walker et al, 1987.) Policy responsibility for the new Housing Benefit was passed to the Department of Social Security and, in this way, social security became an instrument of housing policy, with the intended result that claimant numbers grew markedly. Administration remained with local authorities.

The Housing Benefit caseload grew substantially again, by 600,000 or 15% during the 1992–97 Conservative administration, partly for similar reasons (DSS, 2000a). Central government reduced housing subsidies to local authorities and housing associations that had been designed to keep rents below market levels. The result was that local authority rents rose by almost a fifth, and housing association rents by one third. Rents in the private sector, that had already risen markedly as the result of 1989 legislation to deregulate rents, continued to rise, and rose by 7% over the same period, bringing even more people within scope of Housing Benefit. Caseloads were further boosted by increased claims for unemployment and disability benefits (Chapters 3 and 9).

It is also worth noting that the policy of selling off local authority housing from the mid-1980s substantially reduced the population potentially eligible to receive Housing Benefit in the event of unemployment or disability. Such people would instead have been eligible to have had their mortgage interest paid under Income Support, although, from April 1996, this facility was abolished for the first nine months of any claim.

In total, some 1.4 million families with 2.7 million children received Housing Benefit in 1998. Another 281,000 claimants, probably mostly of working age, received assistance with their mortgage interest payment while in receipt of Income Support. A proportion of these people will be in receipt of benefit solely on account of their housing costs. (Many pensioners in rented accommodation receiving Income Support fall into this category.) Also, the disincentives created by receipt of Housing Benefit have been found to increase the time that people remain on benefit (Shaw et al, 1996b). For example, many Income Support recipients were worried about both the fall in Housing Benefit on returning to work and delays in the processing of Housing Benefit claims that might leave them without income. Likewise, owner–occupiers were fearful of having to pay mortgage interest if they took a job that did not last. While recent policy changes have sought to rectify both these impediments, when viewed historically it is evident that the implications of housing costs, engineered by housing policy considerations, have been imprinted on social security caseloads.

What has been learned

Deliberate, and less deliberate, policy reforms doubled the number of families receiving state financial support for their children, created a new class of benefit recipients – over one million strong – who receive means-tested assistance while working, and massively increased the number of people reliant on mean-tested help with their housing costs.

Reforms were less successful in reducing claimant numbers. It is not clear that the child support policies have significantly cut the number of lone parents on benefit, although caseloads have been falling since 1996. However, New Deal for Lone Parents may have helped around 3% of lone parents to move off Income Support over a period of 18 months.

TWENTY

Reflecting on benefit receipt by families and children

Summary

Changes in attitudes, behaviour and in the labour market outweighed declines in fertility that should have reduced the number of families with children claiming benefit.

Changes in sexual relations and in the stability of relationships led to an increase in lone parenthood, especially lone motherhood.

The declining age of lone parents and their children, perhaps combined with slack labour demand, caused a fall in the proportion of lone parents in paid work and, until 1993/94, a corresponding increase in the proportion claiming out of work benefits.

Unemployment increased the reliance of two-parent families on benefit.

In-work benefits – introduced to offset the work disincentive effects of mean-tested benefits – created a new class of employed social security recipient, mostly comprising one and two parent families.

Figure 20.1: Understanding child and family benefit caseloads

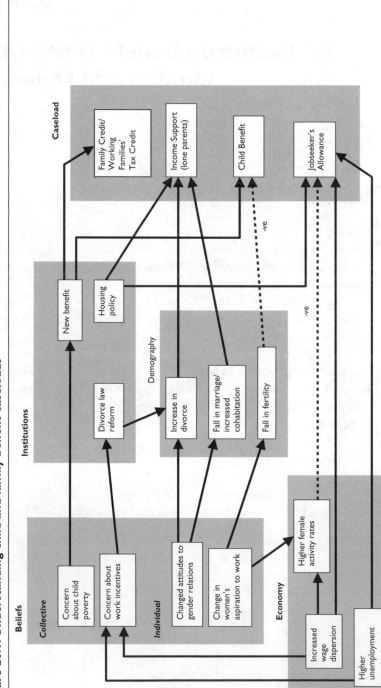

-ve: indicates a negative effect or association

Despite the fact that the number of children aged under 16 fell markedly between 1971 and 1999, far more children and families were receiving benefit at the end of the 1990s than had been doing so at the beginning of the 1970s. Although, as always, the reasons are complex, there is a clear story to tell. Declines in fertility were outweighed by new claims on social security that resulted from new family forms, which in turn reflected a changed morality (Figure 20.1). At the same time, developments in the labour market eroded the self-sufficiency of families, and government sought to alleviate this situation by creating new in-work benefits, which meant that employment no longer ended reliance on means-tested benefits.

Two policy changes – one indigenous to social security, the other exogenous – more or less complete the picture. Introducing Child Benefit effectively guaranteed that every family with children would receive at least one social security benefit (since non-take-up of this universal benefit has always been negligible). The exogenous policy was housing, and the change in strategy from subsidising 'bricks and mortar' towards targeting low-income households. As a result, social security inadvertently became an instrument of housing policy, and families with children were forced to claim social security on account of their housing costs.

Lone parents

The tripling in the number of lone parent families between 1971 and 1998 changed the contours of social security provision. Claiming in negligible numbers in the 1970s, by the end of the 1990s lone parents constituted the largest group of recipients of means-tested benefits other than pensioners. More lone parents received means-tested benefits than either unemployed or disabled people with children.

The upward trend in lone parent numbers was first driven by divorce and then, with the rise in cohabitation, by the breakdown of non-marital relationships. Latterly, there has been a rise in the number of mothers who do not seem to have co-resided with their partners. However, these are not primarily teenage pregnancies, a theme beloved by the tabloid media, which are still running at a much lower level than in the 1970s.

As the number of lone parents rose, so the proportion employed fell. The downward trend in employment is not easily explained by increasingly generous benefit provision. Benefits, net of housing costs, rose in real terms, but did not match earnings growth. If anything, deprivation among lone parents has increased. Rather, it appears likely that the fall in the average age of lone parents – possibly indicating less work experience – together with a corresponding increase in the proportion with young children, have kept lone parents out of the labour market.

But it is important to note that the rate of increase in lone parents began to subside in the mid-1990s and, much more dramatically, the proportion claiming Income Support dropped to levels comparable with those in the mid-1980s. It seems likely that this reflects a migration of lone parents from mean-tested out-of-work benefits into means-tested in-work benefits in response to deliberate initiatives to make Family Credit more compatible with the needs of lone parents. These included a low hours of work threshold, offsetting childcare costs and the partial disregarding of income received from the non-resident parent. It may also reflect a 'maturing' of the lone parent population, with a decline in the proportion of women who have only recently become lone parents, although this hypothesis requires further substantiation.

Whatever the recent developments, it seems clear that a probably irreversible shift in attitudes and behaviour has occurred that has changed the nature of cohabiting relationships. Marriage is visibly less stable than before, if only because dissolution is socially acceptable, though still traumatic. Cohabitation remains, to date, less permanent than marriage, but is increasingly likely to result in children. The risks of lone parenthood are greater than ever, something that may further erode the structures of social control that in the past served to limit them.

Two-parent families

In the case of two-parent families, the consequences of changes in the labour market, especially in the period up to the mid-1990s, exerted upward pressure on claimant caseloads that exceeded demographic factors – later parenting and smaller families – that acted to reduce claims on benefit.

Higher unemployment than in the 1980s and early 1990s reached beyond the old smokestack industries and affected families with children, a group that had previously tended to avoid the worst ravages of unemployment because they typically contained prime age workers. Families were also much affected by the attenuation in the earnings distribution that meant that increasing numbers of jobs failed to pay anything akin to a family wage. In this context, it became imperative for many families to have two earners – a strategy that had become possible given the shifting pattern of labour demand and the changed aspirations of women.

Two-earner families began to set society's consumption standards and were better protected against the impact of unemployment, with the effect that one-earner families began to become a relatively disadvantaged minority. Indeed, an increasing number of one-earner families became reliant on means-tested in-work benefits that had been introduced to tackle the work disincentives created by means-tested benefits that paid more to families with dependent children.

The increasing importance of in-work benefits that serve to supplement low wages, and arguably to subsidise employers, created a new class of welfare recipient that maintained an active relationship with the labour market while continuing to receive benefit, often for long periods. For the most part this new class was comprised exclusively of one and two parent families with children. However, with the exception of working families receiving Housing Benefit, this class of benefit recipient was abolished with the introduction of the Working Families' Tax Credit in 1999. Although now invisible in terms of caseloads and social security expenditure, the newly acquired role of the state in financially supporting private sector employment is to expand to embrace low paid workers without children.

What has been learned

The number of families with children reliant on social security benefits increased between 1971 and 1999. This is explicable in terms of a growth in lone parenthood – itself the consequence of new sexual attitudes and behaviour – higher unemployment, and the creation of in-work benefits designed to counteract work disincentives generated by low wages and means-tested benefits that (partially) take account of the cost of children.

Part 5
Benefits for retirement

TWENTY ONE

Trends in pension provision

Summary

The number of retirement pensioners increased by 44% to 10.8 million between 1971 and 1998. 64% of pensioners are women.

Retirement pensioners constitute the largest group of benefit recipients and in 1998/99 accounted for 46% of social security expenditure. Increased spending on elderly people was responsible for 42% of the total rise in benefits expenditure between 1971/72 and 1998/99.

Virtually all men aged 65 and women aged 60 or older are entitled to a state pension (which can be postponed).

Most pensioners who have no other income, a proportion that has been declining, are eligible for means-tested Income Support.

At least 65% of pensioners also receive private or occupational pensions.

Leaving aside Child Benefit that is paid on behalf of 12.8 million children, retirement pensioners constitute Britain's largest group of benefit recipients (DSS, 1999i). Some 18% of the population (10.8 million people) were over pensionable age in 1998, and the income maintenance benefits that they received, worth £44.6 billion, accounted for 46% of social security expenditure. Approximately 16% of pensioner units also received disability benefits. Women account for 64% of pensioners.

The number of pensioners has increased steadily over the last 30 years, adding 3.3 million people (44%) to the retirement pension caseload between 1971 and 1998 (Figure 21.1). Indeed, social security and social assistance spending on elderly people increased by 103% between 1973 and 1998/99, and accounted for 42% of the total rise in social security expenditure (Evans, 1998). While the growth in numbers was large in

Figure 21.1: The pensioner population (men and women pensioners) (1971-98)

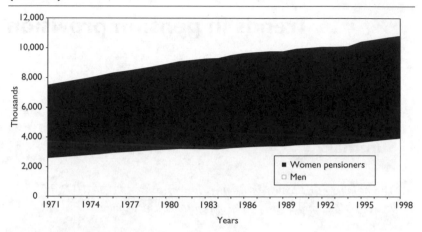

Source: DSS (1999c) and earlier volumes

absolute terms, it was exceeded in proportional terms by rises in the number of unemployed and disabled people claiming benefit.

Pension provision in Britain

Retirement, and the pension provision that underwrites it, are phenomena of the 20th century. In pre and early industrial economies people continued in employment until almost the end of their lives. However, increased longevity, combined with expectations of high productivity in employment that some older workers find difficult to sustain, have created an economic need and social taste for a period of worklessness at the end of life. When pensions were first introduced in Britain for people aged 70, the average period of retirement was less than two years. Now, with pension ages lowered to 65 for men and 60 for women (to be equalised in the decade 2010 to 2020) and greater life expectancies, the average man draws a pension for about 14 years and a woman for 22 years (*Population Trends*, 1999, vol 95, Spring). While demography is the main motor determining the number of older people, institutional frameworks and individual choice, more or less constrained by social and economic circumstances, determine the nature of the pensions that people receive. The economy generates the resources needed to pay for pensions, and often significantly influences the choices open to individuals at different stages in their lives.

Figure 21.2: Numbers receiving state pensions (1971-98)

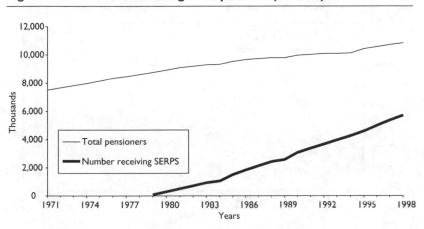

Source: DSS (1999c) and earlier volumes

It is important to recall the different forms of pension provision in Britain. Most significant, in terms of coverage, is the basic state pension, which was largely put in place in 1948 but which had its origins in the 1908 National Insurance Act. Benefits are calculated on a flat-rate basis according to an individual's National Insurance contributions, with a system of credits – and, since 1978, home responsibilities protection – to cover gaps in the contribution record. (Despite linking benefit to life-time contributions, the basic Retirement Pension is essentially a 'pay as you go' rather than a funded scheme.) A total of 10.73 million people received the basic state pension in 1998/99.

A second contributory pension, the State Earnings Related Pension (SERPS), was introduced in 1978, but significantly downgraded in 1988. In 1998 it was received by 53% of pensioners (Figure 21.2) but, whereas someone could theoretically receive as much as £125 per week in SERPS, the average amount in payment was only £23 (DSS, 1999c). The third category of benefit, Income Support, is means tested; it was paid to 1.65 million (15%) pensioners in 1998/99, usually in addition to a basic state pension.

A married woman can claim a basic retirement pension (called a Category B pension) on the basis of the contributions paid by her husband when he qualifies for his own pension and if she has reached retirement age. She can also claim a Category B pension if the pension to which she is entitled on her own behalf is less than she would receive on the basis of her husband's income. The proportion of women claiming pension in their own right has risen only slightly in the last 20 years,

Figure 21.3: Female pensioners with own retirement pensions (1971-97)

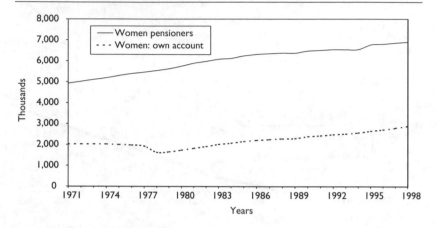

Source: DSS (1999c) and earlier volumes

despite higher employment participation rates among working aged women (Figure 21.3). The reason probably has to do with the high levels of part-time working and low pay among women.

In addition to state pension provision, Britain has pioneered occupational and personal pensions through a panoply of tax incentives and reduced National Insurance contributions. The former are provided by employers, who typically make income-related contributions that match or exceed those of employees. The pensions payable are either fixed in relation to final salary (defined benefit) or, increasingly, on the basis of contributions (defined contribution). Personal pensions are arranged by individuals through insurance companies without the direct involvement of employers, although employers may make contributions if they wish. Legislation was introduced in 1988 that meant that people could opt out of SERPS or occupational pensions in order to acquire a personal pension into which the government also made contributions to guarantee a minimum 'protected rights pension'. Thirty-five per cent of employees belonged to occupational pension schemes in 1995/ 96 (PRG 1998) – down from 41% in 1988/89 – while the proportion of people with personal pensions had grown from effectively nothing to 16% (having peaked at 18% in 1992/93). In 1995/96, 65% of all pensioners had an occupational pension, including 69% of those who had recently retired (ie they were within five years of pension age) (PRG, 1998). On average it was worth £78.40 per week (although the median amount was only £44.10). Less than 5% of people who had retired by 1996/97 had a personal pension (DSS, 2000c).

Figure 21.4: Proportion of pensioners with an occupational pension (1979-95)

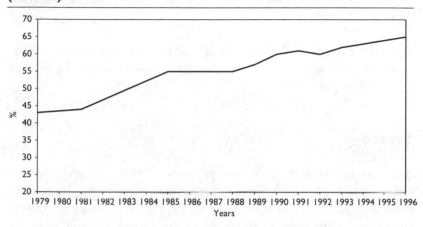

Source: DSS (1999c) and earlier volumes

Despite the growth in the coverage of private and occupational pensions, significant numbers of pensioners still need to claim means-tested benefits. In 1998, 1.7 million or 22% of pensioner units (households) claimed means-tested Income Support to supplement their Retirement Pension, 1.9 million received means-tested Housing Benefit (1998) to help meet their outgoings on rent, and 2.7 million received a means-tested rebate on the local property tax (Council Tax Benefit) (DSS, 1999c). By 1999 the number of pensioners receiving Income Support had fallen to just over 1.6 million.

The Labour government is intent on reforming the British pension provision, recognising that it currently fails to provide adequate financial support for many pensioners who do not have occupational and personal pensions, and that the erosion of SERPS is to perpetuate this problem. Its plans include:

- the introduction of a minimum income guarantee (MIG), comprising the basic state pensions and means-tested Income Support;
- the replacement of the SERPS with a relatively generous State Second Pension (SSP) targeted at the low paid (those earning enough to pay National Insurance contributions [£66 per week] and up to £9,000 pa);
- the introduction of stakeholder pensions, which are to be low-cost, flexible and secure schemes aimed at those on modest incomes (£9,000-£18,000 pa). Employers will have to offer a stakeholder

pension, where there is no occupational pension, and contributions can be collected via the payroll, but employers will not have to make a contribution.

With the exception of MIG, introduced in April 1999, these reforms have yet to be implemented and are not discussed further in this and later chapters.

Strategy

The current structure of pension provision in Britain is such that it is necessary to explain both the increase in the number of people receiving basic state pension, and the change in the number and proportion of pensioners who have recourse to means-tested Income Support. Demographic factors are discussed first, in Chapter 22, since they largely determine the size of the pensioner population before considering, in Chapter 23, the policy developments that have both dramatically changed the incomes of retired people and engineered a radical move away from means testing. Apart from noting the strong popular support for continued state pension provision, discussion of the domain of beliefs in Chapter 24 is limited to those that inform people's decision to plan, or not to plan, for security in their old age. The impact of economic change, considered in Chapter 25, is indirect and less immediate than in the case of either unemployment or even disability benefits. The discussion is summarised in Chapter 26.

TWENTY TWO

The demography of pensions' growth

Summary

The increase in the Retirement Pension caseload between 1971 and 1998 was driven almost entirely by demographic factors.

Increased life expectancy more than offset a 35% fall in the number of births.

Of the total growth in the pensioner population (over the slightly shorter period 1973-94) 46% was accounted for by increased survival after retirement.

Migration had little effect on pensioner caseloads; less than 2% of pensioners were born abroad.

A slight fall in the proportion of female pensioners – who are still less likely than men to have occupational pensions in their own right – *will have slightly eased the pressure on the means-tested Income Support caseload.* So did *reforms in 1993* that *transferred financial responsibility for supporting residential care from social security to local authority social services departments.*

The increase in pensioners living alone, rather than with younger kin, *will have increased claims for Income Support.*

The size of the pensioner population is driven almost entirely by demographic factors. It is determined, first, by the number of people reaching pensionable age, itself a consequence of the number of births 60-65 years earlier and the rates of survival over the intervening years. Second, it is affected by the age-specific death rates of the pensionable population and third, by in-migration and out-migration, although the latter is not very important since pensions are payable to people living abroad. The only non-demographic factor of importance affecting the number of pensioners is the propensity to continue in employment beyond pensionable age. In Britain, people who work after pension age do not receive state pensions, but instead earn increments that are added to their basic pension when they retire or reach the age of 65 for women or 70 for men.

Each of these factors – cohort size and survival, migration and effective retirement age – is considered in turn in this chapter, which ends with a discussion of gender differentials and living arrangements.

Cohort size and survival

It is evident that the increase in the number of people reaching pensionable age is determined more by survival rates than by variations in the size of birth cohorts. Birth numbers fell by about 35% between 1905 and 1935 but the number of people reaching pensionable age 60–65 years later actually increased by about 3% (CSO, 1998). The scale and timing of in-migration has been such that it has only contributed marginally to the growth of the elderly population: in 1993-96 only 1.6% of the elderly population of Great Britain had been born abroad (Haskey, 1997). It would seem, therefore, that improvements in survival rates have offset the decline in the numbers of people reaching retirement age that would have been predicted on the basis of birth cohort size. Whereas 53% of men born in 1906 and so destined to attain retirement age in 1971 would have lived to do so, as many as 73% of those born 27 years later survived long enough to retire in 1998 (Figure 22.1).

The other major factor determining the size of the pensioner population is the length of time that people live after reaching pensionable age. Age-specific survival rates post pensionable age have increased markedly in the last 30 years, adding substantially to the number of pensioners. Life expectancy for men at age 60 increased from 15.3 years in 1971 to 18.5 years in 1996, while that for women rose from 19.8 years to 22.4 years.

To put it another way, 29% of men born in 1918 reached the age of 80 compared with only 15% of those born 30 years earlier (DSS, 2000a; see also Figure 22.1). As a consequence, whereas the total number of pensioners rose by 44% between 1971 and 1998, the number aged over 80 increased by as much as 224% for men and 225% for women. Evans

Figure 22.1: Cohort survival rates

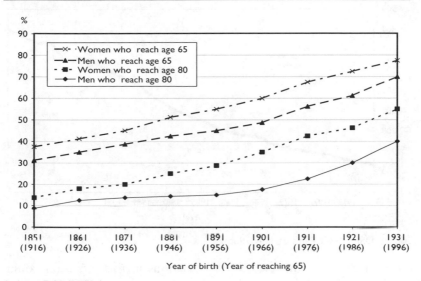

Source: DSS (2000a)

(1998) calculated that over the period 1973-94 rising survival rates contributed 46% to the growth in the pensioner population.

Migration

It is not possible reliably to estimate the effect of net migration on pensioner numbers. As noted above less than 2% of the pensioner population was born abroad. The majority of these will presumably be receiving a mix of pension provision, with perhaps a disproportionately large number being reliant on means-tested assistance. People leaving Britain are generally still able to claim their pension on retirement. Figure 22.2 presents the numbers of British pensioners living abroad, which in 1998 comprised 7% of the total (DSS, 1999c). Numbers have increased faster than the total number of pensioners, with a particular marked rise in the number living in Continental Europe.

In recent years the number of pensioners living in the Caribbean increased markedly above a trend of a 2.1% growth per year; between 1993 and 1998 numbers increased by 32%, which may reflect migrants retiring to their place of birth. Some pensioners residing abroad live in countries that have reciprocal agreements with Britain. Only pensioners living in these countries get their pensions uprated in the same way as

Figure 22.2: Pensioners living abroad (1973-98)

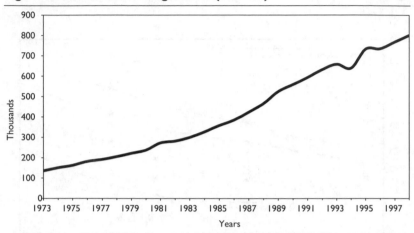

Source: DSS (1988d) and earlier volumes

those in Britain. However, while variations in this provision could determine spending on pensions they do not affect the size of the pensioner caseload.

Early retirement

Although the effective age of retirement has fallen noticeably, this has had only a limited impact on the number of people receiving state pensions (since state pension is not payable to people under pensionable age). In 1971, only 6% of men aged 55-59, and 16% of those aged 60-64, were economically inactive, whereas by 1996 the corresponding figures had risen to 25% and 50% respectively (Figure 22.3). Activity rates among women have varied only slightly, as any trend towards early retirement has been offset by higher numbers who sustained a career in employment.

Around 231,000 men aged 60-64, and 241,000 aged 50-59, were in receipt of means-tested Income Support and Jobseeker's Allowance in 1999. A total of 322,000 and 196,000 respectively claimed Incapacity Benefit. Given that, in 1995, the median stay on Income Support for men aged 60 lasted until retirement age (Shaw et al, 1996a), a significant proportion of all of these groups will already have effectively entered retirement even if they have done so unwittingly. A total of 234,000 women aged 50-59 were in receipt of Income Support in 1999, and 225,000 received Incapacity Benefit.

Figure 22.3: Activity rates between ages 55 and 64 (1971-96)

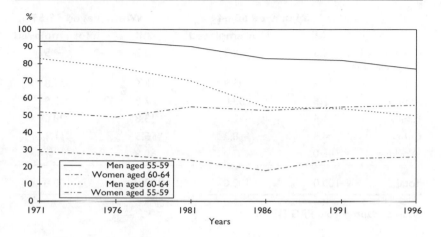

Source: PRG (1998)

The reasons for the fall in economic activity among older men divide into two sets. The first are linked to the rise in occupational pensions which means that some men can afford to retire early, a trend that is thought to have been encouraged by the provision of final salary schemes, allied to the desire of employers to ease older workers out of their employment. While the economic inactivity of this group is in some sense voluntary, this is not true of other people who have been made redundant, have no recourse to occupational pensions, and who are unable to find work. It is often presumed that significant numbers of the latter group have transferred to higher, non-means-tested disability benefits, although the evidence for this is not indisputable (see Chapter 13). There is also the possibility that some people retiring early on an occupational pension do so on health grounds. In 1999 legislation was passed to means test Incapacity Benefit in situations where people receive significant amounts of occupational pension.

In 1996, 46% of men aged 60-64 who were not working said that they were sick or disabled, 33% described themselves as retired and only 8% as unemployed (Table 22.1). Although most of the people describing themselves as either retired or sick will not work again and are de facto retired, their subsistence costs are met from disability and unemployment-related benefits, not retirement pensions (see Chapter 4).

Table 22.1: Reasons for not being active in the labour market (%)

| | Men aged 60-64 | | Women aged 55-59 | |
	All	Not employed	All	Not employed
Unemployed (ILO definition)	4.5	8.3	2.2	4.5
Sick	24.8	45.9	18.6	37.8
Retired	17.8	33.0	7.8	15.9
Family	1.4	2.6	13.8	28.0
Other	4.5	8.3	5.5	11.1
Working	46.0		50.8	
Total	100.0	100.0	100.0	100.0

Source: adapted from PRG (1998)

One aspect of the fall in effective retirement age that does affect the size of the pensioner pool is the decline in the proportion of people deferring retirement until after pensionable age. In 1971, 26% of pensioners received income from employment, compared with 11% in 1998 (DSS, 1999c). Moreover, whereas in 1971 26% of all pensioners were receiving increments due to deferred retirement, this was true of just 11% in 1998. The trend to reduced employment after retirement is, of course, imprinted on the current pensioner population and on the pensions received. In 1998, 19% of pensioners aged 80 and over received increments on account of deferred retirement, compared with 9% of those aged 70-74. However, the impact of this trend on the overall number of pensioners is unlikely to have been very great. On the not altogether realistic assumptions that life expectancy and employment are not related, and that people typically work for two-and-a-half years after retirement age, it can be calculated that under 2% more people are drawing state pension than would have been the case had the fall in post-retirement age working not occurred.

Gender and marriage

Despite a slight narrowing of sex differentials, life expectancy continues to be greater for women than men, with the result that the majority of pensioners are women and the proportion of women rises with increasing age. In 1998, women constituted 64% of all people of pensionable age, slightly less than in 1971, when the corresponding proportion was 69%

(ONS, 2000). Of people aged 65 to 74, 54% were women, as were 74% of the over-85s. Given that female employment rates have traditionally been lower than for males, and that employed women have been less likely to acquire occupational pensions, a higher proportion of women than men have recourse to means-tested benefits in old age. The slight decline in the preponderance of women, and to a small extent their increased attachment to the labour market, is exerting downward pressure on the numbers claiming means-tested Income Support in old age.

On the other hand, there has been a significant growth in independent living among pensioners, which may increase demand for Income Support among pensioners (Grundy, 1996). The growth has been most marked among the oldest pensioners, presumably a reflection of better health, policies for community care and a greater wish for independence. Forty-nine per cent of women age 85 or more lived alone in 1991, compared to just 30% in 1971.

The proportion of pensioners living in 'complex' households – typically with their children – has fallen markedly; for example, for women aged 75-84 the proportion fell from 24% to 9% between 1971 and 1991 (Table 22.2). Although pensioners living with kin are still treated as separate households for the purposes of social security, and so can claim means-tested benefit in their own right, they may be less likely to do so because of economies of scale.

The number of pensioners living as couples has increased somewhat, reducing the number of pensioner units and reducing expenditure on social security because of economies of scale built into benefits. This was the result of marriage becoming both more prevalent and occurring earlier among cohorts born after 1920, and the slight narrowing of sex differentials in mortality; by 1991 married women outnumbered widows until the age of 73, whereas this had only been so until the age of 71 in 1971.

Finally, it is noteworthy that the proportion of people aged over 85 living in institutions also rose between 1981 and 1991. This might suggest that some substitution occurred between private and institutional care, but probably reflects a response to new social care needs created by substantially larger numbers of people surviving to this age. This period witnessed a sizeable expansion in the provision of private residential care homes that until 1993 was funded by the social security system, when responsibility for residential care costs was transferred to local authorities.

Table 22.2: Living arrangements of people aged over 65, England and Wales (1971, 1981, 1991) (%)

Sex	Age group	Year	Family/household type					
			Solitary	Married couple alone	Married couple +others	Lone parent	Complex	Non-private household
Men	65-74	1971	11	58	16	2	11	3
		1981	14	61	14	2	8	1
		1991	16	65	13	1	5	1
	75-84	1971	18	47	10	4	15	6
		1981	22	54	7	3	11	4
		1991	24	58	6	2	6	4
	85+	1971	20	24	6	8	27	15
		1981	29	31	5	5	20	11
		1991	32	36	3	3	10	16
Women	65-74	1971	32	36	7	6	16	3
		1981	35	42	7	5	10	1
		1991	34	46	6	5	7	1
	75-84	1971	40	16	3	8	24	8
		1981	50	20	2	6	16	6
		1991	53	23	2	5	9	7
	85+	1971	30	5	1	12	31	22
		1981	42	5	1	8	25	19
		1991	49	6	0	5	13	27

Source: Grundy (1996) based on OPCS Longitudinal Study

On balance, therefore, the slight narrowing of sex differentials in life expectancy and changes in living arrangements served to slow the rate of growth in pensioners claiming means-tested supplementation to their basic pensions.

What has been learned

For once the story is straightforward. The number of pensioners increased by 44% between 1971 and 1998, primarily as a result of reduced mortality before retirement age and increased life expectancy thereafter. The preponderance of women declined, slightly easing pressure on the pensioner caseload of means-tested Income Support.

TWENTY THREE

Institutional aspects of pension provision

Summary

British pension provision, featuring low National Insurance pensions, helps to create two nations in old age, one characterised by low incomes and means–tested supplementation, the other by relative affluence due to income from occupational pensions.

However, pension reforms enacted until 1978 served to enhance the level and coverage of state provision, leading each new generation of pensioners to be better provided for than earlier ones.

Greater coverage of improved occupational pensions increased average incomes and reduced the need for means testing but created greater income inequality among pensioners.

British pension provision has long been recognised to generate two nations in old age. One comprises people who enjoy continuous prosperous employment and reach retirement with a full state pension and typically also an occupational or personal pension. The second 'nation' includes people who have never worked and those who have had a history of low-paid and intermittent work, and as a consequence need to rely on means-tested supplementation in old age. The image of two nations remains apt, despite various policy developments over the years. Indeed, on occasion, policy changes have tended to reinforce inequalities in old age, with those in secure employment benefiting most from improved pension provisions.

The intention in this chapter is to explore the institutional factors that have forged these two nations: the availability and coverage of the different kinds of pension and the impact of this on pensioners' incomes and on their need to seek means-tested supplementation. Each of these issues is considered in turn. Doing so provides a partial explanation for the division between people arriving in old age with a portfolio of pension provision and those who do not and, hence, of the relative size of the two nations in old age.

State and private pensions

Pension reform exemplifies the history of Britain's welfare state, with an initial growth in state provision and later state encouragement of the private sector to help fund the growing financial burden.

Current pensioners may be receiving state pensions derived from contributions paid under the 1925 Contributory Pension Scheme, the 1948 Insurance Scheme, the 1961 Graduated Pension Scheme (terminated in 1975), and the 1978 State Earnings Related Pension Scheme (SERPS). The original intention of SERPS was that the combination of basic and earnings-related pension would generate a pension equivalent to half a person's wage for people retiring after 40 years of employment. The scheme was intended to be phased in, with the first full benefits being paid to those retiring in 1998, with full maturity attained in 2018. SERPS provided additional pension equivalent to 25% of earnings over the best 20 years of working life, and increased the basic pension in line with the higher of earnings or prices. It also offered better benefits to widows and recipients of invalidity benefits. However, the indexing to wages was removed in 1990 as a result of reforms in 1985/88 that were a response to growing concerns about the viability of funding SERPS when dependency ratios worsened from 2020 onwards. The accrual rate was also reduced from 25% to 20%, the best 20-year provision was dropped and survivors' benefits halved; these reforms to affect pensioners retiring after April 1999.

The effect of all the policy reforms through to 1978 was potentially to raise the state pensions of successive cohorts of pensioners, which, other things unchanged, would have led to a reduction in the proportion of pensioners with means-tested supplementation. Subsequent changes will have had the opposite effect from the date of their implementation. Since the early 1990s, the average SERPS pension will have been sufficient to lift pensioners above the threshold for means-tested supplementation provided they did not have high housing costs that would have made them eligible for Housing Benefit.

The legislation that provided for the introduction of SERPS in 1978 also sought to give further impetus to the development of occupational schemes. It did so by reducing National Insurance contributions for people opting out of SERPS and into schemes that guaranteed to provide a pension broadly equivalent to the state scheme (the Guaranteed Minimum Pension). Moreover, the state accepted responsibility to inflation-proof the guaranteed minimum component of occupational schemes. This responsibility reverted back to occupational schemes with the 1985/88 reforms that also permitted the provision of defined contribution pensions at a time when most schemes offered defined benefits linked to final pay. Compulsory membership of employers' occupational schemes was outlawed, and incentives were introduced to encourage people to acquire their own personal pension scheme.

The intention and result of reforms in the 1980s was to shift the balance of advantage away from defined benefit occupational schemes, some of the most generous of which were provided by the public sector, towards personal pensions and defined contribution (money purchase) occupational schemes, which are cheaper for employers to provide. Occupational and personal pensions both serve to increase incomes in retirement and thereby to reduce the number dependent on means-tested supplementation. The latter, however, place the responsibility for pension planning on employees rather than employers, which may in time result in fewer people acquiring pensions and more becoming dependent on means-tested supplementation.

The present-day importance of these historical developments is that they help to explain the diversity of income received by current pensioners, who accrued or failed to accrue their pension rights under a sequence of different policy regimes.

Coverage of pension schemes

Coverage of pension schemes provides the most obvious key to understanding the relative size of the two nations of pensioners. In 1995, 46% of employees belonged to occupational pension schemes, the lowest proportion since 1983. The peak year of coverage was 1967, when 53% of employees were members. The decline in membership reflects falling public sector employment – where occupational pensions are almost universal – the demise of some of the larger manufacturing companies, and the promotion of personal pensions after their introduction in 1988. The reduced coverage of occupational pensions has exclusively affected men; the proportion of women with occupational pensions continues to grow but, at 42%, still falls short of the 54% achieved by men.

Occupational pensions, are by definition, not available to the self-employed, to unemployed people or to anyone outside the labour market. Moreover, the increased prevalence of unemployment and greater employment mobility means that people are being forced to leave schemes more frequently than in the past, and joining more schemes as they change companies and industries. It used to be very difficult to transfer pension entitlement between different schemes; often the value of pensions was frozen or only partially uprated to take account of inflation, so that the pensions people could expect in retirement were much reduced. Legislation has lessened but not eradicated this problem.

As already noted, occupational pensions are most widespread in the public sector and among large employers. In 1994, pensions were provided by 90% of firms with over 100 employees, but by only 35% of those with five employees or less. Eligibility criteria for membership include length of service (49% of schemes), hours worked (32%), age (56% of defined benefit schemes have a minimum age limit and 44% a maximum age) and grade or salary (14% of defined benefit schemes and 22% of defined contribution schemes) – see Casey et al (1996). Less-skilled, low-paid, part-time workers in casual employment are all less likely than other workers to have occupational pensions. Women are disproportionately represented among these groups of workers, which helps to explain the comparatively small number of women who are members of occupational pension schemes. There has, however, been an increase in pension provision among part-time female workers, doubling to 24% between 1968 and 1995 (PRG, 1998).

Although it was hoped that personal pensions would reach groups not covered by occupational pensions, the kinds of people who do not have an occupational pension are also less likely to have taken out a personal pension. Women, notably when working part-time, are particularly unlikely to have a personal pension, as are employees earning less than £100 per week (1995 prices). Over two thirds of men who have been engaged in self-employment for at least five years had a personal pension in 1995, but this applied to only a third of women in similar circumstances. Taking both occupational and personal pensions, it remains true that low-paid men and women, especially those working part-time, are among the least likely to have any form of non-state pension. Slightly less than a third of people retiring in the next 20 years are likely to have no occupational or personal pension, of whom three quarters are women (McKay et al, 2000).

Even state pensions do not provide universal coverage; in 1998 only 42% of female pensioners drew a Retirement Pension in their own right, and, as recently as 1995/96, 4% of newly retired pensioner units and 2% of all units had no Retirement Pension. In the latter two cases, a proportion of people would have been working beyond retirement age. But it should be noted that there is a lower earnings limit below which National Insurance contributions are not payable, and hence below which pension entitlement does not accrue. Credits are payable in periods of unemployment, sickness and when people have ceased employment to look after dependants, although these are flat rate. Until 1977, it was possible for a married woman to opt to accrue a pension entirely on the basis of her husband's contributions. Indeed, until around 1980 the number of women pensioners receiving a pension in their own right actually fell. However, it has subsequently risen as new cohorts of pensioners have included higher numbers of women who have held jobs for substantial periods of their lives.

The state pension is typically insufficient in itself to lift a pensioner above the level of means-tested benefits. It follows that those groups of people that are least likely to have an occupational or personal pension – the very old, the formerly low paid and many women – are the most likely to rely on means-tested assistance in retirement.

Growth of pensioner incomes

The average income of pensioners is known to have risen by over 70% in real terms between 1979 and 1997, which was noticeably faster than average wages (Figure 23.1). It is also highly likely that incomes increased throughout the previous decade.

However, income inequality among pensioner households, having first decreased in the period up to about 1981, then rose substantially before falling very slightly during the 1990s. The Gini coefficient, a measure of inequality, for the incomes of single pensioners rose from 0.20 to 0.30 between 1979 and 1991, and that for pensioner couples from 0.24 to 0.33, and in both cases remained higher in 1996/97 than in 1979. Whereas the real incomes of pensioner households in the most affluent quintile rose by about almost four fifths between 1979 and 1996/97, those of the poorest quintile grew by only a third (Figure 23.2). These developments markedly reinforced the existence of two nations in old age, while changing their relative size.

Investigating the movements in the relative value of the components of pensioners' incomes helps to explain the increase in inequality and the shift in the pattern of benefit receipt.

Figure 23.1: Growth in average weekly net income of all pensioner units

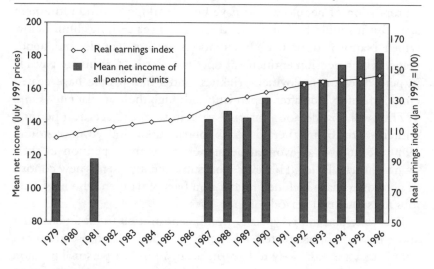

Source: DSS (2000c)

Figure 23.2: Median income of pensioner couples (1979 and 1996/97)

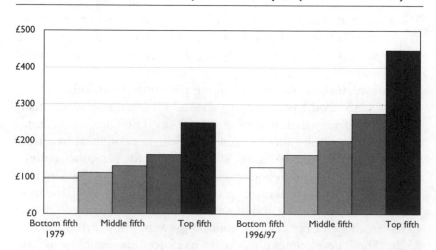

Source: DSS (2000c)

Figure 23.3: Real value of state and occupational pensions (1971-98)

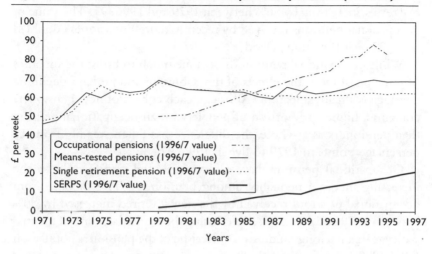

Source: DSS (1998d) and earlier volumes and own calculations

The level of the basic state pension moved ahead of prices over the period until 1979. Thereafter, with the uncoupling of up-rating from wages, the pension for a single person has remained at around £60 per week in 1997 prices (Figure 23.3). Pensions in payment, which reflect the outcome of people's employment histories and their opportunity to acquire earnings-related pensions under the graduated pension schemes (maximum £7 per week for men) and SERPS have continued to increase. The real value of state pensions in payment to single pensioners increased by 42% and those to pensioner couples by 34% between 1979 and 1996/97 (figures include means-tested income). Even so, state pensions in payment did not keep pace with the growth in average earnings which occurred over this period.

It is the growth in occupational pensions that has done most to increase pensioner incomes. Although coverage of occupational pensions within the labour force has fallen back in recent years, the proportion of pensioners receiving income from occupational schemes has continued to increase, albeit at a much slower rate since 1990. In 1979, 43% of pensioners had occupational pensions, and by 1996/97 this figure had reached 65% (DSS, 1999c). Moreover, these global statistics mask a somewhat greater increase – from 32% to 58% – among single pensioners. Such pensioners are predominantly women, and either will have acquired an occupational pension in their own right or will have inherited a survivor's pension of the basis of their husband's contributions. The average size of occupational pension has also increased substantially in real terms, increasing by 86% between 1979 and 1996/97. The value of occupational pensions received by recently retired pensioners doubled to £122 over the same period.

While occupational pensions have done much to boost the incomes of some pensioners, the effects of the stabilising and perhaps declining coverage is already apparent. Although each cohort of new pensioners contains a higher proportion of people with an occupational pension than pensioners as a whole, the difference has fallen steadily from 12 percentage points in 1979 to five in 1996/97.

Occupational pensions have also contributed significantly to the increasing income inequality among pensioners. The income from occupational pensions received by the newly retired increased by 86% between 1979 and 1996/97, exacerbating the marked decline of income with age that is a longstanding characteristic of the pensioner population (DSS, 1999c). So, for example, the average occupational pension received by men retiring between 1990 and 1994 was worth £87 per week compared to the £50 paid to men retiring 20 years earlier (Johnson and Stears, 1995). Newly retired couples in 1996/97 received twice as much income from occupational pensions in 1996/97 as in 1979, in real terms.

In addition, occupational pensions have also been a major motor for carrying inequalities forged in the labour market forward into retirement. Only about a third of full-time employees earning less than £170 per week in 1997 were members of an occupational pension scheme, compared with three quarters of those earning more than £450 a week (PRG, 1998). Whereas the average occupational pension received by pensioner couples in the bottom fifth of the income distribution rose by only about £10 per week in real terms between 1979 and 1996/97, that of couples in the top fifth rose by around £160 (Figure 23.4).

Finally, pensioners' income from investments also rose notably between 1979 and 1996/97 – it nearly doubled in real terms – but again exacerbated inequality. The increase was especially marked among pensioner couples (Figure 23.5) but nevertheless the average investment income received by couples in the lowest two fifths of the income distribution still amounted to less than £10 per week in 1997 out of a total income of about £135. Investments contributed more than £180 to the weekly gross income of richest fifth of pensioners.

Figure 23.4: Average gross weekly occupational pension income

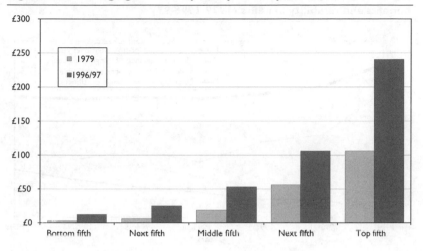

Source: DSS (2000b, Chart 3.2)

Figure 23.5: Proportion of pensioners with occupational pensions and income from investments (1979-1995/96)

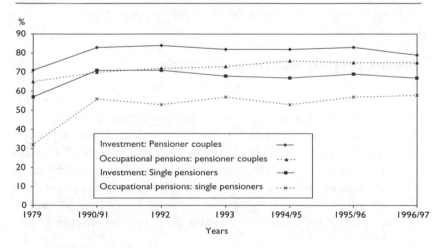

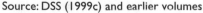

Source: DSS (1999c) and earlier volumes

Taking the period 1971 to 1996/97 as a whole, the net outcome of the processes considered is aptly summarised by the maxim 'unto those who have, more shall be given'. The 1970s were different, and extreme poverty among pensioners – defined as household income less than 40% of the average – virtually disappeared. This advance was undone in

Figure 23.6: Proportion of pensioners with income from means-tested benefits and disability benefits (1979-1996-97)

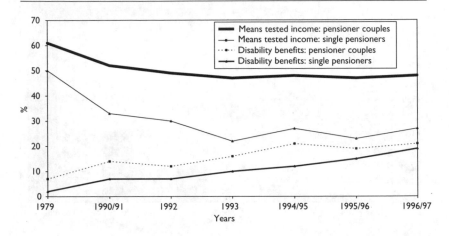

Source: DSS (1999c)

the 1980s and, although the growth in income inequality was not marked during the early 1990s, further polarisation is inherent in the ownership of investments and the possession of occupational pensions.

Means testing and pension traps

The net result of the changes in incomes reported in the previous section is that the proportion of pensioners reliant on means-tested income – Housing Benefit and Council Tax Benefit as well as Income Support – fell markedly from 57% to 40% between 1979 and 1996/97. Over this period the number receiving means-tested supplementary pensions through Income Support (or its predecessor benefit Supplementary Benefit) would have been expected to increase by 19% on account of demographic factors, whereas caseloads grew by only a tenth of this amount.

The numbers receiving means-tested income would have declined still further had it not been for successive governments pursuing housing policies that sought to shift subsidies away from bricks and mortar towards low-income residents. A consequence of this strategy was to increase rents. In 1998, 1.8 million pensioner households received Housing Benefit, virtually the same number as when the current scheme was introduced in 1988 despite rising incomes. (A national rent rebate scheme was first introduced in 1972/73 but no figures on uptake seem to be available until the 1980s.)

The increased importance of Housing Benefit to pensioners is one of the reasons why the average means-tested income of pensioners increased so markedly in real terms between 1979 and 1996/97, almost tripling from £14 to £38.

Having a small occupational pension or some income from investments does not guarantee that a pensioner will not also need to claim means-tested supplementation. In such cases, thrift is penalised since pensioners will receive no financial benefit from their pension contributions. Of more direct import for the main theme of this chapter, they will not be floated off state means-tested benefits.

In 1982, the last known micro-analysis of the pension trap, some 52% of occupational pensioners were affected (Walker et al, 1987). From published information for 1997, it is evident that 345,000 pensioner units receiving Income Support also received superannuation from a pension fund (DSS, 1998d); this suggests that perhaps 8% of pensioner households with income from occupational pensions are still reliant on means testing for basic income maintenance. While the data for 1982 and 1997 are not directly comparable, it is possible to conclude that the prevalence of the poverty trap has reduced significantly as pensions have generated higher incomes and allowed more people to move out of range of means testing.

However, the pension trap created by the interaction between Housing Benefit and Council Tax Benefit is more extensive. In 1997, 857,000 occupational pensioners (20%) received Council Tax Benefit and 546,000 (13%) Housing Benefit, and so lost the full value of their pension income. Moreover, since the Housing Benefit caseload in particular has been increasing in recent years, the prevalence of this variant of the occupational pension trap has probably also been growing. The government's intention to try to develop policies to counteract the worst excesses of the pension trap in the context of promoting the Minimum Income Guarantee for pensioners were announced in the 2000 Budget.

To summarise, the maturation of occupational pension schemes, and to a lesser extent the more widespread ownership of financial assets, has reduced reliance on means testing from 57% to 40% of pensioners over 18 years and decreased the size of Britain's poor nation in old age by about 15%. In relative terms, however, the poverty experienced by this smaller group is more severe than it was in either 1981 or perhaps 1971.

What has been learned

The cumulative effect of numerous pension reforms involving first, expanded coverage and increased benefits provided by the state system and latterly, the encouragement of occupational pensions and most recently personal ones, has been to shift the balance of state provision. Virtually all retired people continue to receive a basic insurance-based state pension, but the number reliant on means-tested supplementation fell by 17 percentage points between 1979 and 1996/97. Had changes in housing policy not occurred, which massively increased average rents, this shift away from means testing would have been even greater.

TWENTY FOUR

Beliefs, opportunities and retirement behaviour

Summary

There has rarely been political consensus on pension policy, but consistent public support for retaining state pension provision has probably helped to protect the incomes of the current generation of pensioners.

People often have limited understanding of how pensions work, lack advice and fail to engage in lifetime financial planning.

Occupational pensions tend first to be acquired by people when aged in either their twenties or their 40s (typically too late).

Retirement has been taking place earlier, although early retirement is frequently not planned long in advance.

Take-up of means-tested benefits is thought to be lower than for other pensions, and may actually have fallen since the 1970s.

This chapter is divided into two parts of disparate length. The first is the shorter, and briefly reviews public attitudes towards state provision of retirement pensions, while the latter considers peoples' responses to planning for their own pensions. The two topics may be reflexive. Support for state provision is strong, if tinged with scepticism about the government's commitment to maintaining generous pensions, while apathy and lack of forward planning typically characterise individuals' approaches to ensuring financial security in old age. Both perspectives have helped to shape the current pattern of provision.

Ideologies of pension provision

It was apparent in Chapter 23 that pension policy in Britain has always been subject to continual review and revision. For seven decades policy sought to provide increasing financial support for ever larger numbers of pensioners within the constraints of financial probity. While Beveridge hoped to implement a fully-funded state pension scheme, political pressure demanded full benefits to be paid ahead of time. The compromise resulted in lower pensions and an unintentionally large role for means-tested supplementation, the reduction of which provided the motive of many subsequent reforms.

Throughout the 1960s and 1970s, pension reform was a topic of much political controversy. Conservative governments were keen to support the burgeoning pension industry, while the Labour party had aspirations to design a more fully comprehensive state scheme, modelled on the social insurance principles that underpinned the more generous provision being developed by social democratic governments in continental Europe. The State Earnings Related Pension Scheme (SERPS) had considerable cross-party support when introduced in 1978, but was overtaken by fears that adverse demography and continuation of the prevailing sluggish economic growth could combine to make the mature scheme financially not viable. Drastic surgery averted any possibility of a 'pensions crisis', but attempts to stimulate alternative provision through the promotion of personal insurance pensions were to some extent frustrated by a furore over the mis-selling of pensions by insurance companies. The 1997 Labour government has made no attempt to reinstate SERPS as a state scheme but has sought instead alternative forms of second tier pensions that are cheaper and yet attuned to the needs of people without occupational or personal pensions. It has also focused on the growing inequality in incomes described in Chapter 23, by providing a means-tested income guarantee, at the same time resisting pressure to return to uprating the basic pension in line with earnings rather than prices on the grounds of cost and prioritising low-income pensioners.

These political machinations have taken place against sustained public support for state pension provision. Elderly people are the most popular of the groups receiving state benefits, and opinion polls have repeatedly registered support for increasing the level of retirement pensions, even when juxtaposed with the need to raise taxation as a consequence. Moreover, the public is generally aware that the value of future state pensions has been eroded (although the extent to which this has happened is less well known), often overstates the importance of the demographic time-bomb, and is generally sceptical about the reliability of state pension provision. Equally, however, many people mistrust private pension companies, citing well publicised scandals, which leaves them with few clear preferences as to the balance between public and private provision.

The pensioner lobby is large and articulate and, while it does not have influence comparable with that of the 'grey panthers' in the US, is capable of orchestrating considerable opposition to government policies. At the time of writing the lobby may be exploiting public ignorance of the extent of the rise in pensioner incomes in arguing for a rise in the basic state pension, when the government would prefer to spend less by targeting assistance to those pensioners with the lowest incomes.

Public support succeeded in protecting the pensions of existing pensioners even at the height of anti-public sector rhetoric. However, it failed to prevent cuts in the incomes of future pensioners or to ensure that all the current generation of pensioners shared in the country's growing prosperity. This last failing will also have contributed to the continued reliance of a large minority of pensioners on means-tested benefits.

Providing for one's old age

Turning from ideology to individual behaviour, the pattern of pension receipt is the cumulative result of a myriad of decisions taken by people over the course of their lifetime. Pensions in Britain are very complex, and the evidence suggests that planning by individuals is limited and belated (Hedges, 1998). In the past little planning was either necessary or undertaken. Occupational pensions were effectively a bonus attached to particular jobs, and their design was almost entirely determined by employers. As discussed already, such pensions were typically restricted to high status employees, but were more wide-ranging in state industries and other public sector organisations. Most people who did not have access to an occupational pension scheme relied entirely on state pension provision. The self-employed constitute an exception since they receive limited state pension provision and the most forward looking of them, or the better informed, took out insurance-based private pensions. More recently, the reduction in state pension provision, through the erosion of SERPS and the promotion of personal pensions for those without an occupational scheme, makes planning necessary, although many people lack the knowledge and understanding to do this effectively.

Career planning

People appear to acquire occupational pensions at two different points in their lives: in their 20s when they first obtain secure employment, and in their 40s. In the latter case it would appear that people either reach a status in their employment career that merits an occupational pension, or they deliberately seek out a job with an occupational pension (McKay et al, 2000). Clearly, delaying joining an occupational pension means that the pension ultimately payable is likely to be small, with a significant proportion merely offsetting entitlement to means–tested supplementation (Walker et al, 1989).

Studies of lifetime pension acquisition have identified distinct behavioural patterns. One fifth of people, predominantly male, join pension schemes early and remain with them. A similar number join later – sometimes after a career break – while another fifth, typically low–status workers, never join a pension scheme. Other groups that rarely join an occupational pension include women who have had caring responsibilities, people with a broken and episodic career, those who have been long-term unemployed, and the self-employed.

People often have a limited understanding of how the different forms of pensions work, and also lack information about their own status, prospects and options (Hedges, 1998). Early in life they feel that they have little spare cash, and the advantages of early investment are only vaguely appreciated, if at all. Typically, they lack advice and the initiative to seek advice. They see personal pensions as risky, and the young are sceptical that the state system will continue. Taking the risk of doing nothing often appears to be the easiest option.

People who are currently retired, and those who have retired since 1971, have lived through many different pension regimes, which, given adequate levels of awareness, may have influenced their approach to pensions and savings. However, the pattern of change has, until quite recently, been one of improving state pension provision and expanding occupational pensions; the effect has been automatically to enhance incomes in retirement over those of previous generations. This may have diminished concern about making provision for old age and reduced personal savings ratios below what they might have been under other circumstances. It might also have inhibited growth of a market to provide for those excluded from state and occupational provision – one reason for government promoting personal pensions after 1988. However, without an appropriate counterfactual, all that can be said for certain is that pensions have low salience for people of working age. This may well cause problems for future generations of pensioners if state provision continues to be reduced and the coverage of occupational pensions slips further.

The retirement decision

There has been a trend towards earlier retirement, but, insofar as this impacts on state provision, it will affect the caseloads of benefits other than retirement pension, since the minimum age at which a pension is payable is fixed (Chapter 25). The link between regulation and behaviour is evident in the fact that 36% of both men and women who retired in the early 1990s did so at the state retirement age (Tanner, 1997). Thirty-one per cent of women continued working after the age of 60, and 8% of men after they had reached age 65. Fourteen per cent of partners retired at the same time, and a further 20% did so within a year of each other. About a quarter of those who retired after retirement age said that they did so in order to improve their financial position, while a similar number reported that they simply enjoyed working. A third of women who continued working did so because their employer had imposed a higher retirement age. One tenth of men retired early for the same reason – often related to the point at which an occupational pension became payable.

There has been a trend towards early retirement (Chapter 25), and this is reflected in people's aspirations, and perhaps in their career planning. People in their 30s who were interviewed in 1994/95 expected to retire around the age of 60, almost two years earlier than people in their late 40s (McKay and Middleton, 1998). However, one cannot be sure that the latter group will not change their minds as they get older. Those with occupational or personal pensions appeared to have a clearer view of when they intended to retire, and expected to do so earlier than those who were entirely reliant on state pensions. Moreover, more people with occupational pensions do retire early, and more do so voluntarily than those who have no occupational pension (Disney et al, 1994; Stears, 1997). One interpretation is that people are increasingly keen to maximise the length of their retirement, provided that they have adequate resources to do so.

However, it is also evident that, for many people, the time of retirement is not fixed long in advance or, if it is, that fate conspires to frustrate people's plans (Tanner, 1997). In the early 1990s, only 37% of people within five years of retirement age were able accurately to predict when they would retire; two fifths of men and a fifth of women retired before they expected to do so. Of those who retired early, less than half seemed to have been forced to do so, 29% did so on health grounds and 19% at their employer's instigation.

Likewise, people are not always able accurately to predict the assets and incomes that they will have at retirement (an impediment to any stylised life cycle savings model that postulates that younger people defer current consumption to provide adequate income in old age). At the end of the 1980s a third of people within five years of retirement overstated their retirement income (Stears, 1997); similarly, a quarter overstated the assets (excluding pension provision) that they would have on retirement, while over 40% underestimated them (Tanner, 1997). The fact that those retiring early were more likely to overstate their assets suggests that they may have been unable to fulfil their retirement savings plan. But a fifth of those who retired when they expected to do so also overestimated their likely assets.

Finally, it is worth noting that even the concept of retirement is not necessarily clear cut. Six per cent of men aged between 59 and 75 who described themselves as retired were working full-time, another 2% were looking for work and, hence, were technically unemployed, and 17% gave primacy to reasons other than retirement, notably health, as the main reason for not seeking work (Tanner, 1997). Nor is retirement necessarily permanent; 7% of men who were retired in 1988/89 said that they no longer were in 1994.

Take-up of benefit

It is generally presumed that the take-up of Retirement Pension is effectively 100%. The reasons given are that notification forms are automatically sent to people as they approach retirement age, that people expect to receive a pension having paid National Insurance contributions, and that it is likely to contribute significantly to the income in retirement.

The take-up of means-tested Income Support is known to be a more serious problem and new mechanisms are to be put in place to boost take-up in the context of the new minimum income guarantee. Measures of take-up are subject to considerable error, since it is necessary to identify eligible non-claimants, and this can only be done on the basis of estimates of income and source of income collected by means of household surveys. The official take-up estimates reproduced in Table 24.1 suggest that the proportion of pensioners claiming means-tested supplementation to which they are entitled has not risen, and may actually have fallen. It follows that a very small part of the fall in the number of pensioners claiming means-tested Income Support could be the result of a decline in take-up. On the other hand, it is possible that expenditure take-up may be higher in the 1990s than it was in the 1970s. This suggests that the proportion of pensioners forgoing large amounts of benefit has fallen over time.

Table 24.1: Take-up of means-tested benefits by pensioners (%)

	Caseload	Expenditure
Supplementary Benefit		
1974	76	65
1979	65	68
Income Support		
1990	n/a	74-83
1994/95	59-66	73-79

Source: Evans (1998)

There is probably also a degree of non-take-up of occupational and personal pensions, which may be generating extra demand for means-tested supplementation. As previously mentioned, prior to 1975 there was no requirement on schemes to provide any benefits to people who left other than a return on the member's contribution. From the 1980s pension funds were obliged to preserve a pension for those who left after two years of service. Measures to improve the portability of pension entitlement between schemes have also been introduced. For the most part, payment of these preserved rights has to be initiated by the pensioner, and it is probable that this does not always happen. Unfortunately there is no systematic measure of the non-take-up of occupational pensions.

What has been learned

Public opinion strongly supports the continued provision of state pensions, and may have served to protect the benefits of existing pensioners when the rights of future pensioners were being eroded in the 1980s. However, it has not been sufficiently powerful to protect or enhance the social insurance component of state provision, and so reduce reliance on means testing and the attendant risk that some of the poorest pensioners will fail to claim all the benefits to which they are entitled.

Pension and retirement decisions are typically more haphazard than their importance demands. In the past there was minimal need to engage in detailed financial planning, since provision was largely determined by the state and employers. It follows that the changed pattern of benefit receipt, with falls in means-tested supplementation partially due to more people having occupational pensions, resulted from the strategic decisions of policy makers rather than the considered actions of prospective pensioners. Indeed, even in current circumstances, when employees are expected to take greater responsibility for financial planning, many seem either apathetic or overwhelmed by complexity or uncertainty. The evidence from decisions about retirement suggests that what planning takes place is quite often overtaken by unforeseen events.

TWENTY FIVE

The economy and pension provision

Summary

Pensioners' incomes, and their claim on social security provision, are largely determined by experiences in the labour market and the financial return on investments. However, the processes involved operate on a historic time-scale.

Half of early retirements appear to be voluntary, but ill-health has been an increasing factor.

People with occupational pensions are more likely than others to retire early, but the decision to retire may be usurped by employers who impose compulsory retirement ages or offer severance packages.

The lower incomes of older pensioners are largely the result of earlier generations missing out on the higher earnings and better pension arrangements available to later generations.

In recent times, and over comparatively short periods, the depletion of assets and depreciation of pension income has not had a large effect on pensioners' living standards nor, therefore, on claims for benefit.

The effect of the economy and economic processes on the size of the pensioner population is likely to be less immediate than in the case of unemployment or even disability. The financial resources that people bring into retirement are clearly in part a function of the economic conditions that prevailed at various times throughout their working lives. Whether they were able to find and sustain employment; whether they were able to save and the level of return on those savings; whether they were able to join an occupational pension scheme; and the state of the financial markets on the date of retirement – are all dependent on the pattern of economic growth and development that accompanied their age cohort. Similarly, the living standards of pensioners are likely to be closely tied to movements in inflation and interest rates following retirement, since a disproportionate proportion of their income is linked to investment. These factors determine the balance between different types of pension provision, notably by affecting the proportion of people who have incomes below the means-tested threshold, rather than the total size of the pensioner caseload. They also take long periods of time – almost an entire lifetime – to shape the pattern of benefit receipt in old age.

It could also be argued that rising life expectancy is a function of economic growth and improved living standards, and that this in turn affects the size of the pensioner population. While there is strong evidence of the relationship between health and economic conditions (Acheson, 1998; Gordon et al, 1999), it is impractical here to attempt to access the relative importance of economic, social and cultural factors in determining longevity.

Rather, the intention in this chapter is to address two specific questions. First, to what extent is the trend towards early retirement, noted in earlier chapters, a consequence of the provision of occupational pensions, and second, what explains the lower incomes characteristic of the oldest pensioners?

Occupational pensions and early retirement

The trend towards early retirement has already been noted (Chapter 18). In the late 1970s and early 1980s, the process was formally encouraged as a strategy to cope with rapidly rising unemployment. The obligation to look for work was removed for men aged over 60, and there is evidence that Employment Service staff encouraged some unemployed older men to move onto benefit. The effect of this policy will have been to increase the number of claimants receiving disability benefits rather than retirement pensions. The decision to retire early also seems to be influenced by whether or not a person has an occupational pension.

Table 25.1 lists the reasons people gave for early retirement in the early 1990s. At that time early retirement triggered by actual or potential redundancy accounted for only about a third of the total for men and one fifth for women. As important was personal ill–health or the sickness of family members, which accounted for about a third of both men and women retiring early. Over the next five years personal ill–heath grew in importance as a reason for early retirement – from 27% to 34% for men and from 30% to 39% for women – at a time when claims for Invalidity Benefit from people close to retirement ages increased by about 21% (Blundell and Johnson, 1996; Tanner, 1997). Even so, half of early retirements occurring in the latter period appeared to be unforced.

Table 25.1: Main reason for early retirement, Great Britain (early 1990s) (%)

Main reason	All	Men	Women
Own ill-health	27	26	27
Ill-health of others	5	4	7
Involuntary redundancy	15	15	14
Voluntary redundancy	18	24	7
Spend more time with family	5	3	11
Enjoy life while young	6	6	5
Fed up with work/want change	5	4	7
Retire with partner	2	0	6
Give younger generation a chance	2	2	2
Other	8	6	12
Fixed retirement age	7	10	1
Number of observations	631	408	223

Source: Tanner (1997)

The reasons given for early retirement varied markedly, between men who had occupational pensions and those who did not, as did the timing of retirement (Table 25.2). (The differences among women were less marked.) Sixty-two per cent of men with occupational pensions instigated the retirement themselves or offered an ill–defined reason for retiring, compared with just 39% of those without. The latter were also twice as likely to be made compulsorily redundant, and significantly more likely to give ill–health as the reason for retirement. The more involuntary, less planned, nature of early retirement for people without occupational pensions is also evidenced by the wider range of ages over which they retired. Seventeen per cent retired before the age of 55, something very rare for those with an occupational pension who, in the case of men, are much more likely to retire at 60 or 62 because of fixed

Table 25.2: Early retirement and occupational pensions, Great Britain (early 1990s) (%)

Sex and reason	All	Occupational pension	No occupational pension
Men			
Firm-instigated[*]	14	12	23
Ill-health	28	26	39
Individual-instigated	36	41	18
Other	21	22	20
Number of observations	433	350	82
Women			
Firm-instigated[*]	13	12	13
Ill-health	32	35	30
Individual-instigated	36	33	39
Other	19	20	18
Number of observations	241	123	118

Note:[*] Includes compulsory redundancy and fixed retirement age.
Source: Tanner (1997)

retirement ages instigated by employers and supported by the rules of the pension scheme.

One possible explanation for the relationship between early retirement and occupational pensions is that people who aspire to retire early deliberately take superannuated employment that facilitates this. However, this seems somewhat unlikely given the evidence in Chapter 24 that long-term retirement planning is the exception rather than the rule.

But occupational pensions certainly seem to facilitate, and sometimes to encourage, people to retire before the state retirement age. Moreover, decisions over the timing of retirement may be affected directly and immediately by the prevailing state of the economy. Equity growth in recent years has been very high – the FT index, for example, grew by 102% between 1990 and 1998. As a consequence, private sector pensions funds have been able to provide better pensions than might otherwise have been the case, especially for those who retired early (DSS, 2000b).

The choice to retire early is not always that of the employee, since fixed retirement ages, and the facility that occupational pensions provide to soften the financial cost of tacit redundancy, can place the initiative with employers. Even so, the fact that in recent years more people have approached retirement age with the prospect of a substantial pension must go some way towards explaining the secular trend towards earlier retirement. Nevertheless, at the turn of the 1990s it was ill-health – rather than a more positive attachment to retirement – that seemed to be triggering more early retirement. Whether this reflects greater pressures at work, stimulated by new expectations and greater insecurity, is a moot point.

Income dynamics

Older pensioners are financially worse off than younger ones, and consequently more are dependent on means-tested income (Johnson and Stears, 1998).

In part, the reason for this is the disproportionate number of women who survive to older ages, and the fact that their incomes are generally less than those for men. However, the incomes of both men and women decline with age, which means a further explanation is required. A number of possibilities exist: older generations will have earned less in work and acquired pension rights at a time when both state and occupational pension regimes were less generous; older pensioners may have less income because their savings and pensions have been inadequately protected against inflation; they may also use up savings so that income from assets declines over time. The evidence of cohort analysis of repeated cross-sectional surveys suggests that the first reason, the higher incomes and greater wealth of later generations, is the driving factor in Britain (Johnson and Stears, 1996).

The generational effect is so strong that it masks the fact that mean incomes of individuals in particular cohorts actually increase as they age – most likely the result of differential mortality, with low-income pensioners dying at younger ages. Figure 25.1, which shows that people with occupational pensions live longer than those without, can be taken as supportive evidence of this effect. Another result of such differential mortality is that the number of people receiving means-tested benefits and SERPS would be substantially higher if death rates were not linked to income.

There is evidence of other processes that serve to counteract the decline in incomes with age. Although occupational incomes did not keep pace with high inflation during the 1970s, they tended to pay above inflation increases in the late 1980s and 1990s. The exact opposite was true of state retirement pensions, which were indexed to the higher of either wages or prices in the 1970s, but only to prices subsequently.

But processes are even more complicated at the level of the individual (Johnson, 1997). The mean incomes of a national sample of married and cohabiting men, aged between 65 and 69 in 1988/89, *increased* over the next five years although median income fell. The reason was that falls in earnings (from a median of £39 to £21 per week) and occupational pensions (from £52 to £42 per week), were offset by rises in state retirement pension and very large rises in state and occupational pensions enjoyed by a small number of men. The incomes of married and cohabiting women initially aged between 60 and 69 moved ahead of prices by about 20%, mainly because 10% more received Retirement Pension, while the incomes of existing widows just about kept up with inflation.

In summary, there is a very powerful imprint of history on the incomes of pensioner households, which seems to explain much of the age-related inequality in living standards. While the depletion of assets and the depreciation in pension income must occur, the studies reviewed suggest that in recent times, and over comparatively short time periods, these factors have not had a profound effect on average income levels.

Figure 25.1: Survival curves for male pensioners born between 1905 and 1914

Source: Johnson and Stears (1996)

What has been learned

Pensioners' incomes necessarily reflect lifelong experiences in the labour market, and carry the imprint of structural economic change on individuals' employment histories and personal finances. The shared economic experiences of successive generations powerfully determine the level of pensions and other incomes in old age, and profoundly influence the pattern of inequality among retirement pensioners. The lower living standards suffered by older pensioners are overwhelmingly the consequence of the fact that they did not experience the higher wages and better institutional arrangements enjoyed by later generations. Occupational pensions are an example of such improved institutional arrangements, which have not only boosted the incomes of later generations but also facilitated, and in some cases enforced, earlier retirement.

TWENTY SIX

Pathways to pensions

Summary

Demography – specifically enhanced life expectancy – *explains the 44% growth in the pensioner caseload.*

Enhanced state benefits – notably SERPS, which ironically has now been abandoned – *and the maturation and greater coverage of occupational pensions account for the fall in the numbers of pensioners claiming means-tested supplementation.*

Means-tested caseloads would have been even smaller had not housing policy driven up rents. They would be greater if universal take-up had been achieved.

Despite the success of past pension reforms *income inequalities forged in the labour market tend still to be largely repeated in old age.*

What were the principal factors leading to the 44% growth in the number of pensioners receiving retirement pensions between 1971 and 1998, and the fall in the proportion receiving means-tested supplementation? The main story is quite straightforward, although again further work would be required to place precise figures on the size of the effects (Figure 26.1).

Demographic change is the main driving factor accounting for the increased number of retirement pensioners. Despite falling birth rates and smaller birth cohorts in the early years of the century, the numbers reaching retirement age have actually increased over the last 26 years. Life expectancy after retirement has also risen, by about one fifth for men and one seventh for women, over the same period. It would appear from existing analysis that the increase in the Retirement Pension population was driven slightly more by the larger number retiring than by improved longevity after retirement. Net in-migration is likely to account for little more than 1% of the increase.

Although there has been a trend towards early retirement that warrants some discussion (see below), this has not affected the number of retirement pensioners, since Retirement Pension cannot be paid until after retirement age. There has been a drop in the number of people deferring retirement that may have increased the number of retirement pensioners by perhaps 2%.

The nine percentage point fall in the number of pensioners with supplementary means-tested pensions, together with the reduction in the proportion of pensioners receiving any form of mean-tested benefit, is a function of rising real personal incomes in old age. (The means-tested threshold has risen relative to prices since 1971, and although its real value has not altered greatly since the end of the 1970s, one would have expected a growth in the means-tested caseload if other factors had held constant.) Two factors explain this change of affairs: the maturing of occupational pensions and the introduction of SERPS. The number of pensioners with an occupational pension increased by 22 percentage points, to 65%, in the 18 years to 1996/97, while the average pension in payment increased by £42 per week (1996 prices). The buoyancy of the stock market during the 1990s ensured that pension payments were generous and that pensions in payment did not lose much of their real value.

The build up of entitlement to SERPS took time, but by 1998, 52% of pensioners had their basic pension topped up from this source, to the tune of an average of £23 per week. As a consequence, comparatively few pensioners – mostly those who retired before 1980 – now have no income beyond a basic Retirement Pension.

Without further micro-analysis it is impossible to determine which was the more important factor in floating pensioners off means testing – occupational pensions or SERPS. The former deliver more income to a larger number of people. On the other hand, employees who remain in SERPS tend to be less well paid and to have less stable employment than those in occupational pension schemes. They might, therefore, be expected to have lower incomes in retirement, and to be more likely to be eligible for means-tested supplementation had it not been for SERPS. It is worth noting that the reduced reliance on means testing could have been greater had it not been for policies to increase the rents of social housing to near market levels.

The success of pension reforms was underwritten by economic growth, boosting the investment income of pension companies and allowing state pensions to be largely funded through economic growth rather than by real intergenerational redistribution. Ironically, a lack of confidence about the sustainability of economic growth, together with concern about future demographic trends increasing demand for pensions, led SERPS to be dismantled, even in the face of continuing public support for generous state provision. As a consequence, future generations of pensioners may become less well protected against financial hardship in old age.

Figure 26.1: Understanding pension caseloads

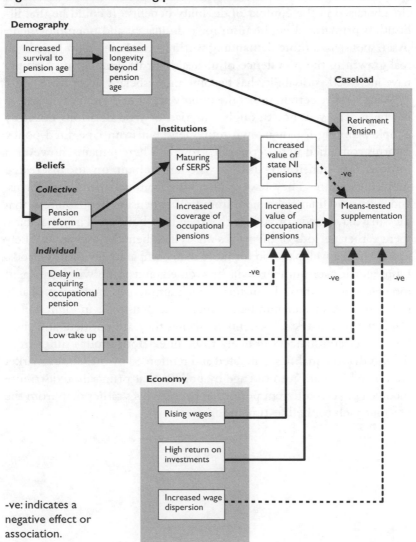

-ve: indicates a negative effect or association.

The factors involved in the trend towards earlier retirement are also complicated. The availability of occupational pensions with provision for early retirement is surely important. It adds to the attractiveness of retirement, given that increasing numbers of people can look forward to a long period in good health without severe financial hardship. But the evidence is that in perhaps half of cases the decision is not one that is freely made. Redundancy may well have been particularly important in triggering retirement during the recession of the 1980s, but the apparent increased prevalence of ill-health is also a significant factor. Why this should be so is unclear, but the finding alerts one to issues already raised in the context of disability benefits. It could be that ill-health is primarily a euphemism for redundancy and unemployment, or a response to a more demanding workplace. There might have been real growth in the prevalence of ill-health, or its visibility may simply have increased as disability has become more socially acceptable.

What is more certain is that the improvement in pensioners' incomes has been achieved, not through a myriad of wise decisions taken by people planning for their own retirement, but from farsighted policy reforms combined with economic growth. There remains, however, a minority of pensioners (40%) who are reliant on means-tested supplementation. They have gained little from past pension reforms, and receive no financial benefit from private pension contributions that they may have made or savings that they have built up. They may have spent earlier periods of their lives on welfare benefits, and are unlikely to have held a well paid job for more than comparatively short periods. Disproportionate numbers will be women, and some will have spent long periods as carers. Their financial circumstances are most probably precarious. A smaller number, perhaps one pensioner in eight, fail to claim the means-tested benefits to which they are entitled, and their financial circumstances are likely to be dire. Both groups suffer from the fact that inequalities generated and reinforced by the labour market are carried forward into old age by policies that primarily redistribute income between different periods in people's lives rather than from the life-time rich to the life-time poor.

Part 6
Towards a welfare class?

TWENTY SEVEN

Understanding the pattern of caseload growth

Summary

Although caseloads of the four recipient groups – unemployed people, disabled people pensioners and families with children – all increased between 1971 and 1998/99, they did so for different reasons. The process of de-industrialisation provided a background for all the changes, but was only implicated as a major direct influence in the case of unemployment-related benefits.

Unemployment caseloads reflected movements in the economic cycle, but increased with the secular decline in manufacturing and a large youth cohort in the 1980s. By 1999, the claimant unemployment was comparable to that in 1971, although changed definitions flatter the comparison, and absolute numbers remained 65% higher because of growth in the labour force – largely on account of higher economic participation by women. Control of inflation replaced full employment as a policy priority in the late 1970s, and from the 1980s active labour market policies began to be implemented.

The number of disabled people claiming benefits rose in response to new provisions, themselves a consequence of growing recognition of the financial needs of disabled people. The reported prevalence of disability increased, while a more competitive economy and labour market may have placed disabled people seeking work at a growing disadvantage. Ill-health associated with increased poverty may also have played a role. An ageing population added to the caseloads of those benefits for people above retirement age.

> *New benefits – notably Child Benefit and means-tested benefits for working families – added to the number of families with children receiving benefit over a period during which fertility fell markedly.* While, at times, unemployment inflated the numbers of families claiming out of work benefits, the three-fold growth in lone parents – reflecting profound changes in sexual attitudes and relationships – was the main cause of growth.
>
> *The increased retirement pensioner caseload was largely the result of higher life expectancy*, but a decline in the means-tested caseload resulted from the maturation of occupational pensions and the State Earnings Related Pensions Scheme.
>
> *The diversity of experience, transience of circumstances, and differences in aspirations worked against the creation of class consciousness and the development of a welfare class.*

The central issue addressed in this book is why, after 50 years of welfare state provision, increasing numbers of people seem still to be financially reliant on receipt of cash benefits. Answering this question has importance beyond mere intellectual curiosity.

The British system of cash benefits is characterised by perpetual reform, a process that is given momentum by shifts in the four sets of necessarily interlinked influences that have been used to organise this book: the economy, demography, institutions and beliefs. However, in choosing the pathway to reform it is self-evident that ideology, beliefs more or less informed by evidence, is paramount. Indeed, it would appear that ideology has not been much influenced by evidence. This is suggested by the fact that, in seeking to explain rising caseloads, it has been necessary to rely on a widely dispersed literature that contains little by way of long-range trend data or rigorous or sophisticated analysis.

Yet, in setting objectives and devising policies by which they might be attained, it is vital to know whether rising caseloads serve as evidence of the success or failure of policy. They could index a positive response to increased need, or be the result of poorly targeted schemes that have created a welfare class, comprising people who either have chosen a life on welfare, or find themselves trapped in economic and social exclusion. The set of appropriate policy responses clearly differs according to what the evidence shows.

The objective of this review, in seeking to provide such evidence, has been to begin to provide a coherent analytic account of the upward trend in social security recipients, taken to include contributory, non-contributory and means-tested claimants, and to assess the role of policy.

The complexity of the British social security system makes it impractical to consider all recipients together as a single set. System is not the right word to describe a collection of at least 39 separate schemes that have disparate objectives, are targeted on different groups of recipients, were implemented at various times over 50 years, and have reached different stages of administrative maturity. British social security has coherence when viewed from a distance – it is principally concerned with the relief of poverty, means-testing is more widely used than in most continental European countries, and the system is heavily centralised, although benefits are increasingly being delivered by interlocking agencies including private and not-for-profit organisations. When studied closely, it is often inchoate, with contradictory objectives and conflicting policies.

The approach adopted, therefore, has been to take an intermediate focus, directing attention to four categories of recipient: unemployed people, disabled people, pensioners, and families with children. Although there is a degree of overlap between categories, in a British context they serve as different domains nested within the national social security structure. This has the advantage of avoiding unnecessary detail and, since the groups have featured in official publications for somewhat over a decade, facilitates comparison over time.

In similar mode, the multifarious factors that conspire to influence the claimant caseloads have been reduced to the four sets of 'drivers' associated with the economy, demography, the welfare institutions engaged in the design and delivery of benefits, and the belief systems that forge politics and influence individual behaviour. The fact that different drivers are pre-eminent in each of the social security domains provides further post-hoc legitimacy to the analytic strategy. Given that the focus of the analysis is on change, wherever possible account has been taken of the dynamics of benefit schemes and of the system in which they are embedded.

The aim in this final chapter is briefly to recap on the processes involved in each domain, but importantly, to draw comparisons between them so as to approach an account of the system as a whole. Perhaps inevitably, the economy is the most important driver. Over time it more or less efficiently delivers the resources that society can choose to spend on social security, while its inefficiencies generate many of the needs to which social security provisions are a response. However, in the making of policy and the evolution of institutions, the impact of the economy has been profoundly mediated by political ideology, while pensioner caseloads have largely been determined by demographic factors. Developments in the domains of the disability and the family have been much shaped by shifts in social values and personal behaviour.

Unemployment

Over almost the last 30 years, Britain has experienced a process of de-industrialisation. Triggered, or highlighted, by the oil crises of the 1970s, traditional production industries declined, manufacturing employment fell by 49%, and the service sector grew to provide 67% rather than 47% of all jobs. Productivity levels rose and production methods changed. Short-term and part-time employment increased and job openings that predominately go to women rose relative to those available to men. The skills required of employees changed and increased. Returns to education grew and median and above median wages rose by at least a third in real terms, while those at the bottom did not change.

Throughout most of this period total employment continued to grow, but many of the jobs created were low waged. Nevertheless, unemployment was driven to unprecedented levels, and changed in nature. The proportion of long-term unemployment rose, and it is probable that 'churning', the process by which people move in and out of short-term unemployment, increased. Caseloads of unemployment-related benefits naturally rose, and the ratio of contributory to means-tested benefits began to change, from 2:1 in 1971 to 1:2 in 1997, as people's entitlement to the former was exhausted and not replenished (and eligibility criteria were altered).

Demography did not ease the transition to a post-industrial society. The potential labour force increased by 8%. But as important, if not more so, an influx of a large cohort of young people coincided with the recession at the beginning of the 1980s, triggering the growth of long-term unemployment comprised of people with little work experience. A disproportionate number of the newly created jobs were taken by women, the result of changing aspirations and priorities, especially among mothers of comparatively young children. A further factor may have been the increasing requirement for families to have two jobs, either in order to make ends meet, or to achieve the standards of living to which they aspire.

These events drove the political agenda, and initially forged policy responses that were pragmatic. The stagflation that gripped Britain in the 1970s caused the Labour government to drop its commitment to full employment, and to adopt unwelcome policies of fiscal restraint. Subsequently, with the 1979 election of the first Thatcher government, a bold experiment was initiated involving the practical application of monetarist theory. The government explicitly sought to use unemployment as a weapon against wage inflation, initially with little regard to the benefits bill. Although earnings-related Unemployment Benefit was abolished soon after the Conservatives assumed power, this yielded few benefit savings, being primarily an ideological gesture which signalled the importance that the government attached to financial incentives. Later, repeated paring of contributory benefits did cut their cost, but added to means-tested caseloads in almost equal measure.

Alongside, and ultimately supplanting, the strong ideological imperative, an interative process was evident in which policy and events interacted, with policy makers sometimes having to respond to the unanticipated consequences of their own policies. Employment advice and benefit administration were separated, and small-scale training and work experience schemes, started in the 1970s, were rapidly expanded in the early 1980s. Older workers were also encouraged to leave the labour market. Both the latter strategies were used to reduce benefit caseloads. In fact, economic activity among men, especially those over 55, fell almost without interruption during 1971-95, recovering slightly thereafter. Increased ill-health was the major reason, at least in the early 1990s, but whether this primarily reflected a deterioration in clinical morbidity or a rise in a social threshold of incapacity is as yet unclear.

Job creation measures were cut back from the mid-1980s for reasons of cost, new ministerial leadership, and changed perceptions of the nature of unemployment. Unemployment came to be seen as a supply-side issue; jobseekers were too rigid in their attitudes and behaviour to capitalise on industry's demand for a flexible, low-cost labour force. Policies were introduced that encouraged and cajoled unemployed claimants to be more enthusiastic and effective in their search for work. Six-monthly interrogatory 'Restart' interviews with unemployed claimants were implemented in 1988, and Jobseeker's Allowance was introduced in 1996, to reintegrate employment and benefit administration and implement a 'stricter benefit regime'. Both measures were credited with initially reducing claimant numbers, but whether the impact has been sustained is unclear. Given that the empirical evidence is that the vast majority of unemployed are positively committed to working, and that the long-term unemployed are trapped by the disadvantages that they take with them into unemployment – low skills, poor education, ill-health, age – the impact of such schemes is likely to have been marginal.

Broadly the same strategy was taken forward by Labour following its election to power in 1997, emphasising the contract between state and benefit claimant and the need for action. However, Labour added compulsory training and work experience for significant numbers of claimants, and sought to enhance the quality of both.

From the mid-1980s onwards, policy focused increasingly on the need to provide and enhance in-work benefits to address the problem of work incentives. This problem was itself partially a consequence of policies that promoted means-testing, and in part the result of the increase in low-paid jobs. As a measure of 'success' the Family Credit caseload rose from 350,000 in 1992 to 788,100 in 1999, partly helped by lone parents being encouraged to enter the labour market. (In 1995/96, however, claimant take-up, another measure of success, was still less than 70%.) The numbers in receipt of Housing Benefit also rose, due largely to a policy of higher rents.

The new Labour government shares the enthusiasm for in-work benefits, although it has begun providing them through the tax system. They certainly boost in-work incomes, and provide a 'parachute' for two-earner families that lose one job. There is, however, little evidence that wage levels are a major constraint on people taking jobs, and some research suggests that in-work benefits may trap people in low paid work (Bryson, 1998). Either way, the policy has created a new class of workers whose income derives from a mix of wages and benefits.

Disability

In Britain over the last five years concern has focused on the extent to which the economy, perhaps interacting with or generating a lower motivation to work, is responsible for the markedly increased number of people receiving incapacity benefits. Taking a longer time horizon, it is clear that the driving factor is a changed level of public awareness and acceptance of disability, and a more heightened appreciation of the personal financial cost involved. There is also an association between poor health, disability, worklessness and poverty although the precise links are unclear. The economy may well be important in terms of increasing the psychological and physical pressures in the workplace, although the evidence in this regard is largely circumstantial.

Of the four kinds of disability benefit in Britain, income maintenance, compensation, additional costs and wage supplementation, the latter two were either rudimentary or non-existent in 1971. In 1998/99 they were received by over 3.3 million people. The number of people claiming income maintenance benefits tripled between 1971 and 1998/99.

Prior to the 1970s there had been no social recognition of the impact of long-term sickness or specific provision for it within the social security system. Disability, particularly that resulting from congenital conditions, was difficult to fit within a social insurance framework, and had largely been overlooked. Growing social awareness, in part stimulated by the emergence of disability rights groups, and a policy concern in the early 1970s to reduce reliance on means-testing, led to the creation of a new kind of non-contributory, non-means-tested benefit. Reflecting social attitudes and the understanding of the day, they were first directed exclusively on physical impairment. Only later, as part of an expansion of coverage, were other forms of disability recognised.

The 1980s policy agendas, developed in response to the rise in unemployment and a political preference for the approaches of business, embraced concerns about financial disincentives and introduced reforms to reduce administration costs and pressures on business. Concerns to tackle sex inequality were also evident, sometimes forced on the British government against its inclinations. The European Court insisted that Invalid Care Allowance – a benefit that acknowledges earnings lost by carers – should be available to women to care for their partners. Most importantly, however, decisions about the restructuring of benefits were deferred until the outcome of large-scale empirical studies of the nature and prevalence of disability.

Research results pointed to the need to extend coverage to groups previously excluded, such as people with learning difficulties. This was done in the 1990s, despite great pressures to restrain expenditure, which, in practice, meant tightening eligibility criteria and greater means testing. The finding that many disabled people expressed the wish to work highlighted the rigidities and work disincentives in the system of income maintenance benefits for disabled people, which provided too sharp a choice between staying on benefit and relying on earnings (Rowlingson and Berthoud, 1996). In-work benefits were considered to be the solution for people with 'partial capacity' for work. This led to the introduction of Disability Working Allowance in 1992.

With the exception of Disability Working Allowance, the caseloads for the newly introduced benefits much exceeded expectations. Because many of the benefits were until recently payable for life, subject to a person's circumstances remaining unchanged, it was inevitable that caseloads would rise and the average length of claim increase as long-term recipients accumulated in the system.

The growth in the caseloads of the established income maintenance benefits for disabled people grew initially from improvements in take-up, perhaps because social attitudes meant that people were more ready to recognise and accept their own status as disabled people. As take-up rose, caseload growth occurred, not so much because of increasing numbers of new cases, but more from extending periods of receipt. This reflected the maturation of benefits designed to meet the needs of long-term conditions, but raised concerns, at a time of high unemployment and fiscal pressure, that disability benefits were becoming a safe haven for the unemployed. In fact, the empirical evidence on a link between unemployment and the receipt of disability benefit is equivocal.

Economic inactivity is rising quickly among older men. Regardless of whether this is unemployment or some form of de facto early retirement, ill-health is often involved, which puts upward pressure on disability benefit caseloads. Caseloads are larger in areas of high unemployment but do not appear to be closely related to cyclical economic fluctuations. It seems more likely that disabled people are marginalised by employers, who enjoy a surplus of labour supply, rather than that they are deterred from wanting work by a deficiency of vacancies. In such circumstances gatekeepers, medical doctors and Employment Service staff might direct people with health problems to disability rather than unemployment-related benefits. The evidence of explicit discrimination by employers is slight, although it is evident that many are not well-informed about issues relating to the employment of disabled people.

This complex interaction between beliefs, behaviour and the labour market presented dilemmas for policy. Malpractice and abuse are suspected, but large-scale reviews of claims did not lead to sizeable reductions in caseload. Moreover, take-up rates remain at only 50%. The current policy response is to emphasise employability, what a person can do rather than what they cannot do. New tests of incapacity are being introduced and, under the New Deal for Disabled People, specialist counsellors are being deployed to assist disabled people to enter the labour market.

Demography has been a less important driver of disability benefit caseloads than the change in attitudes. However, the population did age over the period 1971 to 1999, and this was important in the growth of Attendance Allowance, which has a caseload dominated by people who are in their 70s or older. The closure of long-stay hospitals, the increased prevalence of older people living alone, and medical advances that keep people alive for longer have all added upward pressure to caseloads. Finally, there is also growing evidence that increased regional economic inequalities may generate greater health needs among poor people and in poor localities.

Children and families

The processes that drove the growth in unemployment and disability benefit caseloads necessarily affected the circumstances and interests of families with children. This is inevitable, of course, because many disabled and unemployed people have children, and some children are disabled and receive special benefits as a consequence. It reflects the fact that the domains of social security used in Britain are not mutually exclusive.

Nevertheless, there are separate benefits payable to children in their own right, and as dependants, and distinct issues that arise from their receipt of other benefits. The principal driving force behind caseload growth in this domain between 1971 and 1999 was the change in individual and collective beliefs about ways of living and the nature and role of the family. The economy, too, was important, making it increasingly difficult for families to be sustained by one wage, and increasing the risk of unemployment and worklessness, and of the associated poverty. Indeed, one striking social development that occurred during the last three decades was the replacement of pensioner households by families with children in the bottom quintile of the equivalised income distribution.

In terms simply of caseloads, the biggest growth occurred with the transformation of the family tax allowance into a cash benefit, Child Benefit, in 1977, and at the same time extending coverage to the first-born child. This more than doubled the number of children for whom benefit was received, and reflected a re-focusing of policy objectives. Family allowances were originally introduced to enhance work incentives, with the creation of the first national means-tested safety net. The financial saving achieved by limiting the allowance to second and subsequent children was also consistent with the pro-natalist policies of the time. Work incentives were still an important consideration in the introduction of Child Benefit, but the prime objectives were to tackle child poverty, particularly among working families, and to redirect control of the income to the principal carer, usually the mother.

Declining fertility has since caused the Child Benefit caseload to fall by almost 10%.

The other area of major caseload growth reflected the nearly three-fold growth in lone parenthood. Over one in five families with dependent children was headed by a lone parent in 1997. Originally driven by separation, and, following divorce legislation enacted in 1971, by divorce, the proportion of never-married lone mothers, either separated from a partner or never having resided with a partner, subsequently increased. Moreover, at a time in the 1980s and early 1990s when economic activity rates among married mothers were rising, the employment of lone mothers fell, and the proportion claiming means-tested Income Support grew. In 1999 lone parents comprised almost one in four of Income Support claimants.

The policy response in the 1970s and 1980s was to introduce new benefits to counter the high risk of poverty experienced by lone parents, and especially lone mothers. One Parent Benefit, a non-contributory supplement to Child Benefit, was implemented in 1981, and special treatment accorded to lone parents in the main means-tested benefits. In-work benefits were also tailored to the presumed needs of lone parents and changed again in the 1990s to further assist them to work.

But other influences came into play in the 1990s that stimulated a change in policy objectives towards a focus on reducing caseloads. A cost-conscious government was worried by escalating expenditure. A new moralism emerged: benefits were presented as undermining the traditional family, and the growth in unmarried mothers and the failure of absent fathers to pay maintenance were taken as evidence. Active labour market policies had legitimated coercive policies to change behaviour, and work was beginning to be recognised as the best means to achieve self-sufficiency. Moreover, it had become the norm for married mothers to work. A Child Support Agency was established in 1993, to recover maintenance payments for lone parents on benefit. It proved to be none too successful, as 40% of absent fathers were themselves on benefit. One Parent Benefit was abolished. Employment advice was offered to lone parents on a trial basis in 1995, and in 1997 re-launched by the new Labour government as the New Deal for Lone Parents.

Since benefit levels for lone parents did not rise substantially in relative terms between the 1970s and 1980s, it is difficult to explain the reduced economic participation by lone mothers by reference to benefit levels. On the other hand, the characteristics of lone mothers did change. They became younger and perhaps less able to compete in the labour market. They would also have confronted the same changes in the labour market, increased low pay and unemployment, that caused worklessness and poverty to increase among two-parent families. The fact that the proportion of lone parents on benefit now seems to be falling might indicate a response to the sustained fall in unemployment, perhaps aided by the availability and tailoring of in-work benefits.

Increased worklessness and poverty among two-parent families was the other concern of policy makers, especially from the mid-1980s onwards, not least because of its impact on benefit caseloads and expenditure. The main issues have already been addressed in the context of unemployment-related benefits. Suffice to say, the growth of low pay increased the significance of a second earner as a defence against poverty. Also, in the absence of in-work benefits, it made it essential for two unemployed parents to achieve the unlikely double of securing two poorly paid jobs simultaneously in order to be able to make the transition out of worklessness. Little wonder that the increasing polarisation into 'work-rich' and 'work poor' families so worries the new Labour government and underpins its proposals to extend in-work benefits through the tax system.

Pensioners

Trends in pensioner caseloads between 1971 and 1999 were determined largely by demography. The influence of the economy was indirect, fixing the resources that workers and employees could accumulate for retirement, and influencing the amount that one generation was prepared to pass to another in the form of 'pay as you go' pensions.

The pensioner population grew by 44% between 1971 and 1998, despite a falling birth rate 60-65 years earlier that should have generated declining caseloads. The principal reason was the increased number of people who survived to retirement age, closely followed by the 20% increase in life expectancy after retirement.

The second major development in the last three decades affecting pensioners was a halving of the proportion dependent on means-testing – the mirror opposite of the change in unemployment-related benefits. The main explanation was rising pensioners' incomes, resulting from the development and maturing of occupational pensions since the 1950s, together with the introduction of SERPS in 1978 for those without access to a non state pension. Deciding which was the more important would require further research, since pensions from SERPS (an average

£23 per week in 1998) were less than occupational pensions (£93[1] inflator), but directed at those with less other income. A secondary factor was the differential improvement in longevity that benefited men, and which meant both that fewer women were widowed and that they were widows for shorter periods. The shift away from means-testing would have been even greater had rents not risen in social housing.

The improvement in pensioners' incomes was primarily the result of the foresightful decisions of policy planners and the provision of occupation pensions by employers, rather than judicious behaviour by ordinary citizens. Lay people find the British pension provisions complex and confusing, planning is limited and often belated. Indeed, many people are unable to predict their likely incomes and assets in retirement, even when they are within five years of retirement age.

In the past little planning was in fact necessary, since occupational pensions were a condition of employment, and those without one could look forward to increasingly generous state pension provision. This has no longer been true since the Thatcher government downgraded SERPS, fearful that it would not be affordable when the dependency ratio worsened in the 2020s. In its place, the government promoted personal pensions provided by insurance companies, but, despite tax incentives, these proved inappropriate for the poorly paid workers, including disproportionate numbers of women, for which SERPS catered. (Mis-selling by the insurance companies also lessened the public's faith in personal pensions.) Unless the proposals put forward by the current Labour government come to fruition, the recent shift in the balance between contributory and means-tested provision will be reversed.

Although occupational pensions contributed significantly to the improvement in pensioners' incomes between 1971 and 1999, they also increased income inequality in retirement, carrying over and exaggerating differentials originating in the labour market. Indeed, the imprint of personal history is very strong in old age – the decline in incomes observed among older people, and the greater reliance on means-tested supplementation, results more from the improved working conditions and incomes of later generations than from the depreciation of pension income or the depletion of assets in old age. The interaction of occupational pensions with means-testing generated an occupational pension trap that, in 1997, meant that at least 850,000 occupational pensioners (8%) were not recouping the full value of their pension contributions. (From the perspective of the state, of course, the same means testing generates savings in public expenditure.)

Finally, the marked trend towards economic inactivity observed among men over 50 served to extend the boundary of retirement to younger ages but, because state pensions are only payable at retirement age, this had no effect on Retirement Pension caseloads. Younger generations aspire to retiring at ever younger ages, and occupational pensions often encourage this by offering variable retirement ages[2], but whether this enthusiasm translates into the planning that earlier generations sought to avoid remains to be seen.

On the making of a welfare class

Caseloads increased across the four domains of British social security between 1971 and 1999, but they did so for very different reasons. While the process of de-industrialisation provided an important backcloth to all the changes, it was only implicated as a major direct influence in the growth of unemployment-related benefits. The upward trends in disability benefits were principally due to greater social awareness of the personal costs of disability, possibly to increased morbidity and probably to ill-health related to higher levels of poverty. The increased number of families with children receiving benefit was an indirect result of changing social attitudes and sexual behaviour as much as economic change. Demography, notably increased longevity, explains the observed growth in pensioner caseloads, although the balance between contributory and means-tested pensions was the result of foresighted policy decisions made between the 1940s and 1970s.

The very different reasons for the growth in caseloads that apply in the four domains of British social security suggest that each group occupies a different position vis-à-vis the labour market and class structure. This serves to undermine any contention that economic and social developments in the last 30 years have produced a cohesive welfare class. However, it does not itself mean that the various groups do not have interests in common or could not forge a shared identity. As yet, however, they do not appear to have done so.

Diversity of experience, transience of circumstance, and differences in aspirations are major impediments to the development of class-consciousness. While long-term unemployment has increased, most unemployment is a temporary, if repeated, experience that does not erode people's allegiance to the labour market.

Some sickness and disability is also transient, but once people move onto higher rate benefits, the chances of them ever returning to the labour market have proved to be very low. Disabled people share this characteristic with retirement pensioners, many of whom also become disabled as they get older. Nevertheless, people disabled young or from birth are often very different from people disabled later in life in terms of personal identity and even economic circumstance. Likewise, the experience of lone parenthood, which typically precipitates quite long spells on benefit, is different again. Lone parents may confront similar barriers to employment as other jobseekers, but their prior concerns will typically be to protect their children from further hurt. Moreover, partnering often provides a route both off benefit and frequently into work (Walker and Ashworth, 1998).

Not only are individual experiences diverse, the opportunities and institutions that might foster the collective solidarity necessary to create a welfare class are largely missing. Trade union membership typically lapses with the onset of unemployment and, not surprisingly, trade unions have generally sought to foster the interests of their employed members that may even be in conflict with those of the jobseeker. Claimant unions, informal associations of social security recipients, are not active everywhere, and, except on rare occasions, have not been able to sustain prolonged national campaigns.

Claimants do not even come into contact with each other much during the administration process. Postal claiming replaced personal interviews in the 1970s, and different counters remained long after insurance and assistance activities were integrated at local level, something that many pensioners appreciated, since they felt stigmatised associating with other groups of claimants (Walker and Brittain, 1995). On the other hand, it is just possible that ONE, the single work focused gateway, and the ubiquitous use of personal advisers that characterises Labour's recent reforms, might draw attention to communalities in the experience of claimants and act as a catalyst for collective action.

In-work benefits also had the potential to forge a discrete economic class, one separate from that which currently underpins the bottom of the class structure. Such benefits gave jobseekers and workers with families a vested interest in wage rates below those generally prevailing for entry level jobs, since they had access to subsidies denied people without children. The econometric work on the substitution and displacement effects of Britain's in-work benefits is inconclusive (Walker, 2000), but qualitative research reveals that Employment Service staff felt that jobseekers without children were placed at a marked disadvantage (Vincent et al, 2000).

Postal claiming and the invisibility of Family Credit recipients in the workplace acted against the formation of an interest class, and the current merging of in-work benefits into the tax system removes them as the potential foundation of a benefit class. Wage subsidies, however, will continue to generate different interest groups within the working class in their new guise as tax credits.

Finally, not much evidence has been unearthed in support of a welfare class founded on either cultural or pyschosocial dependency. It did not feature strongly in the empirical research literature and nor, therefore, in the explanations for the growth in claimant numbers. Unemployed and disabled claimants typically retain prior attachments to work, as do many lone parents, and it is other barriers that prevent them from working. Falling caseloads in the context of the buoyant economy of the late 1990s support this contention. So, too, do the programme evaluations that show coercive and active labour market policies working most effectively in areas of low unemployment (Smith et al, 2000; Hasluck, 2000).

Fraud exists, but official figures indicate that it is restricted to a small number of claimants. Likewise, while claimants say that they need to work while claiming benefits in order to make ends meet, few appear to do so, albeit possibly through lack of opportunity (Shaw et al, 1996b). Some qualitative research suggests that abuse of the system is prevalent in certain areas, but there is little evidence to suggest that it is geographically widespread (Dennis, 1997).

The possibility that dependency manifests itself in welfare communities in particular localities, rather than as a welfare class, is not thoroughly investigated in this book and warrants further analysis. The processes involved in generating poor places have been discussed elsewhere, with housing policy often implicated in their formation (Walker and Park, 1998). With the sale of council houses and the decline in new building, need came to exceed supply and allocation policies limited intake to the most disadvantaged groups. The result was that some local authority estates became the refuges of lone parents, pensioners and others receiving welfare benefits. Furthermore, working residents on local authority estates tended to hold jobs that were particularly at risk during the recessions of the 1980s and early 1990s, resulting in a further spatial concentration of unemployment and income poverty.

The extent to which these processes triggered, or were reinforced by, psychosocial or cultural dependency is unknown, but the belief that they are important underpins a number of recent initiatives undertaken by the Social Exclusion Unit established by the Labour government in 1997. However, Lee and Murie (1997) counsel against the danger of poor estates becoming a stereotype; many council estates retain a social mix and the map of deprivation, both at national and local level, differs markedly from a map of tenure. Likewise, as already noted, spatial concentrations of long-term unemployment and incapacity may be explicable in terms of the complex two-way associations between poverty and poor health. Moreover, there is also evidence that spatial concentrations of benefit recipients can, in the right circumstances, be a powerful force for social regeneration rather than a mechanism generating cultural dependency (Holman, 1998).

What has been learned

On the basis of the evidence assembled in this book, the answer to the question 'Is there a welfare class?' must be 'No'. There are, however, large numbers of people who are reliant for varying lengths of time on social security benefits. Many are poor even while in receipt of benefits, and the sense of stigma can add to the social exclusion that some claimants experience. However, poverty and social exclusion would undoubtedly be much worse in the absence of cash benefits.

Increased caseloads reflect the fall-out of 30 years of social and economic change. To the extent that this change has proved to be less painful for specific individuals and families and society as a whole because of Britain's panoply of benefit provisions, then social security deserves to be judged more as a substantial success than as a substantial failure.

Notes

[1] A mean of £91 was recorded for 1996/97 for all pensioner units, inflated in the text to 1998 prices (DSS, 1999c). 1996/97 values for couple and single pensioners were £120 and £63 respectively.

[2] In April 2000 the Labour government announced its intention to introduce a minimum age at which occupational pensions can be paid, although this met with instant opposition from trade unions and the pensioner lobby.

References and further reading

ABI (Association of British Insurers) (1997 and 1998) *Insurance trends – Quarterly statistics and research review*, vols 14 and 16, London: ABI.

Acheson, D. (1998) *Independent Inquiry into Inequalities in Health*, London: The Stationery Office (Committee chaired by Sir Donald Acheson).

Adams, E. (1999) *Incapacity benefit in Glasgow: Comparative study*, Report to Glasgow Development Agency, Glasgow.

Alcock, P. (1999) 'Employment and social exclusion', in J. Lind and I. Moller (eds) *Inclusion and exclusion: Unemployment and non-standard employment in Europe*, Aldershot: Ashgate, pp 149-66.

Amzallag, J. (1996) *Replacement ratios: Comparability and trends*, Reports II-III NUSA DUA 25th General Assembly, 13-19 November 1995, Geneva: ISSA.

Anderson, P. and Mann, N. (1997) *Safety first: The making of New Labour*, London: Granta.

Anderton, B., Riley, R. and Young, G. (1999) *The New Deal for young people: First year analysis of the implications for the macroeconomy*, Sheffield: Employment Service, Research and Development, ESR 33.

Arthur, S. et al (1999) *New Deal for disabled people: Early implementation*, DSS Research Report No 106, London: CDS.

Ashworth, J. (1995) 'The empirical relationship between budgetary deficits and government expenditure growth: An examination using cointegration', *Public Finance*, vol 50, pp 1-18.

Ashworth, K. and Walker, R. (1993) 'How family credit works', *Benefits*, vol 7, pp 27-8.

Ashworth, K. and Youngs, R. (2000) *Prospects of part-time work: The impact of the Back to Work Bonus*, DSS Research Report No 115, London: CDS.

Askham, J., Hancock, R. and Hills, J. (1995) *Opinions on pensions: Older people's attitudes to incomes, taxes and benefits*, London: Age Concern Institute of Gerontology, King's College.

Atkinson, A. (1970) *Poverty in Britain and the reform of social security*, Cambridge: Cambridge University Press.

Audit Commission (1997) *Retiring nature: Early retirement in local government*, Abingdon: Audit Commission.

Audit Commission (2000) 'Retiring nature: Early retirement in local government', *Audit Commission Update*, March.

Bairam, E. and Ward, B. (1993) 'The externality effect of government expenditure on investment in OECD countries', *Applied Economics*, vol 25, no 711.

Banks, J., Blundell, R. and Lewbel, A. (1996) 'Tax reform and welfare measurement: do we need demand system estimation?', *The Economic Journal*, vol 106, pp 1227-41.

Barnett, J. (1982) *Inside the treasury*, London: Andre Deutsch.

Barnes, H., Thornton. P. and Maynard Campbell, S. (1998) *Disabled people and employment: A review of research and development work*, Bristol/York: The Policy Press/Joseph Rowntree Foundation.

Barr, N. and Coulter, F. (1990) 'Social security: solution or problem?', in J. Hills (ed) *The state of welfare* (1st edn), Oxford: Clarendon Press, pp 274-337.

Barrientos, A. (1998) 'Supplementary pension coverage in Britain', *Fiscal Studies*, vol 19, pp 429-46.

Bartley, M. and Owen, C. (1996) 'Relation between socioeconomic status, employment and health during economic change, 1973 - 1993', *BMJ*, vol 313, 24 August.

Beatty, C. and Fothergill, S. (1999a) *Incapacity benefit and unemployment*, Sheffield: Centre for Regional Economic and Social Research, Sheffield Hallam University.

Beatty, C. and Fothergill, S. (1999b) *Labour market detachment in rural England*, Rural Development Commission Research, Report 40.

Beatty, C. et al (1997) *The real level of unemployment*, Sheffield: Centre for Regional Economic and Social Research, Sheffield Hallam University.

Beattie, R. and McGillwray, W. (1995) 'A risky strategy: Reflections on the World Bank Report "Averting the old age crisis"', *International Social Security Review*, vol 3-4/95, pp 5-22, Geneva: ISSA.

Bell, I., Houston, N. and Heyes, R. (1997) 'Workless households, unemployment and economic inactivity', *Labour Market Trends*, September.

Benefits Agency (1997) *Benefit review: Disability living allowance: Report on main study*, Leeds: Benefit Agency Security (Benefit Review Team).

Benefits Agency (1999) *Business Plan, 1999/2000*, Leeds: Benefits Agency.

Bennett, F. and Walker R. (1998) *Working with work*, York: YPS for the Joseph Rowntree Foundation.

Benezeval, M., Judge, K. and Whitehead, M. (1995) *Tackling inequalities in health: An agenda for action*, London: Kings Fund Institute.

Berthoud, R. (1998a) *Disability benefits: A review of the issues and options for reform*, York: Joseph Rowntree Foundation.

Berthoud, R. (1998b) 'Small change: the benefits agenda for disabled people', *New Economy*, vol 5, pp 224-29.

Berthoud, R., Lakey, J. and McKay, S. (1993) *The economic problems of disabled people*, London: Policy Studies Institute.

Beveridge, Sir W. (1942) *Social insurance and allied services*, Cmnd 6404, London: HMSO.

Bingley, P. and Walker, I. (1997) 'The labour supply, unemployment and participation of lone mothers in in-work transfer programmes', *The Economic Journal*, vol 107, pp 1375-90.

Blair, T. (1997a) 'The 21st century welfare state', Speech to the Social Policy and Economic Performance Conference, Amsterdam, 24 January.

Blair, T. (1997b) 'The will to win', Speech on the Aylesbury Estate, Southwark, 2 June.

Blair, T. (1999) 'Beveridge revisited: a welfare state for the 21st century', in R. Walker (ed) *Ending child poverty: Popular welfare for the 21st century*, Bristol: The Policy Press, pp 7-18.

Blundell, R., and Johnson, P. (1996) *Pensions and retirement in the UK*, London: IFS Mimeo prepared for the International Social Security Conference Project Pre-conference.

Blundell, R. and Johnson, P. (1997) *Pensions and retirement in the UK*, Cambridge, MA: National Bureau of Economic Research Inc.

Bone, M. et al (1992) *Retirement and retirement plans*, A survey carried out by Social Survey Division of OPCS on behalf of the DSS, London: HMSO.

Bottomley, D., McKay, S. and Walker, R. (1997) *Unemployment and jobseeking*, DSS Research Report No 62, London: HMSO.

Bradshaw, J. (1998) 'International comparisons of support for lone parents', in R. Ford and J. Millar (eds) *Private lives and public responses: Lone parenthood and future policy in the UK*, London: Policy Studies Institute, pp 154-68.

Bradshaw, J. and Millar, J. (1991) *Lone parent families in the UK*, DSS Research Report No 6, London: HMSO.

Bradshaw, J. et al (1996) *The employment of lone parents: A comparison of policy in 20 countries*, London: Family Policy Studies Centre.

Brown, J. (1984) *The disability income system*, London: Policy Studies Institute.

Browning, M. (1992) 'Children and household economic behaviour', *Journal of Economic Literature*, vol 30, no 3, pp 1434-75.

Bryson, A. (1998) 'Lone mothers' earnings', in R. Ford and J. Millar (eds) *Private lives and public responses*, London: Policy Studies Institute, pp 169-92.

Bryson, A. and Marsh, A. (1996) *Leaving family credit*, DSS Research Report No 48, London: HMSO.

Bryson, A., Ford, R. and White, M. (1997) *Making work pay*, York: YPS.

Bryson, C. (1997) 'Benefit claimants: villains or victims?', in R. Jowell, J. Curtice, A. Park, L. Brook, K. Thomson and C. Bryson (eds) *British social attitudes the 14th report*, Aldershot: Ashgate Publishing Ltd, pp 73-88.

BSA (1984 onwards) *British Social Attitudes*, Aldershot: Dartmouth.

Burchardt, T. and Hills, J. (1997) *Private welfare insurance and social security: Pushing the boundaries*, York: Joseph Rowntree Foundation.

Burgess, S. and Rees, H. (1996) 'Job tenure in Great Britain 1975-1992', *Economic Journal*, vol 106, pp 334-44, London: Royal Economic Society.

Burgess, S. and Rees, H. (1997) *A disaggregation analysis of the evolution of job tenure in Great Britain 1975-1993*, Discussion Paper No 1711, October, London: Centre for Economic Policy Research.

Burtless, G. (1997) 'Social security's long-term budget outlook', *National Tax Journal*, vol L, pp 399-412.

Burton, D. (1997) 'Ethnicity and occupational welfare: A study of pension scheme membership in Britain, notes and issues', *Work, Employment and Society*, vol 11, no 3, pp 505-18, Durham: British Sociological Association.

Campbell, N. (1999a) 'The decline of employment among older people in Britain', in *Persistent poverty and lifetime inequality: The evidence*, CASE Report No 5, J. Hills (chair) London: HM Treasury, pp 52-61.

Campbell, N. (1999b) 'The decline of employment among older people in Britain', CASE Paper No 19, London: LSE STICERD.

Carnegie Inquiry (1993) *Life work and livelihood in the third age*, Advisory Committee of the Carnegie Inquiry into the Third Age, Dunfermline: Carnegie UK Trust.

Casarico, A. (1998) 'Pension reform and economic performance under imperfect capital markets', *The Economic Journal*, vol 108, pp 344-62.

Casey, B., Hales, J. and Millward, N. (1996) *Employer's pension provision 1994*, DSS Research Report No 58, London: The Stationery Office.

Chamberlayne, P. (1992) 'Income-maintenance and institutional forms – a comparison of France, West-Germany, Italy and Britain 1945-90', *Policy & Politics*, vol 20, pp 299-318.

Clarke, A., Craig, G. and Glendinning, C. (1996) *Small change: The impact of the Child Support Act on lone mothers and children*, London: Family Policy Studies Centre.

Clasen, J. (1994) *Paying the jobless*, Aldershot: Ashgate.

Clasen, J., Gould, A. and Vincent, J. (1998) *Voices within and without: Responses to long-term unemployment in Germany, Sweden and Britain*, Bristol: The Policy Press.

Coddington, A. and Perryman, M. (1998) *The moderniser's dilemma: Radical politics in the age of Blair*, London: Lawrence and Wishart.

Commission of the European Communities Directorate-General for Single Market and Financial Services (1997) *Supplementary pensions in the single market – A green paper*, COH (97) 283 final, Brussels: The Commission.

Commission on Social Justice (1994) *Social justice: Strategies for national renewal*, London: Vintage.

Conservative Party (1997) *You can only be sure with the Conservatives: The Conservative manifesto 1997*, London: Conservative Central Office.

Convery, P. (1997) 'Unemployment', in A. Walker and C. Walker, *Britain divided*, London: Child Poverty Action Group, pp 170-97.

Corden, A. (1995) *Changing perspectives on take-up*, York: Social Policy Research Unit, University of York.

Cousins, C., Jenkins, J. and Laux, R. (1998) 'Disability data from the LFS: comparing 1997-8 with the past', *Labour Market Trends*, June.

Craig, P. and Greenslade, M. (1998) 'First findings from the disability follow up to the Family Resources Survey', London: DSS.

Creedy, J. (ed) (1995) *The economics of ageing*, Aldershot: E. Elgar.

CSO (Central Statistical Office) (1998) *Population Trends*, London: The Stationery Office.

CSO (2000) *Economic Trends*, London: The Stationery Office.

Curry, C. (1996) *PENSIM: A dynamic simulation model of pensioners' incomes*, London: DSS, Analytical Services Division.

Dawes, L. (1994) *Long-term unemployment and labour market flexibility*, Leicester: Centre for Labour Market Studies, University of Leicester.

Dawson, A. and Evans, G. (1987) 'Pensioners' incomes and expenditure 1970-1985', *Employment Gazette* (May), London: HSMO.

Deacon, A. (1981) 'Unemployment and politics in Britain since 1945', in B. Showler and A. Sinfield (eds) *The workless state*, London: Martin Robertson, pp 59-88.

Deacon, A. (1997) 'Welfare to work: options and issues', *Social Policy Review 9*, London: SPA.

Deacon, A. (1999) 'The balance of rights and responsibilities within welfare', in R. Walker (ed) *Ending child poverty: Popular welfare for the 21st century*, Bristol: The Policy Press, pp 75-82.

Deacon, A. and Mann, K. (1997) 'Moralism and modernity: the paradox of the New Labour thinking on welfare', *Benefits*, vol 20, September.

Dennis, N. (1997) *The invention of permanent poverty*, Choice in welfare series No 34, London: Health and Welfare Unit, Institute of Economic Affairs.

Desai, M. et al (1999) 'Gender and the labour market', in P. Gregg and J. Wadsworth (eds) *The state of working Britain*, Manchester: Manchester University Press, pp 168-85.

DfEE (Department for Education and Employment) (1998) *Labour market and skills trends 1998/9*, Suffolk: DfEE Publications.

DfEE (1999) *Smith welcomes continued improvement in employment and falling unemployment*, DfEE Press Release, 78/99 17 February.

DfEE (2000) *Labour Market Trends*, vol 107.

DHSS (1985) *Reform of social security*, Cmnd 9517, London: HMSO.

Dilnot, A. and Johnson, P. (1993) *Taxation of private pensions*, London: Institute for Fiscal Studies.

Dilnot, A. and Walker, I. (1989) *The economics of social security*, Oxford: Oxford University Press.

Dilnot, A. et al (1994) *Pensions policy in the U.K: An economic analysis*, London: Institute for Fiscal Studies.

Disney, R. and Stears, G. (1996) *Why is there a decline in defined benefit pension plan membership in Britain?*, Institute for Fiscal Studies Working Paper Series No W96/4, London: IFS.

Disney, R. and Webb, S. (1991) 'Why are there so many long term sick in Britain?', *The Economic Journal*, vol 101, March, pp 252-62.

Disney, R., Grundy, E. and Johnson, P. (1997) *The dynamics of retirement*, DSS Research Report No 72, London: The Stationery Office.

Disney, R., Meghir, C. and Whitehouse, E. (1994) 'Retirement behaviour in Britain', *Fiscal Studies*, vol 15, no 1.

Disability Living Allowance Advisory Board (1998) *The future of Disability Living Allowance and Attendance Allowance*, London: DLAAB.

Dobson, B. et al (1995) *Diet choice and poverty*, London: Family Policy Studies Centre.

DoH (Department of Health) (1999) *Modernising mental health services: Safe sound and supportive*, London: DoH.

Dorsett, R. et al (1998) *Leaving Incapacity Benefit*, DSS Research Report No 86, London: The Stationery Office.

DSS (Department of Social Security) (1974) *Report of the committee on one-parent families (Finer Report)*, Cmnd 5629, London: HMSO.

DSS (1990) *The way ahead: Benefits for disabled people*, Cm 917, London: HMSO.

DSS (1993) *The growth of social security*, London: HMSO.

DSS (1996a) *Memorandum to the Social Security Committee Inquiry into Incapacity Benefit*, HC paper 80-I, November.

DSS (1996b) *The government's expenditure plans*, London: HMSO.

DSS (1997a) *Households below average incomes: A statistical analysis 1979-1994/5*, London: DSS and the Government Statistical Service.

DSS (1997b) *Welfare reform focus files*, London: Central Office of Information.

DSS (1997c) *Pensioners' income series 1995/6*, London: DSS, Analytical Services Division.

DSS (1997d) *Income related benefits: Estimates of take-up in 1995/96*, London: The Stationery Office.

DSS (1997e) *The government's expenditure plans, 1997-98 to 1999-2000: Social Security Departmental Report*, Cm 3613, London: The Stationery Office.

DSS (1997f) *Glossary of terms, abbreviations and acronyms used in social security*, London: DSS.

DSS (1998a) *New ambitions for our country: A new contract for welfare*, Cm 3805, London: The Stationery Office.

DSS (1998b) *Cross benefit analysis: Population of working age on key benefits; provisional analysis*, London: Government Statistical Service.

DSS (1998c) *Second tier pension provision 1995/96*, Newcastle upon Tyne: DSS, Analytical Services Division.

DSS (1998d), *Social security statistics 1998*, Leeds: CDS.

DSS (1998e) *A new contract for welfare support for disabled people,* Cm 4103, London: The Stationery Office.

DSS (1999a) *Cross benefit analysis: Quarterly bulletin on the population of working age on key benefits,* May.

DSS (1999b) *Incapacity benefit and severe disablement allowance quarterly statistics,* August, London: DSS.

DSS (1999c), *Social security statistics 1999,* Leeds: CDS.

DSS (1999d) *Income support, Quarterly statistical enquiry, November,* London: DSS.

DSS (1999e) *Income related benefits estimates of take-up in 1996/7 (rev) and 1997/8,* London: DSS.

DSS (1999f) *Households below average incomes: A statistical analysis 1994/5-1997/8,* London: DSS and the Government Statistical Service.

DSS (1999g) *Opportunity for all: Tacking poverty and social exclusion,* Cm 4445, London: The Stationery Office.

DSS (1999h) *Social security departmental report: The government's expenditure plans 1999/2000,* Cm 4214, London: The Stationery Office.

DSS (2000a) *The changing welfare state: Social security spending,* London: DSS.

DSS (2000b) *Income support quarterly statistical enquiry, November 1999,* London: DSS.

DSS (2000c) *The changing welfare state: Pensioner incomes,* Paper 2 London: DSS.

DSS (2000d) *Disability care and mobility benefits – August 1999 quarterly statistical enquiry,* London: DSS.

DSS (2000e) *Client group analysis: Quarterly bulletin on the population of working age on key benefits – August 1999,* London: DSS.

DSS (2000f) *Incapacity benefit quarterly statistical enquiry, November 1999,* London: DSS.

DSS (2000g) *The results of the Area Benefit Review from April 1998 to March 1999 and measurements for the Public Service Agreement: Fraud and error in claims for Income Support and Jobseeker's Allowance,* London: DSS, Analytic Services Division.

DSS/DfEE (1998) *Discussion paper: Personal adviser service, Paper to consultation meeting 12 May 1998*, New Deal for Disabled People.

Eardley, T. et al (1995) *Social assistance in the OECD countries*, DSS Research Report No 46/47, London: The Stationery Office.

Echevarria, C.A. (1995) 'On age distribution of population, government expenditure and fiscal federalism', *Journal of Population Economics*, vol 8, pp 301-13.

Edgeley, J. and Sweeney, K. (1998) 'Characteristics of JSA claimants who have joined the claimant count for Incapacity Benefit', *Labour Market Trends*, February, pp 79-83.

Elias, P. (1997) *The effect of unemployment benefits on the labour force participation of partners*, Warwick: Institute for Employment Research.

Ellison, R., Tinsley, K. and Housta, N. (1997) 'British labour force projections 1997-2006', *Employment Gazette* (February), London: Government Statistical Service.

EOC (Equal Opportunities Commission) (1997) *Analysis of incomes received by men and women pensioners 1975 and 1994/95*, Manchester: EOC.

EPI (Employment Policy Institute) (1996 and 1997) 'Commentary and key points', *Employment Audit*, Issues 1, 4 and 5 (1996 and 1997) London: EPI.

EPI (1998) 'Britain's "hidden jobless": non-employment and labour market attachment', *Employment Audit*, Issue 7, Spring, London: EPI.

Erens, B. and Ghate, D. (1993) *Invalidity benefit: A longitudinal survey of new recipients*, DSS Research Report No 20, London: HMSO.

Ermisch, J. (1991) *Lone parenthood: An economic analysis*, Cambridge: National Institute of Economic and Social Research.

Ermisch, J. and Di Salvo, P. (1996) 'The economic determinants of young people's household formation', *Economica*, vol 64, pp 627-44.

Ermisch, J. and Wright, R. E. (1991) 'Welfare benefits and lone parents' employment in Great Britain', *Journal of Human Resources*, vol 26, no 3, pp 424-56.

Evans, M. (1995) 'Out for the count: The incomes of the non-household population and the effect of their exclusion from national income profiles: Discussion Paper WSP/111', London: STICERD, London School of Economics.

Evans, M. (1998) 'Social security: dismantling the pyramids?', in H. Glennerster and J. Hills (eds) *The state of welfare* (2nd edn), Oxford: Oxford University Press, pp 257-307.

Family Fund (1999) *Annual report 1998/9*, York: The Family Fund.

Feldstein, M. (1998) 'A new era of social security', *Public Interest*, Winter, pp 102-25.

Feldstein, M. and Samwick, A. (1997) *The economics of prefunding social security and medicare benefits*, National Bureau of Economic Research Working Report 6055, MA: National Bureau of Economic Research Inc.

Ferge, Z. (1997) 'The changed welfare paradigm: the individualisation of the social', *Social Policy and Administration*, vol 31, pp 20-44.

Field, F. (1985) *Making welfare work: Reconstructing welfare for the millennium*, London: Institute of Community Studies.

Field, F. (1996a) *Stakeholder welfare*, Choice in Welfare Series No 32, London: Institute of Economic Affairs.

Field, F. (1996b) *How to pay for the future: Building a stakeholders' welfare*, London: Institute of Community Studies.

Field, F. (1997) *Reforming welfare*, London: The Social Market Foundation.

Field, J. and Prior, G. (1996) *Women and pensions*, DSS Research Report No 49, London: HMSO.

Finch, H. and Elam, G. (1995) *Managing money in later life*, DSS Research Report No 38, London: HMSO.

Finlayson, L. and Marsh, A. (1998) *Lone parents on the margins of work*, DSS Research Report No 80, Leeds: CDS.

Finn, D. (1998) 'Labour's New Deal for the unemployed and the stricter benefit regime', *Social Policy Review 10*, London: SPA.

Fisher Committee (1973) *Report on the abuses of social security benefits*, London: HMSO.

Ford, R. (1998) 'Lone mothers' decisions whether or not to work: Childcare in the balance', in R. Ford and J. Millar (eds) *Private lives and public responses: Lone parenthood and future policy in the UK*, London: Policy Studies Institute, pp 1-21.

Ford, R. and Millar, J. (1998) 'Lone parenthood in the UK: Policy dilemmas and solutions', in R. Ford and J. Millar (eds) *Private lives and public responses: Lone parenthood and future policy in the UK*, London: Policy Studies Institute.

Ford, R., Marsh, A. and Finlayson, L. (1998) *What happens to lone parents: A cohort study 1991-1995*, DSS Research Report No 77, London: The Stationery Office.

Ford, R., Marsh, A. and McKay, S. (1995) *Changes in lone parenthood*, DSS Research Report No 40, London: HMSO.

Forrest, R., Leather, P. and Pantazis, C. (1997) *Home ownership in old age: The future of owner-occupation in an ageing society*, Oxford: Anchor Trust.

Gal, J. (1998) 'Categorical benefits in welfare states: Findings from Great Britain and Israel', *International Social Security Review*, vol 51, pp 73-101.

Gallie, D. (1988) 'Employment, unemployment and social stratification', in D. Gallie (ed) *Employment in Britain*, Oxford: Basil Blackwell, pp 465-92.

Geddis, P., Beatty, R. and Tyrell, M. (1997) *Focus on Northern Ireland: A statistical profile*, London, The Stationery Office.

Gibb, K. (1995), *Housing Benefit: The future*, London: National Federation of Housing Associations.

Giddens, A. (1998) *The third way*, Cambridge: Polity Press.

Giles, C., Johnson, P. and McCrae, J. (1997) 'Housing Benefit and financial returns to employment for tenants in the social sector', *Fiscal Studies*, vol 18, pp 49-72.

Ginn, J., and Arber, S. (1999) 'Changing patterns of pension inequality: The impact of privatisation', *Ageing and Society*, vol 19, pp 319-24.

Glennerster, H. and Hills, J. (1998), *The state of welfare*, Oxford: Oxford University Press.

Golding, P. (1998) 'Reporting welfare', Paper presented to BBC seminar on Reporting Welfare Reform, Mansfield College, Oxford, 8-9 September.

Goodman, A. and Webb, S. (1994) *For richer, for poorer: The changing distribution of income in the United Kingdom 1961-91*, Institute for Fiscal Studies Commentary No 42, London: IFS.

Gordon, D. et al (eds) (1999) *Inequalities in health: The evidence presented to the Independent Inquiry into Inequalities in Health*, chaired by Sir Donald Acheson, Bristol: The Policy Press.

Gosling, A., Machin, S. and Meghir, C. (1996) 'What has happened to the wages of men since 1966?', in J. Hills (ed) *New inequalities: The changing distribution of income and wealth in the United Kingdom*, Cambridge: Cambridge University Press, pp 135-57.

Government Actuary (1999) *Occupational pension schemes: Tenth Survey*, London: The Stationery Office.

Grabiner, Lord (2000) *The informal economy*, London: HM Treasury.

Gregg, P. (ed) (1997) *Job wages and poverty*, London: Centre for Economic Performance.

Gregg, P. (1999) 'The impact of unemployment and job loss on future earnings', in J. Hills (ed) *Persistent poverty and lifetime inequality: The evidence*, CASE report No 5, London: HM Treasury, pp 89-96.

Gregg, P. and Wadsworth, J. (1994) *More work in fewer households*, Social Policy Research Finding No 61, York: Joseph Rowntree Foundation.

Gregg, P. and Wadsworth, J. (1996a) 'More work in fewer households', in J. Hills (ed) *New inequalities: The changing distribution of income and wealth in the United Kingdom*, Cambridge: Cambridge University Press, pp 181-207.

Gregg, P. and Wadsworth, J. (1996b) 'The polarisation of work', *Employment Audit*, Issue No 1, London: Employment Policy Institute.

Gregg, P. and Wadsworth, J. (1997a) 'The changing nature of entry jobs in Britain', in P. Gregg (ed) *Jobs wages and poverty*, London: Centre for Economic Performance.

Gregg, P. and Wadsworth, J. (1997b) 'A year in the labour market', *Employment Audit*, Issue No 4, London: Employment Policy Institute.

Gregg, P., Hansen, K. and Wadsworth, J. (1999a) 'The rise of the workless household', in P. Gregg and J. Wadsworth (eds) *The state of working Britain*, Manchester: Manchester University Press, pp 75-89.

Gregg, P., Harkness, S. and Machin, S. (1999b) *Child poverty and its consequences*, Findings, York: Joseph Rowntree Foundation.

Grover, C. and Stewart, J. (1999) '"Market workfare": Social security, social regulation and competitiveness in the 1990s', *Journal of Social Policy*, vol 28, part 1, pp 73-96.

Grundy, E. (1996) 'Population review: (5) the population aged 60 and over', *Population Trends*, vol 84, Summer, pp 14-20.

Grundy, E., Ahlburg, D., Ali, M., Breeze, E. and Sloggett, A. (1999) *Disability in Great Britain*, DSS Research Report No 94, London: Corporate Document Services.

Hales, J. et al (2000) *Evaluation of New Deal for lone parents: Early lessons from the phase one prototype – findings of surveys*, DSS Research Report No 109, London: CDS.

Halsey, A. H. (1993) 'Changes in the family', *Children and Society*, vol 7, no 2, pp 125-36.

Hancock, R. and Jarvis, C. (1994) *Long-term effects of being a carer*, London: HMSO.

Hancock, R., Jarvis, C. and Mueller, G. (1995) *The outlook for incomes in retirement – Social trends and attitudes*, London: Age Concern Institute of Gerontology.

Hancock, R., Mallender, J. and Pudney, S. (1992) 'Constructing a computer model for simulating the future distribution of pensioners' incomes for Great Britain', in R. Hancock and H. Sutherland (eds) *Microsimulation models for public policy analysis: New frontiers*, London: STICERD, London School of Economics.

Hansard (1991) *Social Security forecasting*, Third Report of the Committee of Public Accounts, 22 May.

Harkness, S. (1999) 'Working 9 to 5?', in P. Gregg and J. Wadsworth (eds) *The state of working Britain*, Manchester: Manchester University Press, pp 90-108.

Harkness, S., Machin, S. and Waldfogel, J. (1997) 'Women's pay and family incomes in Britain, 1979-91', in A. Goodman and S. Webb (eds) *For richer for poorer – The changing distribution of income in the UK 1961-91*, Oxford: Oxford University Press.

Harman, H. (1996) *Getting welfare to work: Opportunities for lone mothers*, London: Labour Social Security Policy Paper.

Hasluck, C. (2000) *The New Deal for young people, two years on*, Research and Development Report ESR41, London: DfEE.

Hasluck, C., McKnight, A. and Elias, P. (2000) *Evaluation of New Deal for Lone Parents: Early lessons from the phase one prototype – cost-benefit and econometric analyses*, DSS Research Report No 110, London: CDS.

Hawkes, C. and Garman, A. (1995) *Perceptions of non state pensions*, In-house report No 8, Social Research Branch, London: DSS, Analytical Services Division.

Haskey, J. (1995) 'Trends in marriage and cohabitation: The decline in marriage and the changing pattern of living in partnerships', *Population Trends*, vol 80, pp 5-15.

Haskey, J. (1997) 'Population review: (8) The ethnic minority and overseas-born populations of Great Britain', *Population Trends*, vol 88, pp 13-29.

Haskey, J. (1998) 'One parent families and their dependent children in Great Britain', in R. Ford and J. Millar (eds) *Private lives and public responses*, London: Policy Studies Institute, pp 22-41.

Haskey, J. (1999) 'Cohabitational and marital histories of adults in Great Britain', *Population Trends*, vol 96, pp 13-23.

Hawksworth, J. (1997) 'Macroeconomic implications of an ageing society', *UK economic outlook*, London: Coopers and Lybrand.

Hedges, A. (1998) *Pensions and retirement planning*, DSS Research Report No 83, Leeds: CDS.

Hedges, A. and Thomas, A. (1994) *Making a claim for disability benefits*, DSS Research Report No 27, London: DSS.

Hills, J. (1995) *Joseph Rowntree Foundation inquiry into income and wealth: Volume 1*, York: Joseph Rowntree Foundation.

Hills, J. (ed) (1996) *New inequalities – the changing distribution of income and wealth in the United Kingdom*, Cambridge: Cambridge University Press.

Hills, J. (1998) *Income and wealth: The latest evidence*, York: Joseph Rowntree Foundation.

Hills, J. and Lelkes, O. (1999) 'Social security, selective universalism and patchwork redistribution', in R. Jowell et al (eds) *British social attitudes: The 16th report*, Aldershot: Ashgate, pp 5-22.

Hirst, M. (1997) 'Variation in the administration of Disability Living Allowance', *Social Policy and Administration*, vol 31, pp 136-56.

Hiscock, J. and Hojman, D.E. (1997) 'Social policy in a fast-growing economy: The case of Chile', *Social Policy and Administration*, vol 31, pp 354-70.

HM Treasury (1997) *Employment opportunity in a changing labour market*, Pre-Budget Report Publications: *The modernisation of Britain's tax and benefit system No 1*, London: HM Treasury.

HM Treasury (1998) *The modernisation of Britain's tax and benefit system*, Budget 98 Publications: *The modernisation of Britain's tax and benefit system No 3*, London: HM Treasury.

HM Treasury (1999) *Tackling poverty and extending opportunity*, The modernisation of Britain's tax and benefit system No 4, London: HM Treasury.

HM Treasury (2000) *Tackling poverty and making work pay – Tax credits for the 21st century*, The modernisation of Britain's tax and benefit system No 6, London: HM Treasury.

Hogwood, B.W. (1998) 'Problems of applying a programme approach to intergovernmental policy delivery', *Local Government Studies*, vol 24, pp 34-44.

Holman, B. (1998) *Faith in the poor*, Oxford: Lion Publishing.

Holmes, P., Lynch, M., and Molho, I. (1991) 'An econometric analysis of the growth in numbers claiming invalidity benefit: A review', *Journal of Social Policy*, vol, 19, no 4, pp 57-105.

House of Commons (1991) *Social security forecasting*, Committee of Public Accounts, Twenty-third report session 1990-1, HC 478.

House of Commons Social Security Committee Fifth Report (1997) *Child Support*, House of Commons Session 1996-7, HC 282.

House of Commons Social Security Select Committee on Social Security (1998) Minutes of Evidence, 21st July 1998, Memorandum from the DSS on Child Benefit Fraud, House of Commons Session 1997-8.

Howard, M. (1999) *Enabling government: Joined up policies for a national disability strategy*, London: Fabian Society.

Howarth, C. (1999) *Monitoring poverty and social exclusion, 1999*, York: Joseph Rowntree Foundation, New Policy Institute.

Howarth, C. et al (1998) *Monitoring poverty and social exclusion: Labour's inheritance*, York: New Policy Institute/Joseph Rowntree Foundation.

Howarth, C. et al (1999) *Monitoring poverty and social exclusion 1999: Labour's inheritence*, York: New Policy Institute/Joseph Rowntree Foundation.

Huby, M. and Walker, R. (1989) 'Social security spending in the inner cities', *Public Money and Management*, vol 9, no 1, pp 39-43.

Hutton, W. (1995) *The state we're in*, London: Jonathan Cape.

Iacovou, M. and Berthoud, R. (2000) *Parents and employment*, DSS Research Report No 109, London: CDS.

IDS (Incomes Data Services) (1996) *The rise of money purchase schemes – Tidal wave or dripping tap?*, London: IDS.

IER (Institute for Employment Relations) (1998) *Review of the economy and employment 1997/98*, Coventry: IER.

Inland Revenue (2000) 'Disabled Person's Tax Credit and Disability Working Allowance', *Quarterly Enquiry*, January, London: Inland Revenue.

IOD (Institute of Directors) (1997) *Pension provision – What employers think*, London: IoD.

Jacobs, J. (1994) 'The scroungers who never were: the effects of the 1989 Social Security Act', *Social Policy Review 6*, London: SPA.

Jarvis, S. and Jenkins, S. (1996) *Changing places: Income mobility and poverty dynamics in Britain*, Working Paper No 96-19, ERSC Research Centre on Micro-social Change, Colchester: University of Essex.

Jarvis, S. and Jenkins, S. (1997), 'Income dynamics in Britain: New evidence from the British household panel survey', in P. Gregg (ed) *Jobs wages and poverty*, London: Centre for Economic Performance.

Jarvis, S. and Jenkins, S. (1998) 'Marriage dissolution and income change: Evidence for Britain', in R. Ford and J. Millar (eds) *Private lives and public responses: Lone parenthood and future policy in the UK*, London: Policy Studies Institute, pp 104-17.

Jenkins, S. and Millar, J. (1989) 'Income risk and income maintenance: implications for incentives to work', in A. Dilnot and I. Walker (eds) *The economics of social security*, Oxford: Oxford University Press, pp 137-52.

Johnson, P. (1997) 'Income dynamics: evidence from the Retirement Survey', in R. Disney, E. Grundy and P. Johnson (eds) *The dynamics of retirement*, DSS Research Report No 72, London: The Stationery Office, pp 132-69.

Johnson, P. and Stears, G. (1995) 'Pension Income Inequality', *Fiscal Studies*, 16, 4. London: Institute for Fiscal Studies.

Johnson, P. and Stears, G. (1996) *Why are older pensioners poorer?*, Institute for Fiscal Studies Working Paper Series No W96/13, London: IFS.

Johnson, P., Disney, R. and Stears, G. (1996) *The retirement income inquiry – Pensions: 2000 and beyond Volume 2. Analysis of trends and options*, Folkestone: Shelwing Ltd.

Johnson, P., Dilnot, A., Disney, R. and Whitehouse, E. (1992) *Income: Pensions, earnings and savings in the third age*, Research Paper No 2, The Carnegie Inquiry into the Third Age, Dunfermline: Carnegie UK Trust and IFS.

Jordan, B. et al (1992) *Trapped in poverty?*, London: Routledge.

Joseph, K. (1975) *Reversing the trend: A critical reappraisal of Conservative economic and social policies*, Seven Speeches by the Right Honourable Keith Joseph, Barry Rose.

Judge, K. (1980) 'Beveridge: past, present and future', in C. Sandford, C. Pond and R. Walker (eds) *Taxation and social policy*, London: Heinemann, pp 172-89.

Karanassou, M. and Snower, D.J. (1998) 'How labour market flexibility affects unemployment: Long-term implications of the chain reaction theory', *The Economic Journal*, vol 108, pp 832-49.

Kiernan, K. and Wicks, M. (1990) *Family change and future policy*, London: Family Policy Studies Centre.

Kemp, P. (1997) *A comparative study of housing allowances*. DSS Research Report No 60, Norwich: The Stationery Office.

Kemp, P.A. and McLaverty, P. (1998) 'Private tenants and perverse incentives in the housing benefit scheme', *Environment and Planning*, vol 16, pp 395-409.

Kemp, P., Wilcox, S. and Bramley, G. (1998) 'Housing policy', *New Economy*, vol 5, pp 157-73.

Kempson, E. (1996) *Life on a low income*, York: YPS for the Joseph Rowntree Foundation.

Kempson, E., Bryson, A. and Rowlingson, K. (1994) *Hard times? How poor families make ends meet*, London: Policy Studies Institute.

Kestenbaum, A. (1997) *Disability-related costs and charges for community care*, London: DIG.

Knight, M. and Fletcher, J. (1996) *Tracking study of former incapacity benefit claimants*, Sheffield: ES RED 110.

Kozak, M. (1998) *Employment, family life and the quality of care services: A review of research in the UK*, DfEE Research Report No 54, Suffolk: DfEE Publications.

Labour Party (1997) *New Labour because Britain deserves better*, London: The Labour Party (Great Britain).

Land, H. and Lewis, J. (1997) *The emergence of lone motherhood as a problem in late twentieth century Britain*, London: London School of Economics.

Land, H. and Lewis, J. (1998) 'The problem of lone motherhood in the British context', in R. Ford and J. Millar (eds) *Private lives and public responses*, London: policy Studies Institute, pp 141-53.

Lazar, H. and Stoyko, P. (1998) 'The future of the welfare state', *International Social Security Review*, vol 51, pp 3-36.

Leadbeater, C. and Mulgan, G. (1994) 'The end of unemployment: bringing work to life', in *The end of unemployment: Bringing work to life*, London: Demos Quarterly Special Employment Issue, pp 4-14.

Lee, P. and Murie, A. (1997) *Poverty, housing tenure and social exclusion*, Bristol/York: The Policy Press/Joseph Rowntree Foundation.

Leeming, A., Unell, J. and Walker, R. (1994) *Lone mothers*, DSS Research Report No 30, London: HMSO.

Le Grand, J. (1990) 'The state of welfare', in J. Hills (ed) *The state of welfare*, (1st ed), Oxford: Clarendon Press, pp 338-82.

Le Grand, J., Propper, C. and Robinson, R. (1992) *The economics of social problems*, London: Macmillan.

Leisering, L. and Walker, R. (eds) (1998) *The dynamics of modern society: Poverty, policy and welfare*, Bristol: The Policy Press.

LGA (1997) 'It's a right ... not a lottery': LGA Benefits take up initiative, London: local Government Association.

Lilley, P. (1993) *Benefits and costs: Securing the future of social security*, Mais Lecture, London: DSS.

Lister, R. (1999) 'A modern party of social justice: achievements and missed opportunities', in R. Walker (eds) *Ending child poverty: Popular welfare for the 21st century*, Bristol: The Policy Press, pp 93-100.

Lonsdale, S. (1987) 'Patterns of paid work', in C. Glendenning and J. Millar (eds) *Women in poverty in Britain*, Brighton: Wheatsheaf, pp 92-111.

Lonsdale, S., Lessof, C. and Ferris, G. (1993) *Invalidity Benefit: A survey of recipients*, DSS Research Report No 19, London: DSS.

Loumidis, J. (1999) 'Survey of participants and non-participants', in S. Arthur et al *New Deal for disabled people: Early implementation*, DSS Research Report No 106, London: Corporate Document Services, pp 65-108.

McCarthy, T.A. and Schmidt, S.J. (1997) 'A vector-autoregression analysis of state government expenditure', *American Economic Review*, vol 87, pp 278-82.

McKay, S. and Marsh, A. (1994) *Lone mothers and work: The effects of benefits and maintenance*, London: HMSO.

McKay, S. and Middleton, S. (1998), *Characteristics of older workers*, DfEE Research Report No 45, London: DfEE.

McKay, S. and Rowlingson, K. (1998) 'Choosing lone parenthood? The dynamics of family change', in R. Ford and J. Millar (eds) *Private lives and public responses: Lone parenthood and future policy in the UK*, London: Policy Studies Institute.

McKay, S. and Rowlingson, K. (1999) *Social security in Britain*, London: Macmillan.

McKay, S., Walker, R. and Youngs, R. (1997) *Unemployment and jobseeking before Jobseeker's Allowance*, DSS Research Report, 73, London: The Stationery Office.

McKay, S., Heaver, C. and Walker, R. (2000) *Building up pension rights*, DSS Research Report No 114, London: The Stationery Office.

McKay, S. et al (1999) *Unemployment and jobseeking after the introduction of Jobseeker's Allowance*, DSS Research Report No 87, London: DSS.

McKendrick, J. (1998) 'The "big" picture: Quality in the lives of lone parents', in R. Ford and J. Millar (eds) *Private lives and public responses: Lone parenthood and future policy in the UK*, London: Policy Studies Institute.

McLaughlin, E., Millar, J. and Cooke, D. (1989) *Work and welfare benefits*, Aldershot: Avebury Press.

Maclean, M. (1994), 'Child Support in the UK: making the move from court to agency', *Houston Law Review*, vol 31, no 2, pp 515-36.

Maclean, M. (1998) 'The origins of child support in Britain and the case for a strong child support system', in R. Ford and J. Millar (eds) *Private lives and public responses: Lone parenthood and future policy in the UK*, London: Policy Studies Institute, pp 226-32.

Macmillan, R. (1999a) 'Moral hazard and the benefits system: Explaining contextualisation and microfoundations in political economy', Unpublished dissertation, University of Sheffield.

Macmillan, R. (1999b) *Getting by: Making ends meet at the back of the queue*, Draft report, July, Sheffield: Centre for Regional Economic and Social Research, Sheffield Hallam University.

Maguire, S. (1993) 'Training for a living? The 1990s youth labour market', *Sociology Review*, September, vol 13, pp 2-6.

Maguire, S. (2000) 'Employers' diminishing demand for young people – myth or reality', *Journal of Education and Work*, forthcoming.

Mandell, M. (1997) 'In defence of social security', *New Politics*, vol VI, pp 21-9.

Mandelson, P. and Liddle, R. (1996) *The Blair revolution: Can New Labour deliver?*, London: Faber and Faber.

Mann, K. (1986) 'The making of a claimant class', *Critical Social Policy*, vol 15, pp 62-74.

Mann, K. (1992) *The making of an English underclass*, Milton Keynes: Open University Press.

Marsh, A. and McKay, S. (1993) *Families, work and benefits*, London: Policy Studies Institute.

Marsh, A., Ford, R. and Finlayson, L. (1997) *Lone parents, work and benefits*, DSS Research Report No 61, London: The Stationery Office.

Martin, J. and White, A. (1988) *The financial circumstances of disabled adults living in private households*, OPCS Disability Surveys Report 2, London: OPCS.

Martin et al (1998) *The prevalence of disability among adults*, OPCS Disability Surveys Report 1, London: OPCS.

Mashaw, J. (1998) 'Disability: Why does the search for good programs continue?', in E. Kingson and J. Schulz (eds) *Social security in the 21st century*, Oxford: Oxford University Press.

Matheson, J. and Pullinger, J. (eds) (1999) *Social trends*, London: The Stationery Office.

Matheson, J. and Summerfield, C. (1999) *Social focus on older people*, London: The Stationery Office.

Matheson, J. and Summerfield, C. (2000) *Social Trends*, London: The Stationery Office.

Mauro, P. (1998), 'Corruption and the composition of government expenditure', *Journal of Public Economics*, vol 69, pp 263-79.

Mead, L. (1986) *Beyond entitlement*, New York, NY: Free Press.

Meager, N. et al (1998) *Employment of disabled people: Assessing the extent of participation*, DfEE Research Report No 69, London: DfEE.

Meager, N. et al (1999) *Monitoring the Disability Discrimination Act (DDA) 1995*, DfEE Research Report No 119, London: DfEE.

Meltzer, I. et al (1995) *OPCS survey of psychiatric morbidity in Great Britain*, London: HMSO.

Merton, R. (1983) 'On the role of social security as a means for efficient risk sharing in an economy where human capital is not tradable', in Z. Bodie and J. Shoven (eds) *Financial aspects of the United States pensions system*, IL: Chicago University Press.

Middleton, S. and Ashworth, K. (1997) *Small fortunes: Spending on children, poverty and parental sacrifice*, York: Joseph Rowntree Foundation.

Middleton, S. and Thomas, M. (1994) 'The "bare essentials": parents' minimum budget for children', in S. Middleton, K. Ashworth and R. Walker (eds) *Family fortunes: Pressures on parents and children in the 1990s*, London: Child Poverty Action Group, pp 9-22.

Middleton, S., Ashworth, K and Walker, R. (1994) *Family fortunes*, London: CPAG Ltd.

Miles, D. (1997a) 'Financial markets, ageing and social welfare', *Fiscal Studies*, vol 18, no 2, London: Institute for Fiscal Studies.

Miles, D. (1997b) *Modelling the impact of demographic change upon the economy*, London: Imperial College and CEPR.

Miles, D. (1997c) 'The implications of switching from unfunded to funded pension systems', *National Institute Economic Review*, London: NIESR.

Moore, J. (1987) 'Welfare and dependency', Speech to the Conservative Constituency Parties Association, September.

Morris, L. (1994) *Dangerous classes: The underclass and social citizenship*, London: Routledge.

Morris, L. and Ritchie, J. (1994) *Income maintenance and living standards*, London: Social and Community Planning Research.

MSC (Manpower Services Commission) (1975) *Manpower Services Commission, Annual report 1974-75*, London: HMSO.

MSC (1986) *Manpower Services Commission, Annual report 1985-86*, London: HMSO.

Murray, C. (1984) *Losing ground*, New York, NY: Basic Books.

Murray, C. (2000) 'Baby beware', *The Sunday Times, Section 5 (News Review)*, London: News International, pp 1-2.

NAPF (National Association of Pension Funds) (1998) *Annual survey of occupational pension schemes 1997*, London: NAPF.

Nichol, C. (1997) 'Patterns of pay: results from the New Earnings Survey', *Labour Market Trends* (November), London: The Stationery Office.

Nickell, S. (1999) 'Unemployment in Britain', in P. Gregg and J. Wadsworth (eds) *The state of working Britain*, Manchester: Manchester University Press, pp 7-28.

Nickell, S. and Bell, B. (1995) 'The collapse in the demand for the unskilled and unemployed across the OECD', *Oxford Review of Economic Policy*, vol 11, no 1, pp 40-62.

Noble, M. et. al (1997) 'The spread of Disability Living Allowance', *Disability and Society*, vol 12, no 5, pp 741-51.

Nomura, M. (1991) 'The displacement effect on government expenditure of two oil crisis', *Manchester School of Economic and Social Studies*, vol LIX, p 408.

OECD (Organisation for Economic Co-operation and Development) (1998) *Employment Outlook*, Paris: OECD.

OECD (1999) *Economic Outlook 66*, Paris: OECD.

Ogus, A., Barendt, E. and Wikeley, N. (1995) *The law of social security* (4th edn), Oxford: Butterworths.

Oldfield, N. and Yu, A. (1993) *The cost of a child: Living standards for the 1990s*, London: Child Poverty Action Group.

Oliver, M. and Barnes, C. (1998) *Disabled people and social policy: From exclusion to inclusion*, London: Longman.

ONS (Office for National Statistics) (1998) *Results from the 1995 General Household Survey,* London: The Stationery Office.

ONS (1998a) *Living in Britain: Results from the 1996 General Household Survey*, London: The Stationery Office.

ONS (1998b) *Abstract of Statistics, 1998*, London: The Stationery Office.

ONS (1999) *Labour Market Trends*, vol 107, no 12, December, London: The Stationery Office.

ONS (2000) *Labour Market Trends*, vol 108, no 4, April, London: The Stationery Office.

Oorschot, W. van (1991) 'Non take up of social security benefit in Europe', *Journal of European Social Policy*, vol 1, no 1, pp 15-30.

Oppenheim, C. (1994) *The welfare state: Putting the record straight*, London: CPAG.

Palley, T.I. (1998) 'The economics of social security: An old Keynesian perspective', *Journal of Post Keynesian Economics*, vol 21, pp 93-110.

Paterson, J. (2000) *Disability rights handbook* (24th edn), April 2000-2001, London: Disability Alliance.

Payne, J. and Range, J. (1998) *Lone parents' lives: An analysis of partnership, employment and housing histories in the 1958 British birth cohort*, DSS Research Report 78, London: The Stationery Office.

PIA (Personal Investment Authority) (1997) *Third survey of the persistency of life and pensions policies*, London: PIA.

Philpott, J. (1990) *A solution to long-term unemployment: The job guarantee*, London: EPI.

Pierson, C. (1998) 'Contemporary challenges to welfare state development', *Political Studies*, vol XLVI, pp 777 94.

Poole, C. (1997) 'Retirement on grounds of ill-health', *BMJ*, vol 314, 29 March.

Powell, M. and Hewitt, M. (1998) 'The end of the welfare state?', *Social Policy and Administration*, vol 32, pp 1-13.

Power, C., and Matthews, S. (1997) 'Origins of health inequalities in a national population sample', *The Lancet*, vol 350, 29 November.

PRG (Pension Reform Group) (1998) *We all need pensions – The prospects for pension provision*, London: The Stationery Office.

Prior, G. and Field, J. (1996) *Pensions and divorce*, DSS Research Report No 50, London: HMSO.

Public Accounts Committee (1991) *Social security forecasting*, House of Commons Paper, 478, May.

Rainford, L. et al (2000) *Health in England, 1998: Investigating the links between social inequalities and health*, London: ONS.

Retirement Income Inquiry (Chaired by Sir John Anson) (1995) *Pensions 2000 and beyond*, Volume 1, Report. Folkestone: Shelwing Ltd.

Ritchie, J. and Snape, D. (1993) 'Invalidity benefit: A preliminary qualitative study of the factors affecting its growth', London: SCPR.

Richards, S. (2000) 'The Prime Mister loses control', *New Statesman*, 7 February.

Roberts, K. (1995) *Youth and employment in modern Britain*, Oxford: Oxford University Press.

Roberts, K. and Lawton, D. (1998) *Reaching its target? Disability Living Allowance for children*, SPRU Social Policy Reports No 9, York: Social Policy Research Unit, University of York.

Rowlingson, K. et al (1997) *Social security fraud: The role of penalties*, DSS Research Report No 64, London: The Stationery Office.

Rowlingson, K. and Berthoud, R. (1996) *Disability, benefits and employment*, DSS Research Report No 54, London: DSS.

Sainsbury, R., Hirst, M. and Lawton, D. (1995) *Evaluation of Disability Living Allowance and Attendance Allowance*, DSS Research Report No 41, London: DSS.

Samwick, A.A. (1998) 'New evidence on pensions, social security, and the timing of retirement', *Journal of Public Economics*, vol 70, pp 207-36.

Schluter, C. (1997) 'On the performance of social benefit systems', *The Economic Journal*, vol 107, pp 489-502.

Seidman, L.S. (1998) 'The case for funding social security', *Public Interest*, Winter, pp 93-101.

Shaw, A., Walker, R., Ashworth, K., Jenkins, S. and Middleton, S. (1996) *Moving off Income Support: Barriers and bridges*, DSS Research Report No 53, London: HMSO.

Shaw, A., Kellard, K. and Walker, R. (1996b) *Barriers, bridges and behaviour*, In-house Report No 18, London: DSS.

Shaw, C. and Haskey, J. (1999) 'New estimates and projections of the population cohabiting in England and Wales', *Population Trends*, vol 95, Spring, pp 1-18.

Shaw, M., Dorling, D., Gordon, D. and Davey Smith, G. (1999) *The widening gap: Health inequalities and policy in Britain*, Bristol: The Policy Press.

Shouls, S. et al (1999) The health and socio-economic circumstances of British lone mothers over the last two decades', *Population Trends*, 95, pp 41-5.

Shropshire, J. and Middleton, S. (1999) *Small expectations: Learning to be poor?*, York: York Publishing Sevices.

Shropshire, J., Warton, R. and Walker, R. (1999) *Unemployment and jobseeking: The experience of people with disabilities*, Research Report No 103, London: DfEE.

Sly, F. (1996) 'Ethnic minority participation in the labour market: trends from the Labour Force Survey 1984-1995', *Labour Market Trends*, July, vol 259.

Sly, F., Thair, T. and Risdon, A. (1999) 'Disability and the labour market: Results from the winter 1998/9 LFS', *Labour Market Trends*, September, vol 455.

Smith, A. et al (2000) *Understanding the impact of Jobseeker's Allowance*, DSS Research Report No 111, London: CDS.

Social Security Departmental Report (1998) *The Government's expenditure plans 1998/9*, Cmmd 3913, Norwich: The Stationery Office.

Social Security Select Committee (1993) *Disability Benefits: The delivery of Disability Living Allowance*, HC 284, April, London: House of Commons.

Social Security Select Committee (1997) *Incapacity Benefit*, HC 80, March, London: House of Commons.

Social Security Select Committee (1998) *Disability Living Allowance*, HC paper 641, May.

Social Security Select Committee (1999) *Disability Living Allowance*, HC 63, February, London: House of Commons.

Stafford, B. (1998) *National Insurance and the contributory principle*, In-house Report No 39, London: DSS.

Stationery Office, The (2000a) *Annual Abstract of Statistics, 2000*, London: The Stationery Office.

Stationery Office, The (2000b) *Social Trends 30, 2000 Edition*, London: The Stationery Office.

Stationery Office, The (2000c) *Living in Britain 1998: Results from the General Household Survey*, London: The Stationery Office.

Stears, G. (1997) 'Occupational and other non-state pensions', in R. Disney, E. Grundy and P. Johnson (eds) *The dynamics of retirement*, DSS Research Report 72, London: DSS, pp 170-93.

Stewart, M. (1999) 'Low pay in Britain', in P. Gregg and J. Wadsworth (eds) *The state of working Britain*, Manchester: Manchester University Press, pp 225-48.

Stuttard, N. (1998) 'The effects of taxes and benefits on household income, 1996-97', *Economic Trends*, no 533, London: HMSO.

Sutherland, H. (1996) *Households, individuals and the re-distribution of income*, DAE Working Papers Amalgamated Series No 9614, Department of Applied Economics, University of Cambridge.

Swales, K. (1998a) *Incapacity Benefit tracking exercise*, In-house Report No 44, London: DSS.

Swales, K. (1998b) *A study of Disability Living Allowance and Attendance Allowance awards*, In-house report No 41, London: DSS.

Sweeney, K. and McMahon, D. (1998) 'The effect of Jobseeker's Allowance on the claimant count', *Labour Market Trends*, April, pp 195-203.

Tanner, S. (1997) 'The dynamics of retirement behaviour', in R. Disney, E. Grundy and P. Johnson (eds) *The dynamics of retirement*, DSS Research Report No 72, London: The Stationery Office, pp 25-72.

Taylor-Gooby, P. (1997) 'European welfare futures: the views of key influentials in six European countries on likely developments in social policy', *Social Policy and Administration*, vol 31, pp 1-19.

Taylor-Gooby, P. (1998) 'Commitment to the welfare state', in R. Jowell, J. Curtice, A. Park, L. Brook, K. Thomson and C. Bryson (eds) *British – and European – Social Attitudes: How Britain differs*, Aldershot: Ashgate.

TC (Training Commission) (1988) *Training Commission, Annual Report 1987-88*, London: HMSO.

Thair, T. and Risdon, A. (2000) 'Women in the labour market: results from the spring 1998 Labour Force Survey', *Labour Market Trends*, vol 107, no 3, pp 102-28.

Thomas, J.M. (1998) 'The role of selective job search in UK unemployment', *The Economic Journal*, vol 108, pp 646-64.

Timmins, N. (1995) *The five giants: A biography of the Welfare State*, London: HarperCollins.

Trickey, H. et al (1998) *Unemployment and jobseeking: Two years on*, DSS Research Report No 87, London: The Stationery Office.

Trickey, H. and Lødemel, I. (2000: forthcoming) *'An offer you can't refuse?':Workforce in international perspective*, Bristol:The Policy Press.

Turnovsky, S.J. (1992) 'Alternative forms of government expenditure financing – a comparative welfare analysis', *Economica*, vol 59, pp 235–52.

Turnovsky, S.J. and Fisher, W.H. (1995) 'The composition of government expenditure and its consequences for macroeconomic performance', *Journal of Economic Dynamics and Control*, vol 19, pp 747-86.

UU (1987) *Hidden unemployment*, London: Unemployment Unit.

Vatter, H.G. and Walker, J.F. (1998) 'Support for baby-boom retirees – not to worry', *Journal of Economic Issues*, vol XXXII, pp 79-86.

Vincent, J. (1998) *Jobseeker's Allowance evaluation: Qualitative research on disallowed and sanctioned claimants, phase two after Jobseeker's Allowance*, DfEE Research Report No 86, London.

Vincent, J. et al (2000) *Piloting change: Interim qualitative findings from the earnings top-up evaluation*, DSS Research Report No 113, London: CDS.

Walford, J. (1998) 'Personal pensions updated, Pensions Survey Update', *Money Management* (March), London: Financial Times Magazines.

Walker, R. (1980) 'Temporal aspects of claiming behaviour: renewal of rent allowances', *Journal of Social Policy*, vol 9, no 2, pp 207-22.

Walker, R. (1998a) 'The Americanisation of British welfare: A case-study of policy transfer', *Focus*, Journal of the Institute for Research on Poverty, University of Madison–Wisconsin, vol 19, no 3, pp 32-40.

Walker, R. (1998b) Talk given to a seminar on the evaluation of the Working Families' Tax Credit organised by Inland Revenue, London, 25 February.

Walker, R. (1999a) '"Welfare to Work" versus poverty and family change: Policy lessons from the USA', *Work, Welfare and Society*, vol 12, no 3, In press.

Walker, R. (1999b) 'Lifetime poverty dynamics', in HM Treasury, *Persistent poverty and lifetime inequality*, London: HM Treasury, pp 9-16.

Walker, R. (ed) (2000) *Ending child poverty: Popular welfare for the 21st century?*, Bristol:The Policy Press.

Walker, R. and Ashworth, K. (1994) *Poverty dynamics: Issues and examples*, Aldershot: Avebury.

Walker, R. and Ashworth, K. (1998) 'Welfare benefits and recession in Great Britain', in L. Leisering and R. Walker (eds) *The dynamics of modern society: Poverty, policy and welfare*, Bristol: The Policy Press, pp 199-210.

Walker, R. and Brittain, K. (1995) *Benefits Agency customers and the 1994 review of the benefits system*, In-house Report No 7, Leeds: DSS.

Walker, R. with Hedges, A. (1985) *Housing Benefit: The experience of implementation*, London: Housing Centre Trust.

Walker, R. and Huby, M. (1989) 'Social security spending in the UK regions: bridging the North-South divide', *Government and Policy*, vol 7, pp 321-40.

Walker, R., Hedges, A. and Massey, S. (1987) *Housing Benefit: Discussion about reform*, London: Housing Centre Trust.

Walker, R. and Lawton, D. (1989) 'The Social Fund as an exercise in resource allocation', *Public Administration*, vol 67, pp 295-317.

Walker, R. and Wiseman, M. (1997) 'The possibility of a British earned income tax credit', *Fiscal Studies*, vol 18, no 4, pp 401-25.

Walker, R., Hardman, G. and Hutton, S. (1989) 'The occupational pension trap: Towards a preliminary empirical specification', *Journal of Social Policy*, vol 18, no 4, pp 575-94.

Walker, R., Lawson, R. and Townsend, P. (eds) (1984), *Responses to poverty: Lessons from Europe*, London: Heinemann.

Walker, R. and Park, J. (1998) 'Unpicking poverty', in C. Oppenheim (ed) *An inclusive society: Strategies for tackling poverty*, London: Institute for Policy Research, pp 29-51.

Walker, R., Shaw, A. and Hull, L. (1995) 'Responding to the risk of unemployment', in ABI (ed) *Risk, insurance and welfare*, London: Association of British Insurers, pp 37-52.

Walton, R. (2000) 'International comparisons of profitability', *Economic Trends*, vol 554, pp 33-46.

Watson, A. et al (1998) *Integrating disabled employees*, DfEE Research Report No 56, London: DfEE.

Webb, S. (1998) 'Crisis: What crisis? Are we really spending too much on social security?', *New Economy*, vol 5, pp 131–35.

White, M. (1991) *Against unemployment*, London: Policy Studies Institute.

White, M. and Lakey, J. (1992) *The Restart effect*, London: Policy Studies Institute.

WHO (World Health Organisation) (1999) *International classification of functioning and disability*, Geneva: WHO.

Wilkinson, R. (1996) *Unhealthy societies: The afflictions of inequality*, London: Routledge.

Williams, D. (1998) 'British social security and taxes: structuring their interactions', *Bulletin for International Fiscal Documentation*, vol 52, pp 440–44.

Williams, T., Hill, H. and Davies, R. (1999) *Attitudes to the welfare state and the response to reform*, DSS Research Report No 88, Leeds: CDS.

Winkelmann, L. and Winkelmann, R. (1997) 'Why are the unemployed so unhappy? Evidence from panel data', *Economica*, vol 65, pp 1–15.

Zarb, G. (1995) 'The dual experience of ageing with a disability', in J. Swain et al (eds) *Disabling barriers-enabling environments*, London: Open University Press/Sage Publications.

Index

Figures/tables are indicated by page references in *italics,* where there is no related text on the same page.

J

K

L

Y

young people
  New Deal (NDYP) xiv, 84, *85,*
    104
  in 1980s: employment problems
    64, 69-70, 82, 104
  and unemployment 25, *61, 62,* 67,
    74
Youth Opportunities Programme
    (YOP) xv, 79
Youth Training Scheme (YTS) xv,
    79, 80-1
Youth Training (YT) xv, 81